7341
JUL 20 1998

HV
1718
028
1997

Debating

⫞ P9-EDF-363

Corporate Crime

INFORMATION RESOURCES CENTER
ASIS
1625 PRINCE STREET
ALEXANDRIA, VA 22314
tel. (703) 519-6200

Edited by

William S. Lofquist
State University of New York—College at Geneseo

Mark A. Cohen
Owen Graduate School of Management
Vanderbilt University

Gary A. Rabe
Minot State University

ACJS Series Editor, Dean J. Champion

Academy of Criminal Justice Sciences
Northern Kentucky University
402 Nunn Hall
Highland Heights, KY 41076

Anderson Publishing Co.
Criminal Justice Division
P.O. Box 1576
Cincinnati, OH 45201-1576

Debating Corporate Crime

Copyright © 1997 by Anderson Publishing Co. and the Academy of Criminal Justice
Sciences

All rights reserved. No part of this book may be reproduced in any form or by any elec-
tronic or mechanical means including information storage and retrieval systems without
permission in writing from the copyright holders.

ISBN 0-87084-185-8
Library of Congress Catalog Number 97-70136

Gail Eccleston *Editor*
Elizabeth A. Shipp *Assistant Editor*
Cover Photography: Tim Grondin Photography, Cincinnati, OH

Acknowledgments

This book represents a collaborative effort in the truest and finest sense. The editors worked closely with one another in developing the framework for this debate, identifying and recruiting our excellent contributing authors, and organizing the individual manuscripts into a provocative text. We would like to acknowledge gratefully the skill, patience, and generosity of each of the contributing authors not only for their individual contribution, but for their considerable efforts in assisting us in forming a coherent whole from many different voices. We would also like to thank Dean Champion, the Series Editor, for his commitment to this project. Gail Eccleston, our Editor at Anderson, has been a tremendous help in coordinating this project.

In addition to these very direct and important contributions, a large number of people have played an important and too often unacknowledged role in shaping the ideas that became this book. Among these people are Dave Ermann, Gerry Turkel, Pan Hao, Valerie Hans, Kurt Cylke, and Gary Green.

Finally, Bill Lofquist wishes to thank Beverly and Sam for their unending support; Mark Cohen thanks Robin and Jenny; and Gary Rabe thanks Kathy, David, and Brian for their dedication, support, and encouragement.

William S. Lofquist
Mark A. Cohen
Gary A. Rabe

Acknowledgments

Foreword

William Lofquist, Mark Cohen, and Gary Rabe have edited a very timely, interesting work about corporate crime, its etiology, persistence, and resilience to legal sanctions. As the last of six commissioned works under my editorship of the ACJS/Anderson Monograph Series in *Issues in Crime and Justice*, this book will provide yet another important dimension to the Series as a representative of its spirit and intent. Thus, it is with more than a small measure of pride that I prepare my last foreword to preface such a noteworthy volume.

We are totally immersed in an era of accountability, especially corporate accountability. Spurred to action by environmentalists and assorted vested interest groups, government at all levels has enacted enabling legislation intended to hold corporations more accountable to the public relating to their business practices, advertising, and diverse uses of natural resources. In 1996, the tobacco industry was subjected to a rigorous assault by congressional investigative committees. Lawsuits filed by victims or relatives of victims of different tobacco products reached an all-time high. Tobacco industry leaders testified before Congress, presenting a fairly systematic diatribe of deniability. Industry whistle-blowers emerged to challenge denials by the tobacco industry that their products are harmless, and allegations of perjury among tobacco industry representatives were widespread.

A nagging question among the citizenry is how these corporate giants can be felled and held accountable for their actions, many of which have been calculated, deliberate, and/or premeditated. How widespread is corporate crime? How much trust should we place in large organizations where tradition is often equated with integrity? Organizations, such as Dow Chemical, have made substantial contributions to many charities and non-profit enterprises whose sole functions are to improve the quality of life in society and a safer natural environment. At the same time, Dow Chemical has polluted the nation's rivers with toxic wastes that have long-term effects on water quality and the safety of persons living in close proximity to such waterways. How is the "good" to be weighed against the "bad," as corporations make concerted efforts through their lobbyists and advertising campaigns to bolster their public image?

It is often assumed that regulatory agencies will detect and punish wrongdoers, whether such wrongdoers are persons or corporations. But scandalous actions and corruption within virtually every government regulatory agency have caused the public to become increasingly skeptical about the effectiveness of government regulation. The monetary sanctions imposed in civil actions are often tokens and function as episodic bandages that disguise the true disease debilitating the system.

Not all corporate misconduct is environmentally relevant. In the 1980s and 1990s, stock brokerage firms were rocked with scandals concerning insider trading. Many banks and financial institutions failed because of monumental embezzlement and fraudulent schemes calculated to maximize profits for a powerful few at the expense of a multitude of investors. Thus, there are multiple dimensions to the corporate crime phenomenon. No single theoretical explanation exists to cover every corporate crime event. Many creative solutions abound among professionals and the legal community about what should be done to remedy corporate crime in its many guises.

Professors Lofquist, Cohen, and Rabe have decided to examine the multifaceted issue of corporate crime in an "issues" context. Their plan is fairly simple, and thus, many persons unfamiliar with the intricacies of corporate deviance can read this work with interest and understanding. They have divided each of several important topics into parts, each consisting of scholarly, dialectic essays by noted experts. Some of these essays have transcended national interests to include international ones, inasmuch as much corporate crime occurs in a global context.

These editors provide some helpful, detailed introductory remarks intended to present their rationale and framework for the discourses to follow. The successfulness of their efforts is evident through the intricate blending of sociological, criminological, economic, and legal thought. The different chapters systematically explore why corporate crime exists and persists; the nature of corporate liabilities in different organizational contexts; the myriad of real or proposed sanctions imposed against corporations and their agents; and a reassessment of corporate criminality and the need for change.

Section I, "The Causes of Corporate Crime," contains alternative explanations to account for corporate misconduct. One view, argued by Mark Cohen and Sally Simpson, is that corporate crime is an organizational phenomenon, where agency goals dictate a course of conduct which may or may not be achieved by lawful means. The confluence of subparts of the whole act in ways to serve utilitarian ends. Individual responsibility is minimal, where department goals channel and distribute organizational decisionmaking in ways that make it difficult to fix any given department with specific liability whenever corporate misconduct is detected. Nevertheless, an element of foreseeability exists, so that actions of individual actors in organizations are deliberate and intended. David Ermann and Gary Rabe suggest a similar scheme, although they suggest that the element of foreseeability may not be as prominent. This is because the complex interactions of organizational subunits and decisionmaking by individual departments make it extremely difficult to anticipate an overall organizational outcome with high predictability.

Section II examines the issue of corporate liability. Jeffrey Parker views organizations and corporations as abstract entities which are punished for the actions of individual actors. Parker notes that many corporate sanctions are inappropriate for corporations per se, and that the law is better-applied to specific individuals in organizations where certain laws are knowingly violated. Nico Jörg counters in Chapter 5 by arguing that organizations *are* entities deserving of criminal sanctions. Although various individual actors in corporations are often responsible for organizational crime, the organization itself must be sanctioned. Such sanctioning will facilitate greater self-regulation and compliance with government-imposed standards.

Section III, "Corporate Criminal Sanctioning," includes chapters by Thomas Ulen and Richard Gruner. Ulen favors sanctions in the form of fines imposed that far outweigh any gains realized by corporations. Thus, a deterrent effect is caused that may diminish corporate deviance. An alternative, espoused by Gruner, is to attack the internal structures of organizations and effect inside cures for organizational problems. Changes in organizational policies and incentive systems that operate to reward regulatory compliance rather than deviation are recommended. The logic of both fines and internal policy and operational changes is explored by both authors.

Section IV, "Regulatory Relations," includes chapters by Leo Barrile and Bridget Hutter. Barrile suggests that the state should act aggressively toward organizations whenever wrongdoing or corporate crime is detected. Strict imposition of criminal penalties are logical outcomes against individual organizational actors. The economic market itself is viewed as less effective in dealing with corporate crime, since it is so centrally implicated in the generation of social harms. However, Hutter suggests a negotiation model, whereby government agencies collaborate in positive ways with corporations to encourage the enactment of compliance plans for self-governance. In effect, the government uses the expertise of corporate actors who know best how their business is transacted and how it can best be modified.

As a resource, this work will be advantageous to scholars interested in doing research about corporate deviance. The list of references is especially current and consists of many cites not ordinarily encountered in traditional journal outlets. Given the unique professional mix of chapter contributors, these references are valuable research tools and contribute greatly to the book's pedagogy. Endnotes are included at the end of each article, and a Bibliography is located at the end of the book, for reader convenience. My editorship has been personally and professionally rewarding, and it is with great pleasure that I conclude with such a creative volume replete with theoretical and substantive insights about corporate crime. I wish my successor, Joy Pollock, the same good fortune I have enjoyed in receiving such an abundance of quality volume proposals from which to choose.

Dean J. Champion
ACJS/Anderson Monograph Series Editor
Minot State University

Contents

1

A Framework for Analysis of the Theories and Issues in Corporate Crime

William S. Lofquist
SUNY College at Geneseo

AGENCY AND STRUCTURE AND CORPORATE CRIME

The debate over the roles of agency and structure in shaping social action is longstanding and central to the social sciences. Advocates of the agency perspective emphasize the role of putatively rational human action (agency) in shaping social institutions and in explaining individual and organizational actions. Advocates of the structural perspective place primary emphasis on social, political, and organizational structures as not only the location but also the source of social activity. These two perspectives cannot be placed in complete opposition to one another because of the inevitably intertwined and dialectical nature of the relationship between the individual and society, though they do resolve the question of causal primacy in different ways.

Well before the term white-collar crime was coined by Edwin Sutherland and academic attention was turned toward the study of the crimes of business, this central and persisting question in the now recognized study of corporate crime was debated. In an exchange published in the legal monthly *The Green Bag* in 1906 and 1907, Frederick N. Judson (1906) and Donald R. Richberg (1906, 1907) offered opposing views on the behavioral and legal status of organizations, with Judson favoring an agency-based, individual-centered view and Richberg arguing in favor of a structural, organization-centered view of corporations. Recent expressions of the former position can be found in rational choice theory in sociology and criminology, and in the law and economics movement among legal scholars and economists. The latter view is most often articulated by organizational theorists in sociology, criminology, management, and law.

1

Despite the centrality of this theoretical debate to the burgeoning study of corporate crime, there remains a need for a systematic effort to organize the contributions of economists, sociologists, criminologists, and legal scholars. This requires identification of the central issues in the study of corporate crime and the application of each of these theoretical perspectives to these issues. Doing so provides a framework in which the literature on corporate crime can be organized and evaluated. That is the project of this book; we have applied these two theoretical perspectives, identified herein as the agency model and the structure model, to each of the four issues of central importance in corporate crime: the causes of corporate crime; the appropriate legal standards of liability in cases of illegal corporate conduct; the appropriate sanctions for adjudicated corporations; and the types of regulatory relations most effective in corporate crime control (see Table 1.1). This schema is ideal typical, as the complexities and nuances of the application of theories to issues throughout this book makes clear. In many cases, the different logics shade into one another, with agency and structure theorists each calling on the other logic to provide a fuller understanding of the issue at hand. Nonetheless, we believe this schema and this book provide an analytically useful, comprehensive, and much needed framework for the study of corporate crime.

In the present literature, the existence of, and interrelationships between, these issues and theories is often unarticulated, resulting in the growing literature in the field lacking focus. Points of divergence and contact between different issues and theories often remain unseen, obscured by disciplinary boundaries and by barriers between practitioners and scholars. For example, the growing debate on corporate criminal sanctioning, a debate fueled by the efforts of the United States Sentencing Commission to develop and implement organizational sentencing guidelines,[1] often occurs without consideration of underlying theories of the causes of corporate crime, the theoretical linkages between these different issues, or how these theories may impact sanctioning policy.

Similarly, corporate criminal liability has a long history in the United States, though it is not widely available in other nations. Its existence provides a greater diversity of legal responses to illegal corporate conduct than is available elsewhere, making it possible for criminal sanctions to target organizations rather than to be limited to their agents. This is consistent with the structure model. However, because corporate criminal liability derives from the application of individual-based common law jurisprudence to organizations, the distinct features of organizations are not recognized by the existing principles of corporate criminal liability. Full explication of the structure model and its application to the issue of corporate criminal liability makes this clear.

As the above examples suggest and the subsequent chapters detail, identifying the theories of corporate crime and its control, and applying them to the different issues in the field elucidates the theoretical logic (or absence thereof) underlying academic and policy debates surrounding these issues. This effort also provides a consistent theoretical basis for offering and evaluating policy proposals, clearly necessary in light of the Sentencing Commission's work. Most fundamentally, identifying and interrelating the major theories and issues in the field provides a level of clarity, maturity, and common currency to a field still largely on the margins of each of its contributing disciplines. Using representatives of these different disciplines and theoretical perspectives in writing this book allows each chapter to be presented in its own theoretical voice, avoiding some of the limitations of secondhand treatments of issues and theories often found in the corporate crime literature. It is our hope that this book accomplishes its goal of providing a degree of integration, organization, and comprehensiveness heretofore unavailable to those interested in corporate crime.

EXAMINING THE ISSUES

The purview of the study of corporate crime stretches from the occurrence of an offense through the detection of that offense by regulatory officials to the imposition of individual or corporate, civil or criminal liability and ends with sanctioning. Why the offense conduct occurs, with particular attention to the relative importance of individual actors and organizational structures, is an issue of considerable importance and debate. Whether, what type, and under what circumstances liability should be imposed on organizational conduct is interesting because of the vastly different international standards of legal liability of corporations, and an even more vast theoretical chasm in recommended standards of liability. Sanctioning illegal corporate conduct, whether through fines, community service, restitution, probation, or adverse publicity, and whether through civil, criminal, or administrative law, is also of interest. Finally, the appropriate regulatory posture, be it largely market-based or state-based, and be it largely self-regulatory, negotiative, or adversarial, is controversial and of interest independent of the types of sanctions employed.

ALTERNATIVE LOGICS OF CORPORATE CRIME

There are two logics or models that tie together these issues and the many different criminological, organizational, economic, and legal approaches to corporate crime. Applied and debated under many different headings over the years, these logics run throughout the law's encounter with corporations. All too often, these logics are left unrecognized or unarticulated by scholars focusing on some issue within the study of corporate crime or by policymakers engaged in the pragmatics of constructing and passing legislation. Nevertheless, these logics are present in the study of corporate crime, and may be read as alternative narratives on the cause and control of corporate crime (see Table 1.1). After outlining these logics, an effort is made to further illustrate their presence and implications for the study of corporate crime by detailing their application to each of the four issues in the study of corporate crime.

Agency logic, which clearly dominates corporate crime control policy, is underlaid by market logic. This paradigm conceptualizes organizations and the individuals within them as rational, unitary, well-informed actors, much like the idealized consumer in the marketplace. By this logic, corporate crimes are the product of individual or organizational utility maximizing decisions,[2] criminal liability is best directed toward identifiable decisionmakers, sanctioning operates primarily through deterrence, and sanctions impose organizational and social costs as well as benefits and thus must be implemented with an eye toward both overdeterrence and underdeterrence (Coase, 1960; Elzinga & Breit, 1976). Though prominent throughout the study of corporate crime, among theorists ranging from classical to Marxist, the most active and sophisticated source of this logic is in the law and economics movement that emerged in the 1960s and which gained substantial academic and applied prestige in the 1980s.

Statutory law has favored market logic. For historical, cultural, and political reasons, statutory actors are almost exclusively natural persons. Judicial interpretations of these laws have introduced juristic persons into the law (see Bernard, 1984; Coleman, 1974, 1982), though the law has accommodated little to this new circumstance. Standards of liability, particularly *mens rea,* are rooted in individual criminal law and assume rationality. Strict and vicarious liability provide a legal means to circumvent these assumptions, though they do so without suggesting a theoretical alternative to agency logic. Available corporate sanctions are those designed for individuals, with only very recent modification to address the distinct characteristics of organizations (see Lofquist, 1993b). The predominance of fines, through which criminal actors are required to return some, all, or even more than the financial gains they sought through crime, best illustrates this point.

In recent years, a well-developed theoretical and empirical critique of, and alternative to, agency logic has emerged. Based in structural logic, at the center of this critique is a rejection of the view of corporate criminality as a rational, profit-driven activity and the corporation as an anthropomorphized entity. Succinctly stated, the primary theoretical criticism of agency logic is that it "is blind to organizational theory and practice" (Fisse, 1978:366). The structure model conceptualizes organizations as complex, differentiated entities, with numerous, often competing goals, limited information, and imperfect communications. As a result of these characteristics, organizations do not directly and unitarily pursue clear and specific goals. Rather, organizational behavior is better characterized as multidimensional; complexity reigns, interests compete, and outcomes are the product of a range of situationally rationally intended but imperfectly interpreted or implemented communications and goals. Analyses of the *Challenger* space shuttle disaster (Kramer, 1987, 1992; Vaughan, 1996), the

My Lai massacre (Kelman & Hamilton, 1989), and the Dalkon Shield contraceptive device case (Perry & Dawson, 1985) well illustrate this approach.

The legal expression of structural logic would explicitly, rather than indirectly, recognize organizations as actors and would identify them as distinct actors in statutory law. Standards of liability would also explicitly provide for organizations as actors, perhaps by attaching liability to particular organizational structures and practices, rather than to individuals or the organization as a whole, in cases of wrongdoing. The Sentencing Commission's recently articulated components of an adequate compliance plan (United States Sentencing Commission, 1991) provide a starting point for these efforts. Finally, corporate criminal sanctioning based on this model, which has been realized in practice in the development of organizational probation (Lofquist, 1993a; Gruner, 1988; Coffee, Gruner & Stone, 1988; Metzger, 1984), involves the use of sanctions designed to alter or rehabilitate organizational characteristics associated with wrongdoing.

Table 1.1
The Logics of Corporate Crime

	Causes of Corporate Crime	Corporate Crime Liability	Sanctioning	Regulatory Regulations
Agency Logic	Rational individual and organizational decisionmakers in pursuit of overarching corporate goals	Prosecute responsible individual agents, with limited support for corporate criminal liability	Punishment of responsible individuals or the organization as a whole through monetary mechanisms geared toward weakening the incentives for crime.	Successful regulation requires striking the appropriate balance of sanctioning power between business and state
Structure Logic	Organizational structures, cultures, and policies create situations in which crime is an outcome of business operations absent identifiable individual intent	Target the organization as a whole or perhaps even locate liability within particular organizational structures and policies	Reform problematic organizational structures through regulatory interventions of various types	Successful regulation is achieved through the structure of relations between business and state

INTEGRATING ISSUES AND THEORIES: AN OVERVIEW OF THE STUDIES OF CORPORATE CRIME

Causes of Corporate Crime

The earliest studies of corporate crime were dominated by sociologists and criminologists, most notably Edwin Sutherland (1949/1983) and his student, Donald Cressey (1950, 1953, 1989). These founding contributions focused on explaining offense conduct, with theoretical foundations rooted in the dominant individual-based criminological theories of the time. Personal financial and psychological motivations and behaviors learned from co-workers and superiors dominated these early explanations (see also Clinard, 1946; Hartung, 1950; Newman, 1958; Geis, 1967). Little consideration was given to the possibility of the distinctive causal contributions of the organization qua organization; rather, outcomes were explained through the actions of employees or by uncritically anthropomorphizing the organization.

The next generation of sociological and criminological theorists moved from a micro to a macro level of analysis, but continued viewing corporate crime as the product of rational, unitary actors. Consistent with the conflict theory ascendant in the 1960s and 1970s, these theorists (see Quinney, 1974a, 1974b, 1977; Nader & Green, 1973; Nader, Green & Seligman, 1976; Simon & Eitzen, 1982) viewed corporate crime as the product of organizations driven to maximize profits in a lax or captured regulatory environment. At the same time, but divided by disciplinary boundaries that had not yet been overcome, economists entered the debate, beginning with the pioneering work of Gary Becker (1968). This approach shared the assumptions of rational agency favored by sociologists and criminologists of the time, but used the vocabulary and ideology of free market economics rather than conflict and Marxist theory, providing a foundation for the emerging law and economics movement. The theoretical common ground found by these otherwise diametrically opposed perspectives provides evidence of the pervasiveness of agency logic and the inattention to structural considerations in understanding our organizational society.

Most recently, a third wave of sociological and criminological theorists has taken a middle-level, organizational approach to explaining corporate crime (Yeager, 1986, 1991; Ermann, 1986, 1991; Ermann & Lundman, 1978, 1982, 1987; Kramer, 1992; Vaughan, 1982, 1996; Rabe & Ermann, 1995). Beginning with the work of legal scholar Christopher Stone in the 1970s (Stone, 1975), with considerable debt to previous theorists working outside the study of corporate crime (Simon, 1945; Cyert & March, 1963; Allison, 1969, 1971), and spreading throughout the growing multidisciplinary inquiry into corporate crime, the structure model was developed and refined. By the 1980s, the debate was fully engaged and disciplinary boundaries were being scaled, with law and economics enjoying considerable academic and applied strength and structural theory coming to dominate sociological and criminological discussions of corporate crime. At present, a rich literature can be found in each of these theoretical traditions, providing grist for an active debate on the roles of agency and structure in understanding corporate crime.

Agency Model. Agency logic has as its starting point a rational actor view of organizations. From this perspective, organizational decision-making processes are analogized to resource-rich individuals. Organizations and the individuals within them are viewed as rational, calculating, unified, and value-maximizing entities, able to make fully-informed and strategic responses to circumstances based on known alternatives. Organizational behavior is thus understood as the product of carefully calculated measures designed to maximize individual and/or organizational benefits relative to costs (Posner, 1985; *Harvard Law Review*, 1979). Crime is among these possible behaviors; where market incentives exceed market and state-imposed disincentives, rational actors will pursue criminal courses of action. A straightforward statement of this logic is Shavell's (1985:1235) assertion that:

> Whether or not a party will actually commit an act . . . .
> depends on his perception of the possibility that he will suf-
> fer a sanction, either monetary or nonmonetary. A party
> will commit an act if, and only if, the expected sanction
> would be less than the expected private benefit.

No distinction is made for actions taken within an organizational context; all actions are individual actions.

Beyond this starting point, applications of agency logic become more complex and differentiated. The purest expression of this logic is in law and economics, a highly economistic approach to organizational behavior (Posner, 1980, 1985; Parker, 1988; see also Byrne & Hoffman, 1985; Fisse, 1986; Horwitz, 1980; Kelman, 1983). From this perspective, organizational behavior is understood as the behavior of discrete and identifiable individual decisionmakers acting within political and economic contexts organized to minimize the potential economic, social, and environmental costs of corporate misconduct. Stated otherwise, a pluralist view (Skocpol, 1980; Skocpol & Finegold, 1982) of American and Western European politics predominates. Within this context, agents pursue criminal courses of action when firm, market, and state incentives toward crime exceed the associated disincentives. Advocates of this view can also be found among classical theorists in sociology and criminology; in this case, the economic vocabulary of costs and benefits is replaced by the psychological vocabulary of pain and pleasure, but the underlying logic is the same (see Hirschi & Gottfredson, 1987; Gottfredson & Hirschi, 1990).

Suggesting the ideal typical nature of the agency/structure dichotomy, this approach provides some role to structure, in this case incentive and control structures. For example, numerous researchers (Macey, 1991; Baysinger, 1991; Alexander & Cohen, 1995) have identified corporate governance structures as important in explaining when agents break the law. However, these remain agency theories in that organizational structures are background considerations; rational actors act with knowledge of these structures and their likely consequences, and shape their behavior to optimize outcomes within these structures. Outcomes are thus foreseeable in a probabilistic sense.

A second group of agency theorists is found among conflict and Marxist-oriented social scientists. Though differing sharply from law and economists on political and ethical questions relating to the propriety, legitimacy, and location of political power within a market economy, these leftist theorists identify rational individual and organizational agency as the source of corporate crime in a capitalist economy. Indeed, from this perspective, capitalism is itself criminogenic, inevitably producing managerial decisions to circumvent legal controls in the pursuit of profits (Simon & Eitzen, 1993). For example, in an effort to explain how "U.S. corporate capitalism has reproduced corporate crime," Barnett (1981:157, 158) invokes classical school theory, stating:

> Corporate crime will occur when management chooses to pursue corporate goals through circumvention of market constraints in a manner prohibited by the state . . . . One can thus expect that a corporation will be more likely to engage in crime when the expected costs of its illegal action are acceptably low relative to the perceived gains.

The theoretical logic is identical to Shavell's, though the views of the political context in which this decisionmaking occurs differ sharply.

Structure Model. To say that corporations are motivated by monetary interests is an obvious truism in a capitalist economy. However, structure theorists argue that this is not necessarily to say that organizations are able to directly and clearly translate this motivation into behavior. Having profitability as a goal at the highest level is far different from pursuing that goal through organizational actions at the level of each division, work group, and employee. Organizational structure and complexity, actions of employees at different levels and places within the organization, unclearly communicated or misunderstood directives, the absence of oversight, and many other circumstances seriously confound the ability of an individual or organization to unitarily pursue organizational goals. These organizational variables are central to the structure model (Allison, 1971; Stone, 1975).

The development of the structure model began with Simon's (1945; March & Simon, 1963) earliest works. In these works, Simon questioned the classical view of the firm (Barnard, 1938), arguing organizational behavior is characterized by "bounded rationality." In describing the work of Cyert and March (1963), which was also instrumental in the development of the structure model, Allison (1971:75) writes that:

> [i]n contrast to traditional theories that explain the firm's behavior in terms of market forces, Cyert and March focus—as organization theory would suggest—on the effect of organizational structure and conventional practice upon the development of goals, the formulation of expectations, and the execution of choice.

Support for and elaboration of this view of organizations as complex, non-optimizing structures has grown substantially over subsequent years.

Christopher Stone has gone so far as to suggest that instances of corporate crime always involve defective organizational procedures (Stone, 1975, 1977). Subsequent commentators have developed from this theoretical orientation the concept of structurally-induced crime (Geraghty, 1979; Conklin, 1977; Needleman & Needleman, 1979). Drawing the linkage between liability and sanctioning, and pointing out the deficiency of market logic in both cases, Geraghty defines "structural crimes" as cases "in which a corporation commits a criminal offense but no criminally culpable individual can be identified" (1979:359).[3] Such identification is difficult because organizational features may shield culpable individuals or because in complex organizations "cumulative individual inadvertence alone can generate criminal violations by the corporation" (1979:359).

This cumulative inadvertence, by which outcomes emerge as byproducts of the process of production rather than as a planned product, is more fully captured by Ermann's concept of escalating commitments (Ermann, 1991; Rabe & Ermann, 1995). In this view, corporate crime often occurs when employees and organizations become committed to initially legitimate courses of action which lead to criminality only after investments of time and the involvement of numerous employees make recognition and control of this emergent criminality difficult. Accordingly, the Ford Pinto case, probably the most widely studied example of corporate crime (see Dowie, 1977; Cullen, Maakestad & Cavender, 1987; Kunen, 1994), can be understood as a consequence of the inability of the compartmentalized concerns of engineers to be heard in the midst of the commitment of Ford's marketing division and top management to developing a competitive, low cost, fuel-efficient automobile. This organizational explanation contrasts sharply with the rationalistic, unitary, bottom line-based explanation of this case (Dowie, 1977) that has entered into popular understandings of corporate crime.

A lay statement of structure logic is found in Representative George Miller's (D-CA) description of defense contractor fraud. In testimony before the House of Representatives during hearings on defense procurement fraud, Miller stated:

> I am sure in many instances systems that were brought to
> the Congress were overpromised and underengineered, if
> you will, in terms of their success. So that started a
> process of shaving corners, looking the other way, substitu-
> tion of materials, falsification of tests, because, in fact, you
> wanted to deliver on the promise that you made to the
> Department of Defense and to the Congress (U.S. House of
> Representatives, 1990a:26).

Identifying the linkage between structure theories of corporate crime and structural approaches to sanctioning, Miller went on to note that given these circumstances, sanctions must be designed to "come to grips . . . with the corporate structure" (1990:27) by seeking to remediate the organizational structures and processes that contributed to criminal activity.

CORPORATE CRIMINAL LIABILITY

The extension of the criminal law to corporations followed the earlier imposition of corporate civil liability (Stone, 1975). The landmark criminal case was *New York Central & Hudson Railroad Co. v. United States* (212 U.S. 481) in 1909, in which the United States Supreme Court upheld a finding that organizations were able to form criminal intent, and were thus subject to criminal liability, though only for economic offenses.[4] The legal basis for this finding was the juristic person standard (see Coleman, 1974, 1982; Stone, 1975; Bernard, 1984; Belbot, 1993), a long-standing common law principle which holds that organizations are persons under the law. Organizations are thus treated as legal individuals, liable through strict and vicarious liability (the common law doctrine of *respondeat superior*) for the acts and omissions of all the natural persons in their service. This liability pertains regardless of the disposition of cases involving individual agents and employees, the state of knowledge of management regarding the alleged offense, and the existence of organizational policies and directives specifically prohibiting the alleged conduct.

The juristic person standard has since been repeatedly upheld by judges and established in statute, with the result being that corporate and individual criminal liability are "nearly coextensive" (Brickey, 1984:8n). Title 1, Section 1 of the United States Code establishes that in acts of Congress, the terms "person" and "whoever" include corporations, "unless the context indicates otherwise" (1 U.S.C. Section 1, 1970). This limitation on the juristic person standard is a substantial one. It has been used to limit application of common law felonies to corporations and to limit the imposition of probation on corporations (Gruner, 1988; Lofquist, 1993a). Nonetheless, and despite the uniqueness of corporate criminal liability in comparative perspective (Mueller, 1957; Leigh, 1982; Laitinen, 1991; Brickey, 1984), continuing questions about its appropriateness by some (*Harvard Law Review*, 1979; Elkins, 1976; Cressey, 1989; Clarke, 1990; Parker, 1991), and substantial efforts to limit its applications (Orland, 1980; American Law Institute, 1985; National Commission on Reform of Federal Criminal Laws, 1970), corporate criminal liability is by now firmly institutionalized as a matter of law (Brickey, 1984).

At the same time, the legal framework for corporate crime control is rooted in individual criminal law. Through judicial interpretation and the juristic person standard, these laws have been extended to corporations. However, they retain their individualistic, classical school assumptions, a point often unrecognized even by structural theorists. These assumptions have provided numerous hurdles to the practical application of the criminal law to corporations (Coleman, 1974; Fisse, 1983; Bernard, 1984; Friedman, 1979). Brickey characterized this situation by remarking about the juristic person standard that "the simplicity of such notions lay only in their inspiration, not in their execution" (Brickey, 1984:14n). This is particularly true in the area of liability. *Mens rea* is at the heart of criminal liability, and courts have been reluctant to characterize organizations, despite the legal fiction of personhood and the absence of legal barriers, as possessing the rationality at the basis of traditional understandings of intent. The concepts of strict and vicarious liability borrowed from tort law have only partly overcome this conceptual barrier.

The implications of this barrier are well documented in research by Frank (1983, 1984; see also Benson, Maakestad, Cullen & Geis, 1988; Benson, Cullen & Maakestad, 1990; Blum-West & Carter, 1983; Clinard & Yeager, 1980). These researchers have found that concern about the appropriateness of corporate criminal liability on the part of prosecutors, rather than issues related to corporate power, limit the extent to which criminal prosecutions are chosen over civil proceedings. Case law also provides ample evidence of the practical limitations on corporate criminal liability and sanctioning, despite their formal availability. The Pinto case, in which Ford was acquitted in large part because of issues of intent, is the best known example.

Agency Model. Some agency theorists, most notably Donald Cressey (1989; see also Parker, 1991; McVisk, 1978), argue that corporate criminal liability is a misnomer, made impossible by legal rules and behavioral realities. Corporate criminal activity is ultimately and inevitably the result of individual actions, and should be theoretically and legally responded to as such. As Cressey stated in this regard, theorists must "recognize that only real persons have the psychological capacity to intend crimes, and then focus their analytical and theoretical skills on these persons" (1989:48). Individual criminal liability is thus advanced as the appropriate legal response to wrongdoing within organizations.

In a more provocative statement of this position, law and economics scholar Jeffrey Parker (1991:1) stated that "corporate criminal liability is a potentially dangerous kind of nonsense suggesting that there is something to be gained from collectivizing criminal responsibility and 'punishing' the complete abstraction that is a corporation." Continuing, Parker echoed Cressey's point that crime can exist "only in the mind of an individual" (*Corporate Crime Reporter,* 1991:19), leading to the conclusion that liability must focus on responsible individuals (see also Mueller, 1957; G. Williams, 1961). Lederman elaborates this point, asserting that:

> the corporation is merely an economic and social enterprise, namely a tool for perpetrating offenses. The possible manipulation of the corporate body by human offenders does not

transform it, however, into a criminal. Criminal law, therefore, should concentrate on the responsibility of the individuals operating the corporate entity and should determine
that only an individual who commits or is involved in an
offense can be considered an offender (1985:338).

The law and economists' theoretical argument is again paralleled by conflict-oriented agency theorists, though with important differences. Glasbeek
(1984:431-435), for example, argues that individual criminal liability must
always be favored over corporate criminal liability, with liability focusing
specifically on identifiable responsible parties or, in cases in which such parties cannot be identified, on senior corporate managers or important shareholders. However, while rejecting corporate criminal liability on theoretical
grounds, he contends that it is business influence over lawmaking and
enforcement, not conceptual problems, that have been the primary obstacle to
greater use of this legally available form of liability. Individual criminal liability in corporate cases faces neither legal nor conceptual barriers, though the
same political power issues pertain, likely limiting its future use.

Other agency theorists concede the legal appropriateness of corporate liability while arguing that corporate criminal liability is incapable of accom-
plishing anything not already achievable through noncriminal enforcement
measures (Posner, 1976, 1980, 1985). Thus, while organization-targeted measures are the most efficient means to ensure the disciplining of agents, specifically criminal forms of liability add little to this equation. Still other agency
theorists favor both individual and organizational criminal liability, arguing that
the availability of both maximizes opportunities for deterrence by empowering
both state- and firm-based monitors (Kraakman, 1984). One variation of this
approach (Carney & Arlen, 1992) is to support individual agent liability, making corporate criminal liability available only in cases of organizational failure
to adequately monitor its agents. Finally, still others argue that efficiency is
obtained by placing criminal liability on the organization, providing it the
incentive to more closely monitor its employees. Absent adequate incentives,
lax monitoring and a greater likelihood of organizational crime result. Whatever the preferred location and type of liability, the unifying assumption of
agency logic as applied to corporate criminal liability is that the imposition of
liability can and must be directed toward efforts to utilize putative individual
and organizational rationality to promote lawful behavior by creating appropriate incentives and disincentives. It is the absence of the appropriate form
and location of liability, in both the law and the organization, not the culture or
the structure of the organization more generally, that is implicated in organizational wrongdoing.

Structure Model. Recognizing the above-discussed legal, cultural, and political
limitations on the use of corporate criminal liability, structure theorists are left

in a difficult position. While the juristic person standard and the practice of judicial interpretation have facilitated the development of corporate criminal liability, they do so by suspending assumptions of rationality rather than replacing them with an organization-specific definition of behavior. This limits effective application of the criminal law to corporations to the extent that fundamental differences exist between individual and organizational actors, with an irreducible organizational component identified in cases of corporate crime. Though American corporations have come under the purview of the criminal law to a greater extent than in nations both within and outside of the common law tradition (Laitinen, 1991; Mueller, 1957; Lansing & Hatfield, 1985), the underlying logic of the juristic person standard has hindered effective legal control of corporations. Though judicial interpretation is a principal source of legal development in common law systems, application of old laws to new legal actors provides for only incremental legal changes (Thomas & Bishop, 1987). Rather than viewing corporations as fundamentally different social actors than individuals, and therefore necessitating a distinct legal regime, application of the criminal law to corporations has resulted in a legal regime in which corporate activities are defined, processed, and sanctioned based on principles derived from individual criminal law (*Yale Law Journal,* 1982).

The result of the tension between corporations as actors and traditional understandings of crime and culpability is that:

> corporate criminal liability is in such a weak and undeveloped state that many commentators urge that corporate criminal sanctions be displaced by civil monetary penalties, injunctions and negotiation and guidance, backed up when necessary by individual criminal sanctions (Fisse, 1983:1143-1144; for examples, see Cressey, 1989; Kriesberg, 1976; Posner, 1985).

The problem in this debate is that the juristic person standard is often unquestioned as the basis for the corporate criminal law. As a result, the choice is often posed as either pretending that corporations are merely big people, and treating them as such, or pretending that individual action within an organization is identifiable, and that offenses that primarily benefit the organization are adequately punished by focusing the criminal justice system's attention on individual employees. Rejecting this conclusion, structure theorists return to their core assumption of the centrality of the organization itself to corporate crime, and derive from this the view that corporate criminal liability must be fundamentally transformed to become consistent with the operational realities of organizations.

Applying this logic, organizations are most effectively controlled when subject to distinct, organization-specific criminal laws, characterized at least in part by sanctions directed toward the alteration of internal organizational structures and processes in cases of wrongdoing (Friedman, 1979; Stone, 1975; Rourke, 1990; *Yale Law Journal*, 1982). In their discussion of Dutch corporate criminal law, which most closely approximates the structural model of corporate criminal liability, Field and Jörg (1991; see also Chapter 5 herein) describe a system in which institutional practices of the organization and characteristics of organizational culture are potential locations of *mens rea* and corporate criminal liability.

This is consistent with measures proposed by Coleman. In his discussion of the asymmetry between individual and organizational actors that has developed with the proliferation of corporate actors and the use of the juristic person standard as the basis of legal control of these actors, Coleman suggests two remedial steps. They are: "either an explicit unbalancing of rights, in order to balance the realization of interests among unequal parties, or else somewhat more direct intervention of the law into the exercise of rights" (Coleman, 1974:77). Steps such as holding organizations to an alternative, higher standard of liability than individuals would be an example of the first approach, while interventionist sanctioning strategies would be included in the second approach.

By this logic, continued adherence to the market model impedes corporate crime control by masking the need for types of legal changes associated with political logic. As Christopher Stone (1975:1) stated in this regard:

> [t]he problems we face in controlling corporations today have their roots in legal history; they are a legacy of the law's failure to search out and take into account special features of business corporations as actors that make the problem of controlling them a problem distinct from that of controlling human beings.

It can be argued that the United States Sentencing Commission has, in its lengthy and detailed definition of an effective compliance plan, developed an organization-specific model of criminal liability. This was not their intention. Nonetheless, the structural characteristics associated with effective compliance plans could be used to inform determinations of organizational criminal liability. While this is not necessary due to the availability of strict liability, an organization-specific approach to culpability would provide a stronger theoretical rationale for imposing liability on organizations.

CORPORATE CRIMINAL SANCTIONING

In his classic book, *Politics and Markets,* Charles Lindblom (1977:ix) identifies the market and political sectors as primary and competing locations of social policy:

> aside from the difference between despotic and libertarian
> governments, the greatest distinction between one govern-
> ment and another is in the degree to which market replaces
> government or government replaces market.

As a location of social policy, the market sector, whether used to control crime, limit pollution, or distribute health care, shapes outcomes by manipulating the relative costs and benefits to agents of behavior, goods, and services in an environment with minimal state involvement. Drawing on agency theory, recently popular school choice or voucher programs (Chubb & Moe, 1990), workfare and other welfare-privatization proposals, and pollution credit plans are examples of efforts to affect behavior by externally manipulating the choices available to actors. In the case of corporate crime control, to the extent that such control occurs through market mechanisms, such as fines, it is said to be the result of the introduction of an unfavorable economy of criminal action.

The political mechanism, on the other hand, enlists state action to structure to some degree the social, political, economic, or organizational environment in which behavior occurs, and to direct action within that environment. Politics-based social policies thus involve the use of state power to directly pursue ends only indirectly pursued through market action. Establishment of best technology available (BTA) pollution control programs, collective bargaining laws, and industrial policy boards with mandated labor and business participation, such as those associated with corporatism (Schmitter, 1974, 1985; Panitch, 1980), are examples of politics-based controls over corporations. In this case of corporate crime, organizational probation makes available state power to create organizational structures that do not produce crime.

The distinction between politics and markets as locations of social policy is ideal typical. As a result, its practical application is somewhat less clear than in theory. State power is inevitably used to shape market structures and relations, meaning that pure markets do not exist. Similarly, politics-based policies are never completely divorced from market-based considerations. Organizations placed on probation, for example, are not removed from market relations. Organizational changes are imposed only with substantial input from the defendant. These changes are further informed by the state's assessment of market-related issues. Despite these limitations, the markets and politics distinction captures the essential difference between focusing on agency and structure as locations of corporate crime control.

Moreover, by identifying corporate crime control policies as either market-based or politics-based, a theoretically and politically more relevant distinction is introduced into the corporate crime control debate. Past discussions of regulatory and corporate crime control strategies have identified the distinction between intrusive and non-intrusive sanctions, but have not linked this distinction to broader theoretical traditions and political processes. Rather, the distinction is posited in descriptive or legalistic terms, such as between direct and indirect controls (Stone, 1977); preventive, reparative, and structural approaches (Fiss, 1978); penetrating and non-penetrating controls (Ermann & Lundman, 1982); liability and intervention (Stone, 1980); economism and legalism (Braithwaite, 1981-1982); and economics and structural reform (Wray, 1992). Zald (1978) developed the distinction between market, hierarchy, and polyarchy as types of organizational controls, but did not apply them to organizational crime.

The markets and politics distinction allows recognition of the crucial differences between, for example, the use of fines and the use of organizational probation in terms of the larger social processes and structures through which they operate. This distinction also provides for links between corporate crime control policies and the whole range of social policies. Further, by focusing on the means by which sanctions are implemented rather than the precise ends to be achieved by them, this distinction provides a means-based mechanism for organizing corporate crime control policies. Whether rehabilitation or deterrence or deserts is achieved is uncertain. That these sanctions are fundamentally and importantly different, however, is clear when their origins are understood theoretically and when they are linked to larger social policy categories.

Much like the development of corporate criminal liability, the historical relationship between the juristic person standard and corporate criminal sanctioning is characterized by innovation and limitation. As organizations were increasingly subjected to the criminal law throughout this century, judges and legislators chose from among the sanctions available for individuals those deemed appropriate for organizations. New criminal sanctions were not developed for these new offenders, thereby continuing the legal anthropomorphism of organizations. Existing agency-based sanctions included fines, imprisonment, and probation, and until quite recently only fines were deemed applicable to organizations by academic commentators and legal policymakers (Newman, 1958; G. Williams, 1961; Harvard Law Review, 1979; National Commission on Reform of Federal Criminal Laws, 1970, 1971). The result is underdevelopment of structure-based corporate crime controls. As G. Robert Blakey, former Senate Judiciary Committee Counsel and an active participant in criminal law reform efforts, stated: "If you look at the American criminal law experience, sentencing has not been our finest hour. There has been virtually no thinking about what to do with organizations" (Blakey, 1991).

Exemplifying this and taking a position shared by many, Clinard and Yeager stated that "a case cannot be made for the arguments that the criminal sanction can incapacitate or rehabilitate a corporation" (1980:90). The use of probation, imprisonment, or other non-market interventions on organizations involved legal innovations beyond the imagination of the judiciary and most academic commentators. More fundamentally, reliance on fines, individual criminal liability, and other deterrence-based agency sanctions was consistent not only with the pattern of development of corporate criminal law, but also with prevailing theories of the causes of corporate crime. Giving policy strength to this theoretical position, business has historically preferred market-based social policies of all types (Galbraith, 1985; Martin & Lodge, 1975; Silk & Vogel, 1976), and has strongly opposed organizational interventions as a threat to its autonomy and an invitation to a judicially managed economy (DeMott, 1977; Toensing, 1990; Heider, 1991).

Agency Model. In identifying rational individual agency as the source of corporate crime, agency theorists have advocated a sanctioning regime that supports or at least concedes the legal inviolability of the corporate form and emphasizes the ability of market forces to discipline corporations and their agents. More specifically, corporate crime control strategies focus on reliance on extant market forces and the simulation of these forces by the regulatory or criminal law to deter illegal conduct. Since money is in this view literally and figuratively the currency of relevance in capitalism, rational actors will respond to its manipulations, if properly gauged, in ways that will maximize their return. In classical school terms, if crime control is sought, fines and other penalties must be designed to ensure that the costs of crime exceed the benefits, factoring in the likelihood of detection. The legal response to corporate crime thus involves confronting corporations with a negative profit contingency in cases of law violation, usually through directly assessed monetary penalties, to which rational actors respond through general and specific deterrence (Dershowitz, 1961; Kadish, 1963; Becker, 1968; Ball & Friedman, 1965/1977; *Harvard Law Review,* 1979; Posner, 1980; Parker, 1988; Friedman, 1962; Thompson, 1991; Wray, 1992; Polinsky & Shavell, 1992).

Agency logic can be seen in the approach taken by *Harvard Law Review* (1979). In a lengthy article calling for reliance on civil and individual criminal liability, it was asserted that:

> [s]ince corporations are primarily profitseeking institutions, they choose to violate the law only if it appears profitable. Profit-maximizing decisions are carefully based upon the probability and amount of potential profit, so a corporate decision to violate the criminal law would generally include a calculation of the likelihood of prosecution and the probable severity of any punishment. Making these costs sufficiently high should eliminate the potential benefit of illegal corporate activity and hence any incentive to undertake such activity (1979:1365).

Stated more concisely, "the optimal fine equals the harm, properly inflated for the chance of not being detected, plus the variable enforcement cost of imposing the fine" (Polinsky & Shavell, 1992:133).

Empirical support for the deterrent effect of fines is widespread (Simpson & Koper, 1992; Cohen, 1989a, 1991, 1992; Paternoster, 1987), with the central thrust of this research being that organizations are indeed responsive to monetary threats. In their research on antitrust defendants, Easterbrook, Landes, and Posner found that "a firm will choose to comply with or violate the [law] depending on whether its anticipated gain from the violation is greater or less than its expected liability" (1980:345). At the same time, some of this research identifies limits to the explanatory power of rationality (Simpson, 1992) and the deterrent effect of fines alone (Simpson & Koper, 1992), leaving us with an empirical picture in which the boundaries between agency and structure and between sanctioning and regulatory relations are sometimes shaded.

In addition to reliance on monetary sanctions, the policy implications often drawn from economic analyses of corporate sanctioning are that organizations should face strictly limited government intervention and that even traditional external regulations should be approached with caution based in fear of overdeterrence (Polinsky & Shavell, 1992; Lott, 1991; Block, 1991; Cohen, 1991, 1992). Some critics of interventionist sanctions, such as organizational probation, invoke images of collectivism and central planning (Parker, 1991, 1993) in opposing any government intrusion into the internal operations of organizations. The regulation that does occur should mimic market mechanisms, thereby maximizing the efficiency of the criminal law. Ermann and Lundman (1982) refer to this as a "beneficiary-choice" approach to controlling corporate crime because free and competitive markets are proposed to force corporations to serve their beneficiaries, particularly stockholders, consumers, and employees.

More recent innovations in corporate criminal sanctioning have often been based in market logic. Their innovativeness is located in the means by which they invoke market logic and harness market forces, not directly as in the past, but through sanctions designed to affect the corporation's market strength. This latter approach includes publicity (Fisse, 1971, 1986; Cullen & Dubeck, 1985; Fisse & Braithwaite, 1983), restitution (Abel, 1985; Yeager, 1984), notice to victims (National Commission on Reform of Federal Criminal Laws, 1970), federal chartering (Nader, Green & Seligman, 1976; Conley, 1977), and alternative fines (Coffee, 1977, 1979-1980, 1990; Kennedy, 1985). Corporate social responsibility, though sometimes presented as involving substantial organizational changes (Nader, Green & Seligman, 1976; Stone, 1975), and criticized as subversive (Friedman, 1970), is also ultimately voluntary and market-based (Engel, 1979; Stone, 1975). Whatever remedial ends it may seek, this approach relies on moral exhortations (Stevenson, 1974) mediated by market considerations. The likelihood of organizational change is thus quite limited (see Mathews, 1984, 1989; Brenner & Molander, 1977). A final sanctioning strategy that has received increased attention in recent years is to rely wholly on existing market mechanisms, rather than supplementing them with state-based, market-modeled penalties. Karpoff and Lott (1993; see also Karpoff, 1991; Garbade, Silber & White, 1982; Bosch & Eckard, 1991), for example, have argued that reputational losses and declining stock values adequately sanction antitrust violations.

With each of these recently developed sanctions, the organizational response to market threats is discretionary to management, and therefore private. To do otherwise, by providing for politics-based sanctioning, creates an "inexorable tendency" toward the establishment of a "huge edifice of government regulation of doubtful efficacy" (Parker, 1990:445-446; see also Parker, 1993). Emphasis should instead be placed on creating incentives for management to respond to agent behavior in the manner it determines is most appropriate. Stone (1980:8) described this situation by stating that, in agency-based sanctioning strategies, such as fining:

> the outside world remains indifferent to how the enterprise participants—its investors and managers, in particular— adapt to the law's threats and distribute among themselves the law-driven losses that occur.

The likelihood and structure of organizational reform is entirely a function of these adaptations, though market logic suggests that the organization will respond to the sanction by sanctioning the responsible individuals. Simply stated, market logic suggests punishing the principal and letting the principal take care of the agent and itself (Coffee, 1986).

Conflict-oriented agency theorists share these theoretical assumptions, but differ in their view of the political context in which sanctioning occurs. While favoring the rational agency view that corporate crime is the product of well-informed and profit-directed managerial decisionmaking (Barnett, 1981), necessitating widely available corporate criminal liability and severe criminal fines (Barnett, 1981; see also Hopkins, 1980; Nader, Green & Seligman, 1976), these theorists identify political forces as the major impediment to effective corporate crime control. Corporate influence over the state suppresses market forces by sharply limiting lawmaking and enforcement efforts,[5] thereby socializing the costs of corporate misconduct. Effective corporate criminal law enforcement requires that market forces be allowed to operate, which in turn requires a political effort to substantially reallocate power among business, state, and public actors.

Structure Model. Due to the predominance of markets as the primary mechanism for the distribution of opportunities and rewards in the United States, as well as to their ideological predominance, the availability of alternative conceptualizations of and locations for state action is often unexplored. This inattention to politics-based crime control suggests that criminal justice policies reflect and reproduce larger social relations. While market-based strategies accept traditional managerial prerogatives and impose only external restraints on those prerogatives, structural sanctions, as with politics-based social policy more generally, confront and potentially exceed the historical limits of law by constraining organizational actions and providing for externally-introduced organizational changes.

As a result, academic and legal attention to structure-based sanctions is new. After a lengthy period of exclusive reliance on market-based sanctions, and a period of difficulty in drawing out the implications for sanctioning of the structure model:[6]

> criminal law scholars [have] begun seriously to consider that the criminal law could also intervene directly by interjecting the court or its agents into the corporation's decision-making process in an attempt to remedy dysfunctions that seem causally related to the criminal behavior (Coffee, 1981:448).

Accompanying the elaboration of the structure model of corporate criminal sanctioning has been a theoretically and empirically based critique of reliance on market-based sanctioning. Criticisms of the agency model center on the ability of corporations to absorb fines; the belief that fines, because they are easily externalized and nonspecifically applied, impact the wrong parties within an organization; the "deterrence trap" of excessively high fines that develops as fines are increased to the point necessary to provide deterrence given the fractional likelihood of apprehension; and the perception that among corporations fines are viewed as merely a cost of doing business (Coffee, 1977, 1981; Fisse, 1985, 1986).

In theoretical terms, the agency model is criticized as viewing the organization based on its stated goals rather than its operational realities. As Ermann and Lundman (1982:vii) note, corporate wrongdoing is:

> seldom produced by single-minded commitments to financial gain compelling the corporation to violate norms whenever rationally calculated corporate interests indicate that profits for stockholders would be increased.

Rather, organizational crime is more often a product of the interactions among the complex of role relations within an organization (*Yale Law Journal*, 1982), a view for which there is growing empirical support (Stone, 1975; Hopkins, 1979; Kramer, 1987; Ermann, 1991). As a result, the impacts of sanctions such as fines are diffused within the organization itself.

Recognizing the extent to which markets are shaped by law (Fligstein, 1990), market logic is also criticized as "curiously one-sided" (Jones, 1982:176). Business seeks out and depends on the state to assure capital accumulation in the face of business-generated accumulation and legitimation crises

(O'Connor, 1973; Habermas, 1973), and in this way develops an interdependent relationship with the state. At the same time, business seeks full autonomy within these markets, rejecting as anathema restrictions on its autonomy (Galbraith, 1985), even after wrongdoing. The resulting state of affairs is one in which "the role of the state is to ensure the conditions of economic freedom and not to eliminate its unacceptable consequences" (Jones, 1982:175). Structural sanctioning rejects this state of affairs, and seeks to remediate and reduce the likelihood of criminal consequences of capital accumulation.

In discussing the aims of structural sanctioning, Stone (1975:120) states that:

> traditional legal strategies have only limited success in bringing about, within the organization, the internal institutional configurations that are necessary if some problem is to be remedied, that is, to induce the ideal authority structures, patterns of information flow, and the like, without which the corporation is not likely to "go straight" in the future . . . . what seems to be needed as a "remedy" is some institutional analogue to the role that responsibility plays in the human being.

The extent to which organizations can be manipulated, particularly when viewed from a structural perspective, suggests that these rehabilitative efforts may have a better chance of success than individual rehabilitation (*Corporate Crime Reporter*, 1987).

Consistent with this approach, remedial interventionist sanctions have been proposed. Organizational probation is the best known and most widely available interventionist sanction. It has been used since the early 1970s (Baldwin, 1974; Levin, 1984; Rush, 1986), though only recently has it gained remedial potential (see Lofquist, 1993a, 1993b; Gruner, 1988, 1993) as a prominent component of the federal organizational sentencing guidelines. In taking this step, the Sentencing Commission made progress in efforts to clear away "the massive underbrush of doctrine stemming from the too-facile application of notions of individual responsibility to corporations" (Friedman, 1979:173) and develop instead organization-specific criminal law to deal with organizational misconduct. As Geraghty (1979:364-365) argued "judicially ordered restructuring of limited, discrete corporate decisionmaking procedures can better achieve the goals of corporate criminal prosecutions than can fines." More specifically, organizational probation encourages or mandates as conditions of probation that defendant organizations address the structural sources of crime within the organization by, for example, establishing a compliance program, conducting a performance audit, or improving internal communication and reporting structures.

Thus, rather than positing a relationship between government and business that protects the decisional prerogatives of business, but seeks to control crime by externally influencing these decisions, structure-based sanctions seek to control crime by altering organizational structures and processes directly (Rush, 1986; Curran, 1986; Gruner, 1988; Coffee, Gruner & Stone, 1988; Metzger, 1984; Metzger & Schwenk, 1990). Their central theoretical logic is that in those cases where organizational misconduct is linked to the structural characteristics of the organization rather than to the motives of particular individuals within the organization, changing those structures holds promise for controlling misconduct.

Though organizational probation is the only politics-based sanction to be made part of American sentencing law, other such sanctions have been proposed. Many of these proposals center on expansion of stakeholder rights (Kelley, 1991; Stevenson, 1974; Stone, 1975; Rothschild-Whitt, 1984; Rothschild & Russell, 1986; Gautschi & Jones, 1987; Barnett, 1981). Arising out of Coleman's observation that a key characteristic of corporate society is the asymmetrical power enjoyed by corporations relative to individuals, these latter approaches seek to create and/or empower countervailing organizations (Galbraith, 1956). These organizations may be community, labor, environmental, or consumer-based, to name only the more likely possibilities. Suggested approaches to stakeholder empowerment include granting stakeholders representation on boards of directors and requiring management consultation with stakeholders in certain specified areas of decisionmaking (Stone, 1975). Such requirements are more intrusive than those usually associated with organizational probation, and have not met with success in the political arena despite some advocacy, particularly in the 1970s (*Los Angeles Times*, 1979; Stone, 1975; Carnoy & Shearer, 1980; Kelley, 1991).

REGULATORY RELATIONS
IN CORPORATE CRIME CONTROL

The final issue in the study of corporate crime is the role of state-business relations in corporate crime control. This is the most recent and least studied of the four issues, emerging as a focus of debate only within the last decade or so. Prior to that time, agency logic was unrivaled in its approach toward explaining and designing regulatory relations. Since then, alternative approaches deriving from different paradigmatic conceptions of the nature of corporate behavior have been recognized (see Table 1.2). Among those who advance agency logic, assumptions of rationality and optimality on the part of state and corporate actors lead to a view of regulation as a matter of striking the appropriate balance of power between business and state actors. The central variable in these analyses, providing the axis along which the views of agency theorists are arrayed, is the size of the state regulatory apparatus. Market-oriented agency theorists, who view the state as adequately or excessively aggressive in its posture toward business, favor a small regulatory state and greater reliance on market mechanisms as a means to facilitate efficient capital accumulation. Conflict-oriented agency theorists, who view the state as subservient to the interests of business, favor a larger regulatory state as a means to exercise necessary control over the profit-oriented designs of capitalists.

In the view of structure theorists, the issue is not so much the amount or severity of existing regulations, but rather the posture of state actors toward regulated corporations. More specifically, structure theorists assert that because corporate structures and cultures, rather than rational actors, are the source of corporate crime, regulation is improved to the extent that regulators take a negotiative, educative, and reformist posture toward regulated corporations. This posture allows regulators to steer corporations toward compliance, minimizing the antagonism that accompanies adversarial relations, while maintaining a viable state presence in the case of corporate recalcitrance. This distinction parallels the larger distinction between corporatism, which is characterized by cooperative, planning-oriented relations between business, labor, and the state (King, 1986; Panitch, 1980; Schmitter, 1985), and free market capitalism or state-centered socialism, which presume more adversarial relations between business and state actors.

Agency Model. Edwin Sutherland, the dean of American criminology and of the study of white-collar crime, stated that effective corporate criminal law enforcement:

> calls for a clear-cut opposition between the public and the government, on the one side, and the businessmen who violate the law, on the other. This clear-cut opposition does not exist and the absence of this opposition is evidence of the lack of organization against white-collar crime. What is, in theory, a war loses much of its conflict because of the fraternization between the two forces. White-collar crimes continue because of this lack of organization on the part of the public (1949/1983:257).

This statement nicely illustrates the agency approach to regulatory relations, though using the vocabulary of a conflict-oriented agency theorist. In it, Sutherland contrasts an adversarial regulatory posture to a captured regulatory posture, arguing that regulatory relations necessarily represent a conflict between opposing business and state actors and interests.

As noted above, this conflict can be viewed from opposing positions within the agency perspective. Market-oriented agency theorists view the state as an impediment to the efficient and effective operations of individual businesses, the economy, and society more generally. Efforts to minimize state regulation of business are thus advocated because these efforts improve the regulatory functions of the market (market discipline), thereby reducing corporate misconduct, while also delivering economic and social goods (Friedman, 1962; Parker, 1993). Recent federal efforts to provide regulatory relief, such as President Bush's Council on Competitiveness (Shute, 1991), exemplify this argument. To the extent that a state regulatory apparatus remains, it is argued that this regulation should mimic as much as possible the operations of the market, relying on fines and other financial incentives and disincentives, and minimizing the use of the criminal law due to its failure to provide a meaningful alternative to noncriminal adjudication. This classical statement of free market economics has enjoyed considerable resurgence in recent years with the growth of the law and economics movement.

Table 1.2
Regulation and Sanctioning

State Posture Toward Business	
Adversarial	

Small Fines
Weak Enforcement
	Large Fines
	Aggressive Enforcement
	Parallel Proceedings Against
	    Individuals and
	    Organizations

State Sanctioning Limited ——————————————————— Substantial Capacity	
Voluntary Compliance Corporate Social Responsibility Negative	Enforced Self-Regulation Organizational Probation

Advocates of this view also often support negotiative relations between business and the state in the event of regulation (Sigler & Murphy, 1988, 1991), a position identified herein as consistent with the structure perspective. To clear up this potential inconsistency, it should be noted that support for negotiative regulatory relations without accompanying support for the ability of the state to meaningfully intervene in the event that negotiations do not bring an end to corporate misconduct is in fact an argument for deregulation. Such arrangements ultimately rely on voluntarism. By leaving the state without the means to sanction corporations, underlying assumptions of rationality and conflicting interests are being made while also being masked behind the essential powerlessness of the state. Negotiation cannot truly occur between such asymmetrical parties.

Conflict-oriented agency theorists, such as Sutherland, view extant regulatory relations as excessively skewed towards the interests of business. Improved regulation, it is argued, can only come by increasing the power of the state to reign in the excesses of corporations (Nader, Green & Seligman, 1976; Snider, 1987, 1990; Pearce & Tombs, 1990; Barrile, 1993, 1994). Consistent with agency logic, these theorists support substantially higher fines as a means to divest the corporation of increased profits sought through corporate crime. Pearce and Tombs, for example, explicitly reject the view that "where regulations are violated, such violations are the result of factors other than pure economic calculation on the part of the corporation" (1990:424). Efforts to increase the distance between regulator and regulated are also supported through laws limiting "revolving door" personnel movement (Simon & Eitzen, 1993; Waldman, 1989). Negotiative relations are rejected as incapable of adequately reigning in the profit-motivated designs of corporate actors, particularly in a capitalist state, where state actors enjoy, at best, only limited autonomy from business (Snider, 1990). Imprisonment of managers, harsh individual and organizational fines, and other measures are favored (Barrile, 1993; Pearce & Tombs, 1990).

Structure Model. All too often, structure theorists argue, the primary distinction in regulatory enforcement is between more enforcement and less enforcement or deregulation. Former EPA Administrator William Ruckleshaus recently made this point. Discussing the deregulatory efforts of the early 1980s, he stated:

> [t]he public got the message by every kind of language—body language, everything else—that we were going to abandon the ends of clean air, clean water. That had the unfortunate result of discrediting the argument over means, which is where the debate ought to be (quoted in Harris and Milkis, 1989:265).

As Ruckleshaus suggests, the importance and variability of the form of the relationship between state and business is lost in traditional approaches to regulation.

In recent years, there has developed a sizable theoretical and empirical literature on the relationship between the form and the effectiveness of regulatory law enforcement (Reich, 1981; Frank, 1984; Braithwaite, 1982; Snider, 1990; Sigler & Murphy, 1988, 1991; Pearce & Tombs, 1990; Hawkins, 1984, 1990, 1992; Hutter, 1988, 1993; Hawkins & Hutter, 1993). Drawing from this literature, structure theorists suggest that corporate compliance is most likely where state-business relations are negotiative and where corporations are involved actively in the creation and monitoring of compliance strategies (Bardach & Kagan, 1982; Braithwaite, 1984, 1985a; Shover, Clelland & Lynxwiler, 1986; Braithwaite & Fisse, 1985). Under such circumstances, it is argued, business resistance is minimized, state resource expenditures are reduced, and important business input is provided. Also, because corporations generally have greater resources than regulators (Frank & Lombness, 1988; Bardach & Kagan, 1982; DeVos, 1985), a cooperative approach combats information scarcity and resource imbalance.

In his work on what he terms "enforced self-regulation," Braithwaite has developed the most fully elaborated and investigated model of negotiative regulatory relations (Braithwaite, 1982, 1985c, 1989b; Braithwaite & Fisse, 1985; Braithwaite & Pettit, 1990; Fisse & Braithwaite, 1993). His primary point is that cooperative regulatory relations, modeled on enforced self-regulation, are the most effective and realistic means to control corporate conduct. The policy implications of this approach are that corporations should be granted the power and the burden to develop compliance strategies for regulations, and that the adequacy and efficacy of these strategies should be approved and monitored by regulators. By "allowing each organization in advance to register principles of accountability consonant with its unique corporate culture" (Braithwaite & Fisse, 1985:336), business input is maximized and subsequent business opposition is minimized. State oversight and approval of these plans increases the likelihood that they are good faith programs and that they will be implemented in a manner that results in organizational change.

Additionally, as developed by Braithwaite, effective compliance monitoring involves ensuring that internal compliance officials enjoy autonomy from production and marketing managers, receive mandatory periodic compliance reports, and conduct inspections. These inspections are limited in number and focus on education, persuasion, and open communications rather than on reporting violations and punishing violators. This approach reduces enforcement costs, establishes clear lines of responsibility for wrongdoing, tailors regulations to specific industries and firms, and increases company commitment to compliance. In the event of continued violations, Braithwaite (1982) proposes that escalating penalties be available to regulators. Application of these penalties, including individual criminal liability, fines, and structural reforms, is facilitated by the identification of lines of communication and locations of responsibility contained in the compliance plan. As a rule, however, persuasion should be the first regulatory approach; punishment being used only in cases of continued noncompliance.

After having developed this approach, Braithwaite analyzed the pharmaceutical (1984) and coal mining (1985a) industries to evaluate the relative effectiveness of adversarial and negotiative regulatory strategies. In the coal mining industry, he found that adversarial regulatory efforts did not improve compliance rates. In fact, compliance and productivity were highest where nonadversarial regulatory relations predominated. Braithwaite explained this by noting that because enforcement resources are limited, punishments are easily absorbed and nonconstructive, and violations are not always intentional, an adversarial approach creates resistance among industry without providing the state adequate resources (material or political) to tightly control business. He concluded that regulators should have the flexibility to choose between persuasion and punishment as the situation warrants. Through further research, Braithwaite (1985c) argues that law abiding corporations do not share a general compliance structure. Rather, they develop compliance systems based on their own culture, structure, environment, and personality. This provides evidence that effective compliance systems cannot be imposed externally by formula. Law abiding structures are better developed by the corporation and then approved externally. Further theoretical elaboration and empirical support for this model can be found in the large body of research generated by the Oxford Centre for Socio-Legal Studies, particularly the works of Hawkins (1984, 1992) and Hutter (1988, 1993).

The empirical origins of negotiative regulatory strategies, then, are twin recognitions: that corporate crime is largely organizational in origins and that corporate crime control is a political endeavor. From this, structure theorists develop a regulatory scheme that is both amenable to the "moral resources" of American society, which holds business in high regard and imposes sanctions on business only reluctantly (Lipset & Schneider, 1987; Hans & Lofquist, 1992) and consistent with the way organizations operate. Too often, justifiable outrage at the excesses of corporate conduct leads to impractical and likely ineffective control strategies. Large fines fall victim to the "deterrence trap" (Coffee, 1979-1980) and punish the wrong parties; adversarial relations misuse limited resources, place punishment above restitution, remediation, and other community benefits that may be gained through negotiation, and create cultures of regulatory resistance (Bardach & Kagan, 1982; Braithwaite & Pettit, 1990); externally developed structural reforms may excessively impinge on business activity and foster strong opposition not only among business, but also within the courts (Braithwaite, 1982; Braithwaite & Fisse, 1985).

Despite understandable retributivist sentiments, structure theorists argue that crime control, in particular corporate crime control, is a fundamentally social activity which must, to be effective, conform to social conditions. Where business is strong and regulatory resources are limited, control efforts that emphasize negotiated remedies and maximize persuasion are more likely to influence organizational behavior. Punitive measures, necessary in cases of continued noncompliance, should be finely tuned to impact the corporation without excessively harming stakeholders. This is the approach taken in the organizational probation provisions developed by the Sentencing Commission. Organizations are granted the power to develop compliance plans, but the development and implementation of this plan are monitored by the courts to assess its adequacy for the task at hand and to assure its meaningful implementation.

CONCLUSION: POINTS OF DIVERGENCE
AND CONTACT

This introduction has provided the framework and rationale for the organization of this book, while also offering a framework for the larger study of corporate crime. In the absence of an overarching theoretical schema such as that provided herein, the linkages between separate issue-based analyses of corporate crime and separate theoretical understandings of these issues are largely unseen. This insularity is to some extent the product of disciplinary boundaries, with legal scholars most interested in issues of liability and sanctioning, economists most concerned with sanctioning, and sociologists most attentive to explaining criminal conduct and exploring regulatory relations. Supplying a common theoretical framework and allowing contributors from different disciplines and theoretical perspectives to use their own voices in articulating their positions provides a way to unite these separate analyses and disciplines in a common effort to improve our understanding of corporate crime.

NOTES

[1]   Federal Organizational Sentencing Guidelines went into effect on November 1, 1991 (U.S. Sentencing Commission, 1991a), and govern offense conduct occurring after that date.

[2]   In some of this literature (see for example, Polinsky & Shavell, 1992; Shavell, 1985, 1990), the organization vanishes from the analysis. The individual becomes the sole unit of analysis, and therefore the sole location of agency and the sole target of control strategies.

[3]   Orland (1980:503n) points out that a number of the most important and innovative works in the area of corporate crime have been notes written by law students. This pattern can be dated at least to Dershowitz (1961), and includes Kriesberg (1976), Geraghty (1979), Katzmann (1980), *Yale Law Journal* (1982b), and *Harvard Law Review* (1979), suggesting greater willingness on the part of the students to venture to the margins of corporation and criminal law.

[4]   Application of criminal liability to corporations for non-economic offenses has been slower to develop and is still often rejected by judges and juries (see Swigert & Farrell, 1980-1981). Recent research on civil jurors involved in corporate cases found that jurors had difficulty in conceptualizing the civil liability of organizations (Hans & Lofquist, 1992).

[5]   See Kunen (1994) for a detailed description of the largely successful efforts of automakers, particularly Ford, to use connections at the highest levels of government to weaken and delay auto safety regulations.

6   Despite the growth of organizational theory and of the study of corporate crime beginning with the works of Simon and Sutherland, respectively, in the 1940s, the theoretical linkages between the fields have been only recently explored. In an article entitled "Decision Making Models and the Control of Corporate Crime," Kriesberg (1976) took the important step of applying Graham Allison's (1971) models of organizational decisionmaking to corporate crime control. Though path-breaking, this analysis was limited by its failure to fully develop structural alternatives to agency-based sanctions (see Fisse, 1978; Lofquist, 1992). Since this initial effort, the structure model of corporate crime control has been steadily elaborated (Orland, 1980; Stone, 1975, 1981; Katzmann, 1980; Ermann & Lundman, 1982; Fisse, 1978; Moore, 1987; Baucus, 1989; Simon, 1979; Schrager & Short, 1978).

Section I

THE CAUSES OF
CORPORATE CRIME

The formal study of corporate crime began with the efforts of sociologists to explain its causes, largely through the application of prominent individual-based theories. The study of its causes remains at the center of concern regarding corporate crime, though the debate has been broadened by the entrance of economists, legal scholars, and organizational theorists. These efforts have generated a large number of case studies and theoretical discourses. The following two chapters provide alternative theoretical approaches, broadly representative of the agency and structure models, to the causes of corporate crime.

In Chapter 2, Cohen and Simpson argue that corporate crime is largely a product of rational individual agency in pursuit of organizational utility. In the classical school tradition, crime is largely an administrative problem; understanding corporate crime should thus proceed from an effort to understand individual decisionmaking and the failure of organizational and legal constraints on this decisionmaking. However, through consideration of a number of non-pecuniary and organizational structural influences on decisionmaking, Cohen and Simpson provide a broader understanding of the agency model than used elsewhere in this volume (they include a formal model of rationality). Drawing from criminological control and opportunity theories, the roles of community bonds, reputational considerations, and other sources of containment on individual behavior are considered. Stated otherwise, if agency and structure perspectives were arrayed on a continuum, this chapter more closely approximates a structure model that do many other works within the agency model. Although they view corporate crime as being the result of rational individual decisions, those decisions are influenced by many of the "structural" characteristics identified as being of most importance to structuralists.

In Chapter 3, Ermann and Rabe develop a specifically organizational structural model of corporate crime. The causes of corporate crime, they argue, are located in complex organizational structures and simultaneous pursuit by organizational subunits of different and sometimes conflicting organizational goals. These structures effect organizational decisionmaking, communication, and control efforts to such an extent that it becomes difficult to think of the organization as a coherent, unitary entity. What most clearly distinguishes this approach from the structure-influenced agency model of Cohen and Simpson is the substantial skepticism Ermann and Rabe express about the foreseeability of organizational outcomes. Whatever the constraints on rationality identified by Cohen and Simpson, organizational outcomes are largely foreseeable to decisionmakers in their model, at least in a probabilistic sense. For Ermann and Rabe, however, foreseeability is compromised by the complex web of sub-units, sub-goals, and sub-decisions that comprise such organizational outcomes as work conditions, factory emissions, and new products.

Despite these differences, as the foregoing suggests, these two chapters clearly identify one of the central points readers are likely to draw from this book: the points of contact and divergence between agency and structure theories. Different theories rarely fully diverge from one another; particularly in practice, neat theoretical distinctions often weaken to reveal the role of insights common to an opposing theoretical tradition. For example, while Cohen and Simpson argue that economic utility maximization is constrained by environmental and individual nonmonetary considerations, insights suggestive of organizational considerations not always explored by classical theorists, Ermann and Rabe view rationality and profitability as important but poorly operationalized goals, hindered by the extent to which escalating commitments to particular courses of actions shape organizational decisions toward these actions.

2

The Origins of Corporate Criminality: Rational Individual and Organizational Actors

Mark A. Cohen
Vanderbilt University

Sally S. Simpson
University of Maryland—College Park

INTRODUCTION

The purpose of this chapter is to provide a comprehensive and testable model of rational choices to explain why corporate crime occurs. The basic premise is that corporate crime occurs as a result of choices made by managers or other individuals within an organization. Our approach is grounded in the economic theory of rational choice under uncertainty. However, we take a more expansive view of the traditional economic model in order to incorporate many of the non-pecuniary components of an individual's well-being. That is, we allow individuals to have qualities such as moral inhibitions, concern for family and community reputation, and so forth. Our approach is also informed by a structuralist position in that the choice of crime occurs in the context of a business organization and is influenced by organizational factors that may affect the costs and benefits of individual actions.

Before examining the causes of corporate crime, it is important to define the boundaries of "corporate crime" itself. Unlike street crime, which often requires traditional *mens rea* components, corporations may be charged with strict and/or vicarious liability crimes without any requirement of intent. The most expansive definition of corporate crime would include any corporate activity (or outcome) that society has deemed to be illegal. This is the approach taken by many empirical researchers in this field (e.g., Clinard et al., 1979), where "corporate crime" often includes regulatory violations that were never charged under criminal laws and probably never could have been charged as crimes. A more restrictive definition would define corporate crime to be only those incidents in which a firm has been prosecuted and convicted of criminal wrongdoing.

For our purposes, we are more interested in explaining behavior than in explaining why society has deemed a certain action to be criminal or why a prosecutor has decided to bring criminal charges instead of relying on a regulatory agency to control corporate activities. There is often little difference between corporate criminal behavior and corporate regulatory noncompliance. As Reiss and Tonry (1993:7) note, the main difference between the two tends to be in the purpose of government enforcement and the nature of remedies. Civil and administrative violations are generally dealt with through attempts to control organizational behavior and to ensure compliance, not to punish past actions or deter future activities. In contrast, criminal violations tend to be those in which enforcement agencies are more concerned about deterrence and/or punishment. But these distinctions are driven by the legal system—not by any inherent differences in the violation themselves. Thus, we can mostly ignore this debate and concentrate on the theory and empirical evidence of why corporate actions (or inactions) occur that are contrary to society's rules. If forced to be explicit, we would define corporate crime to be any act that *could* be charged under criminal laws, under the theory that many crimes go undetected or unprosecuted for lack of evidence, lack of government resources, *or* because they are simply deemed by government authorities as better handled through civil remedies. However, as will be discussed below, there is nothing magical about the label "crime." The model we present can be applied to almost any corporate action.

UNDERLYING THEORETICAL MODEL
AND EMPIRICAL IMPLICATIONS

This section provides a unifying theoretical framework in which corporate crime is the outcome of decisions by rational, utility-maximizing individuals who have the ability to incur criminal liability on behalf of the corporation. However, unlike traditional street crime or white-collar crime, there is often an additional layer of control and decisionmaking that affects the decision to commit crime. That layer of control is the corporation itself, which may provide incentives or disincentives to commit (or prevent) criminal activity within the corporation. The model we present is thus one of individual decisionmaking in the context of external constraints. It combines many features of the "rational choice theory of corporate crime" described in Paternoster and Simpson (1993) with the "principal-agency theory" explanation described by Alexander and Cohen (1995). Thus, we assume that individuals weigh the expected costs against the expected benefits of illegal behavior (which may include nonpecuniary costs and benefits such as self-respect and moral behavior), *and* that owners and/or managers of corporations weigh the expected costs and benefits of monitoring their employees to deter (or encourage) corporate crime.[1]

INDIVIDUAL DECISIONMAKING

Although we are interested in actions (or inactions) taken on behalf of a corporation that may be deemed criminal, we focus on individual decisionmakers within the corporation. There are various individual decisionmakers within any organization, including owners, managers, and employees. Individuals are assumed to be rational-expected utility maximizers. "Utility" is nothing more than an economist's jargon to represent the personal satisfaction one receives from various pecuniary and nonpecuniary pleasures in life. Utility may depend on many nonpecuniary factors besides monetary income and wealth. In particular, utility functions are likely to include components such as: (1) monetary income, (2) leisure time and activities that enhance one's quality of life, and (3) reputation and stature in the family, community, and among peers. One reason this characterization might seem too restrictive is that it precludes individual behavior that is simply deemed to be "moral" without conferring any of the above benefits (see, e.g., Etzioni, 1988). However, moral behavior can be incorporated into this analysis either by adding an explicit constraint on individual behavior, by making it part of the collectivity via concerns of the family, community and peers (Etzioni, 1988:253), by introducing a fourth factor, "self-respect" or moral inhibitions.[2] Following Paternoster and Simpson (1993), we adopt the latter approach.

Even in the absence of moral inhibitions, there are various constraints on individual behavior that are likely to reduce the chance that crime will occur. These constraints include both formal and informal sanctions offered by institutions such as the criminal justice system, employment contracts, extraorganizational normative controls (Reichman, 1993), religious doctrines, and family or peer pressure. As noted by Paternoster and Simpson (1993), it is not the actual probability of punishment that matters from the individual's perspective. Instead, it is the perceived certainty and severity of punishment that matters. Thus, expected utility depends on the individual's expectations of these parameters, not necessarily the objective measures that researchers might observe *ex post facto.* Closely related to this concept of perceived certainty and severity of punishment is the fact that there are limits to the amount of information and experience brought to the decision process by decisionmakers, i.e., knowledge is bounded.

Formally, the individual's utility maximization problem can be character-ized as:

Maximize Expected Utility (Income, Quality of Life, Reputation, Self-Respect) subject to:

Income = f (Wage Rate, Hours of Work, Probability and Severity of Penalty if Crime is Committed)

Quality of Life = f (Value of Time, Hours of Work, Value of Freedom, Probability and Severity of Prison and Expected Incarceration Time if Crime is Committed)

Reputation = f (Existing Reputation, Expected Reduction in Reputa-tion if Crime is Detected)

Self Respect = f (Existing Self-Respect and Loss in Self-Respect if Crime is Committed)

Given the above scenario, why do some people commit corporate crimes while others do not? Rational individuals weigh the expected benefits from com-mitting a crime against the expected costs. The expected costs of committing a crime might include both formal sanctions (probability of detection, severity of punishment, etc.), informal sanctions or "psychic" costs to the individual (lack of self-respect, loss of reputation, etc.), and the cost of executing the crime itself. The expected benefits of the crime are increased income (or preserving income that might otherwise be lost through job dislocations), more leisure time, higher status within the organization, etc. Thus, corporate crime is the result of individual decisions made in the face of various opportunities and constraints.

Although the general utility maximizing model applies to all individuals, not every person has the same propensity to commit a crime—even if they face the same external constraints. Some people have more moral inhibitions than others; some are extremely averse to going to jail while others are less concerned about the consequences of such punishment. Put differently, individ-uals may place different weights on the various arguments in their utility func-tions. Some individuals may place virtually zero weight on moral inhibitions (and thus be likely to commit a crime if it appeared profitable), while others place a very high weight on that factor (and will almost never commit a crime even if it is profitable). Similarly, the constraints we identified above may be more or less binding for different individuals. Individuals will differ in their current job status, their economic status, stature within the community, etc. For example, individuals with little reputation in the community may find this con-straint less binding; they have little reputation to lose if they are caught com-mitting a crime, and thus the "cost" to them in lost reputation is very small. Those with extremely high reputations in the community will have a lot to lose and thus pay an extremely high price for committing a crime.[3]

Another important factor that affects the choice of crime is opportunity. The opportunity to commit crime will vary by firm, industry and managerial position within a firm. Potentially, every transaction made by a manager or a firm within an industry carries the opportunity to act criminally. For instance, every sale that is contracted carries with it the opportunity to illegally tie the sale of one product to another. Every accounting entry may be fraudulent or not. Day-to-day production can meet emission standards or violate them. These opportunities will vary, obviously depending on firm size, type of business, regulatory environment, and so forth. Opportunities also carry different detection risks. It may be easier to violate emissions standards for one day and avoid a random emissions audit than it is to set up a price-fixing conspiracy and risk that one of the potential co-conspirators will report you and your firm to the Justice Department. Thus, some crime opportunities are qualitatively "better" than others.

Despite the fact that the above model assumes the individual "chooses" a level of illegal activity, we do not require that there be any actual "intent" to commit the crime. Instead, strict liability crimes can be accommodated by realizing that all business decisions involve some degree of risk and hence there is at least some probabalistic chance that a strict liability crime will take place. Instead of "intending" to commit the crime, we might think of the individual decisionmaker as having chosen a level of care designed to prevent the crime from occurring. Thus, the individual's action becomes a "causal factor" in the strict liability crime, but not necessarily the only factor. For example, although nobody at Exxon intended to cause an oil spill, some employees might have taken actions that increased the likelihood that such an accident would eventually happen. Although there was no one decision point whether or not to "spill oil," there were many decision points by many individuals—all of which increased (or decreased) the probability that a spill would occur. Choices were made by the captain of the ship about whether or not he should drink prior to commanding the ship, whether or not to delegate responsibility to a second mate on the ship, etc. Choices were made by top management about how much monitoring should be done on employees who are reformed alcoholics, how many layers of control should be in place on an oil tanker, what safety and oil spill containment equipment should be on board or nearby a tanker, etc. Thus, even though we have formulated this model in terms of illegal activities, it applies equally to actions that raise or lower the probability of an illegal activity occurring. Throughout the chapter, when we refer to individuals as having chosen to commit a crime, we really mean that they have chosen an action (or inaction) that leads to criminal liability.

CORPORATIONS AS DECISIONMAKERS

Instead of focusing on individual actions, we can also model crime as being the outcome of company-level characteristics. If we assume for a moment that corporate policies and decisions are perfectly carried out by employees, then the corporation can be examined in this manner. In particular, assuming the goal of the corporation is to maximize long-run profits, we can easily write down a model of expected profit maximization. The expected costs of committing a crime are compared to the expected benefits and the firm commits the crime if it is in its best interest to do so. As in the previous section, the expected costs of committing the crime depend on the probability and severity of corporate punishment. There is a natural analog to individual reputation as the firm's reputation with consumers, the government, suppliers and buyers (among others) may also be hurt by a criminal conviction, which in turn may hurt future sales/profitability (see, e.g., Karpoff & Lott, 1993).

Formally, the firm can be characterized as an expected profit-maximizing unit subject to various constraints on their activities:

Maximize Expected Profit (Price of Product x Total Sales of Product, Net Benefit from Illegal Activity, Cost of Production/Distribution, Sanction for Illegal Activity) subject to:

Price x Sales = f (Market Demand Curve Facing Firm, Moral/Social Responsibility of Firm, Existing Employee Morale and Loss of Morale if Crime is Committed)

Net Benefit from Illegal Activity = f (Benefits from Crime, Cost of Committing Illegal Activity, Cost of Avoiding Detection)

Cost of Production/Distribution = f (Price of Inputs, Technology; Existing Employee Morale and Loss of Morale if Crime is Committed)

Sanction for Illegal Activity = f (Probability & Severity of Monetary Penalty if Crime is Committed, Probability and Severity of Organizational Probation if Crime is Committed, Existing Reputation and Expected Reduction in Reputation if Crime is Detected and Resulting Loss in Sales, Profits, etc.)

The model of corporate decisionmaking we presented is general enough to allow for the case where the firm ignores any social responsibility of business unless the firm finds that its interest (i.e., long run profitability) is best served by being socially responsible, as well as the case where social responsibility is assumed to be one of the constraints on profit maximization itself. For example, a firm that has an effective monopoly on a product might decide not to charge the "monopoly" price solely on moral grounds, or because doing so will hurt the firm's reputation and ultimately lead consumers to find alternatives, lobby for government antitrust actions, etc. In the first case, the "social responsibility" operates as a direct constraint on the price charged. In the latter case, there may be little or no inherent "social responsibility" constraint on firm behavior; instead, the firm is simply recognizing the fact that "socially irresponsible" behavior is likely to be punished by society in one manner or another.

Thus far, our model of corporate decisionmaking works if the policies and decisions of the company are perfectly carried out by employees. This is obviously true when the company is a sole-proprietorship, and is likely to be true in small closely held companies, where the owner is the manager, the firm management structure is flat, and there are few employees (e.g., Braithwaite & Makkai, 1991). As discussed in the next section, however, as the size of the firm expands and the cost of monitoring the actions of managers and employees increases, the owner's desires might not be carried out. In that case, a divergence of interests between the owners and managers (or employees) of the firm might result in more or less crime than the above model would predict.

INDIVIDUAL DECISIONMAKING WITHIN A PRINCIPAL AGENT CONTEXT

Hidden from view and exogenous to our earlier discussion were other choices being made by decisionmakers that directly affected the constraints that our individual faced when determining whether or not to commit a crime. Although there may be varying degrees of "explicit choice" involved, the government ultimately chooses the probability and severity of punishment and society chooses what social norms to adopt and hence how illegal activities will be viewed in the family and community.[4]

Similarly, added complexity arises when we introduce the corporation into the model. As noted in the previous section, there may be a divergence of interests between the owner of the firm and its employees. This "principal-agent" relationship between owners and managers of the firm may be an important element of the cause of corporate crime. This relationship causes a divergence of interests between the owner and manager of the firm that may result in more (or less) corporate crime than the owner would prefer (Alexander & Cohen, 1995). It is similar to the divergence of interests between an individual who is contemplating the commission of a crime and society or the government. Because of this divergence of interests, the owners of the corporation will decide what rewards and punishments its managers and employees will receive, including monetary compensation, promotions or firings, and non-pecuniary benefits of the job. The corporation will also decide the probability of internal detection and punishment.

To illustrate, assume there is only one owner and one manager of the firm.[5] The owner (principal) hires the manager (agent) with the expectation that she will earn a reasonable profit for the owner after receiving an agreed upon wage. Suppose further that there are two ways to achieve a given level of profit: a legal method (competition) and an illegal one (price fixing). The legal method requires more work on the part of the manager, as she has to compete in the marketplace. The illegal method allows the same level of profits but requires significantly less time and work. Thus, the manager can increase "leisure time" and not work as many hours, while at the same time keeping the owner's profit levels the same. However, suppose that if the manager is caught price fixing, the firm will be fined by the government and perhaps lose some customers as its reputation is diminished. In that case, the owner would clearly prefer the competitive method to the illegal price fixing one. Thus, there is a divergence of interests between the owner and manger. In the extreme, where the owner cannot observe the manager's actions (unless they are uncovered by the government), and the manager is not held personally liable for the price fixing arrangement, the outcome is clear: the manager will commit the crime despite the fact that the company owners do not want the crime committed. This example is obviously a simplification that ignores some of the other constraints on the manager's action, such as moral inhibition, reputation in the community, etc. However, the point is that as long as the owner cannot perfectly monitor the daily actions of the manager, there is the risk that the expected utility of illegal activity to the manager exceeds the expected utility of legal activity and that the reverse holds for the owner. The opposite might also hold, of course, where the owner prefers illegal activity but the manager does not.

Given the above scenario, we would expect the owner of the firm to put mechanisms in place to encourage managers to conduct business in a legal fashion (or illegal manner if that is in the owner's self interest). These mechanisms might involve costly monitoring devices such as internal audits, requiring extra layers of management approval for certain actions, or random inspections by third parties. They might also include monetary incentives such as promotions to managers whose units are crime-free and demotions or dismissals of managers whose units commit corporate crimes. Of course, if owners want to encourage crime, the opposite incentives might be put into place.

Even if owners of firms had no direct contact with corporate criminal behavior, their internal corporate policies might encourage or discourage corporate crime. In that sense, corporate owners can easily be linked as a causal factor in criminal activity. Although they may not explicitly choose to commit a crime, their decisions on the size and intensity of internal compliance programs, compensation and performance evaluation processes, strategic plans, and so on may be thought of as choosing a "probability" that crime will be committed by one of their agents. Indeed, this principal-agent relationship provides some theoretical justification for "vicarious liability" of corporations for their employees actions. Although the discussion has thus far focused on the owner-manager relationship, there is also a principal-agent relationship between managers and employees with the same fundamental characteristics. Managers might encourage or discourage corporate crimes that are committed by employees on behalf of the firm.

EMPIRICAL IMPLICATIONS OF MODEL

The models described above are complex and involve many interactions that make empirical specifications and testing problematic. Since we have specified several different decisionmakers (government, firms, managers, and employees), the same criminal event may be jointly determined by decisions made at several (or all) of these levels. Thus, a fully integrated empirical model would simultaneously account for each decisionmaker's problem and attempt to estimate reduced form equations for each choice variable. Not only are we unaware of any fully integrated attempts to test such a model, but the full theoretical implications have not been fully explored.[6] For example, although deterrence theory tells us that increasing the penalty to corporations convicted of crime is likely to reduce the incidence of crime, it is possible that just the opposite will happen when firms are held strictly liable for their employees actions. Since the expected cost of punishment is based on both the penalty and the probability of detection, if increased corporate monitoring of employees results in higher detection levels (and not much lower crime), it is possible that the firm is better off decreasing internal monitoring, thereby lowering the chance of being detected for a crime (see Arlen, 1994). In practice, since criminal sanctions tend to be mitigated when firms are shown to be acting in good faith, this may not be a problem.[7]

In theory, many perverse results like the one described above are possible, even if they are unlikely. Although this section describes the empirical implications of a rational decision-making model, whether or not these implications really follow from the model depends on the exact specification, functional form, and parameter estimates that one assumes in writing the model down. At this very theoretical level, we ignore some of these perverse results and concentrate on the "main effects" we expect from the model.

Starting with the firm-level analysis, the model predicts corporate crime to be *negatively* correlated with the probability of detection and the severity of punishment if detected. This includes both government-imposed sanctions and those imposed by the market itself (e.g., loss in firm reputation). The model also predicts that crime rates will vary by industry according to the opportunities to commit crime with "better opportunities" being equivalent to lower costs. Finally, it predicts that firms facing extreme economic disruptions and a higher risk of bankruptcy (or other pernicious financial consequences) will have higher crime rates, as firms that were previously "risk neutral" will now act as though they are "risk loving" and be willing to take less care to prevent crime in exchange for the certainty of higher profits (Cohen, 1987:34).

Returning to the model of individual choice, it is clear that we would expect more corporate crime (all else equal), the less binding various constraints are in the individual utility maximization problem. Thus, we expect crime to be *negatively* correlated with the probability and severity of criminal justice-imposed punishment. If employers do not want corporate crime to take place, we would also expect crime to be negatively correlated with the probability and severity of punishment imposed by employers on employees who take actions that might increase the probability of crime.[8] We also expect there to be less corporate crime when social norms are stronger and when the potential loss to individual reputation is larger. For example, an individual in a high profile professional career may experience a significant loss in reputation and subsequent earnings if forced out of a career through formal debarment or less formal sanctions, whereas a low-level worker who follows a manager's instructions to illegally dispose of a hazardous waste may have little problem finding a job as a blue-collar worker elsewhere. We also expect there to be less crime when individuals perceive the regulatory process to be "fair."

Prior criminal (and non-criminal regulatory) behavior may also be an important explanatory variable in understanding a firm's likelihood of committing a crime. However, this factor may have a positive or negative effect on subsequent criminal behavior. The fact that a firm has previously committed a wrongful act (or has a lack of adequate internal monitoring or prevention programs) may increase the likelihood of subsequent illegal behavior. In addition, prior criminal behavior may serve as a proxy for some underlying explanatory variable that we cannot necessarily observe, such as lack of corporate culture conducive to moral behavior. In a model that does not control for government enforcement levels, prior criminal behavior may simply serve as a proxy for government enforcement to the extent that the government more closely scrutinizes past violators. On the other hand, if sanctions are sufficiently harsh, they might have a "specific deterrence effect" on violators, resulting in less criminal behavior for prior offenders.

There are also several empirical implications of the principal-agency relationship between owners and managers of organizations. If owners do not want crime committed, we expect less crime when owners and managers interests are more aligned (and more crime when they are less aligned). Thus, for example, we would expect less crime when managers of the corporation have a relatively high percentage ownership of the company. (In the extreme, where the owner is the manager, this problem simply disappears.) Similarly, characteristics of the firm or industry that make it more or less costly for companies to monitor their employees will affect the crime rate. Thus, larger firms may have higher crime rates due to the high cost of centralizing internal monitoring and enforcement efforts. Firms also may have higher rates because they operate in markets that are subjected to greater law. Unfortunately, it is virtually impossible to theoretically derive strong hypotheses about many of these factors that might affect the crime rate, since they depend heavily on technology and costs. For example, it is also quite possible that larger firms experience economies of scale in certain monitoring technologies, have more sophisticated personnel management practices, etc. and are thus able to lower their probability of committing a crime relative to their smaller competitors. Thus, the theory does not tell us whether large firms are more or less likely to commit crimes. (By virtue of their size and exposure to criminal opportunities, we would expect there to be more crimes, but not necessarily more crimes on a per employee or per dollar sales basis.)

REVIEW OF EMPIRICAL EVIDENCE

This section reviews the existing empirical evidence on the causes of corporate crime. To empirically validate any theory of the causes of corporate crime would require far more data than we will ever be able to obtain. Ideally, one would like to obtain a sample of firms (along with their employees and management) that committed crimes and compare them to those that did not. Obtaining such a sample is itself problematic, since researchers are only able to observe crimes that are detected and punished by government authorities. Thus, beginning with a sample of convicted corporate offenders introduces a bias in the sample, although the nature of that bias is not obvious. Perhaps these are firms that are easy to catch, perhaps they are firms that are targeted by government authorities for enforcement. Even if one can obtain a random or representative sample of firms that committed corporate crimes, it is not always possible to obtain a comparison group of firms that did not commit crimes, since those firms might have committed crimes that went undetected. Finally, few researchers have been able to obtain comprehensive data on corporations, employees, or managers involved in criminal activities.[9]

Although the previous section outlined a model of rational decisionmaking as opposed to a "structuralist" model (the subject of the next chapter), it is important to keep in mind that our theoretical model includes many organizational and structural variables, as they are important constraints that increase or decrease the costs and opportunities for crime. Thus, our review of the empirical analysis necessarily includes studies that purport to test a structural approach. First, we review studies that have looked at corporate behavior. Next, we examine the little empirical evidence that exists on individual decisionmaking.

EMPIRICAL EVIDENCE ON CORPORATIONS

Prior empirical studies of corporations have been able to explain only a small percentage of the variation in crime rates. Most studies attempting to explain corporate crime rates have focused on a particular type of crime or regulatory violation, such as antitrust (Staw & Szawajkowski, 1975; Simpson, 1986; Jamieson, 1994), OSHA or environmental violations (Hill, Kelley, Agle, Hitt & Hoskisson, 1992). However, following Sutherland's lead (1949), a few studies have examined an entire set of companies over time, such as the Fortune 500 companies (Clinard et al., 1979; Baucus & Near, 1991), or all publicly traded companies (Alexander & Cohen, 1996). Most of these studies include structural variables such as size and financial strength of the organization and its market. Others specify how "results-oriented" internal controls (e.g., incentive systems, divisional evaluations based on rate of return criteria) act as catalysts for corporate wrongdoing (Hill et al., 1992).

For example, Baucus and Near (1991) propose three types of antecedents to corporate crime. First, some factors are external to the firm ("environmental") and involve the growth, uncertainties, complexity, etc. of the industry. Second, some factors are internal characteristics of the firm, such as financial health and size of the firm. Third, some factors are related to the specific crime type itself, such as industry (e.g., differences in corporate culture), prior violations and type of violation (e.g., government procurement fraud may be easier to commit than other forms of fraud). Baucus and Near find only limited support for the hypothesis that environmental factors are associated with corporate crime, with there being some indication of a U-shaped relationship, i.e., more crime at the most scarce and most abundant resources and at the most and least turbulent environments. Beyond that, only size of firm is significant, with larger firms engaging in more crime. The latter result is difficult to interpret, however, since they do not control for size of firm when measuring the crime rate. Larger firms are "exposed" to more opportunities to commit crime and more individuals that need to be monitored. Thus, the larger crime rate may be due to differences in the culture of large firms, or it may be due to the difficulty of monitoring in large organizations. The former argument is a structural one, while the latter is based more on the agency-relationship and individual decisionmaking.

Although most of the variables in the Baucus and Near paper have a "structuralist" foundation, they are also consistent with our model. For example, we indicated that firms in periods of extreme economic uncertainty (which may occur during episodes of extreme decline or growth, see e.g., Simpson, 1986; Yeager, 1986; Jamieson, 1994; Alexander & Cohen, 1996) may act risk loving as they are less concerned by the prospect that their criminal actions will force a bankruptcy.

Other studies, also consistent with our framework, examine more explicitly the nature of internal organizational characteristics and how managerial philosophies, strategies, and evaluation criteria affect corporate misconduct. Hill and his associates (1992) studied 174 Fortune 1000 manufacturing companies and matched reported OSHA and EPA violations with internal organizational data collected in a 1986 mail survey. Results show that the greater the importance top management attached to rate of return criteria in evaluations of divisional performance, the greater the incidence of both OSHA and EPA violations. In a similar vein, Simpson and Koper (1995) examined the antitrust offending of 46 U.S. manufacturing firms between 1963 and 1984 to see whether managerial turnover, CEO background and power, firm decentralization, and product strategy affected offending levels. Offending levels were highest when firms: (1) were headed by CEOs from finance and administrative backgrounds (indicating, potentially, a greater likelihood of "management by numbers" evaluations), (2) had prior offending records, and (3) pursued product-dominant strategies. Offending significantly decreased when there was a change in top management. In general, decentralization was unrelated to offending except for poorly performing companies. The coupling of poor performance with decentralized organizational structure significantly increased antitrust offending.

A few studies have gone beyond organizational and structural characteristics and examined behavioral variables. For example, there is some evidence that corporations respond to government enforcement activities. Block, Nold, and Sidak (1981) found increased antitrust enforcement and the prospect of private legal actions had the deterrent effect of reducing markups in the bread industry. Simpson and Koper (1992) found that recidivism among antitrust offenders was related to the severity of the sanction—suggesting that corporate crime might be the outcome of a rational cost-benefit calculation. Similarly, Cohen (1987) found that the size of oil spills was related to government enforcement intensity, and Magat and Viscusi (1990) found a similar result for water pollution levels of pulp and paper mills.

Finally, Alexander and Cohen (1995) examined how the principal-agency relationship between owners and managers of firms may affect the crime rate. They hypothesized that firms where managers have more at stake in the firm (as measured through higher percentage ownership of the firm's outstanding shares) are more likely to work for the best interest of shareholders. In a matched sample of known criminal and noncriminal publicly traded firms, they found that firms that are more closely held were less likely to commit a crime, which is consistent with the view that owners (shareholders) did not generally prefer crime to be committed on their behalf. Thus, some corporate crime appears to be committed by individuals within a firm despite the fact that it is not in the firm owners' best interest to commit the crime.

EMPIRICAL EVIDENCE ON INDIVIDUALS

There is little direct empirical evidence on the reasons that individuals commit crimes on behalf of their organizations. Most of the evidence to date has been limited to asking potential criminal offenders why they might or might not take criminal actions. Although some of these studies are primarily anecdotal, a handful of studies are based on extensive surveys with business executives, business students, or actual employees or officers. For example, Fisse and Braithwaite (1983) interviewed corporate managers and concluded that the negative effects of publicity weighed heavily on the managers' self-esteem and social relationships, and were more of a deterrent than formal sanctions. Simpson's (1992) interviews with top- and mid-level managers also indicated the greater deterrent value of informal and stigmatic sanctions over criminal justice interventions. Clinard (1983) interviewed retired middle managers of Fortune 500 companies concerning why some corporations were more ethical than others. More than 50 percent stated that top management behavior was the main reason for ethical behavior (or lack thereof), while only 3 percent believed it was due to financial difficulties (Clinard, 1983:54).

Braithwaite and Makkai (1991) surveyed over 400 nursing home managers in Australia and studied the factors these managers claim are important in their decisions about whether or not to comply with the law. Cross-sectional (1991) and over time (Makkai & Braithwaite, 1994) analyses revealed that nursing home executives were undeterred by formal legal sanction threats. Among a myriad of potential sources of legal sanctions, only one had any significant effect on nursing home regulatory compliance (the probability of state level detection) and this effect was dependent on manager's low ranking on an emotionality scale (1994). The cross-sectional data found that managers were less likely to deviate from compliance when they believed in the regulatory standards (moral belief), did not profess belief in a "subculture of resistance" that undermined the legitimacy of the standards, and their organization was not constrained financially (1991:207-211). The panel data, however, failed to replicate the significant effect of belief in standards (1994:358), but did uncover a significant "guilt" effect. Nursing home directors who thought persons responsible for meeting compliance standards should feel guilty when that standard was not met generally scored higher on compliance.

Most of the above studies fail to consider the full range of individual-level influences that we have included in our principal agency/rational choice model of corporate offending. One study that incorporates morality, a full array of formal and informal sanction threats, and perceived benefits into a model of corporate offending is that of Paternoster and Simpson (1995). They administered a factorial survey to business students and business executives taking an executive education seminar. Respondents were given four corporate crime scenarios in which levels of structural and individual-level factors predicted to affect offending decisions (e.g., different managerial level and crime benefits for the manager) were randomized across vignettes. In a series of questions following each scenario, respondents were asked how likely it was that they would offend given scenario conditions and their perceived level of formal and informal sanction costs. Results indicate that intentions to offend are a function of perceived firm benefits (e.g., save a large amount of money, challenge an existing law, and increase firm revenue), the moral climate of the company (the act was common in the firm), the threat of foreign competition, and managerial power (respondents were more likely to offend when ordered to do so by a supervisor).

Additionally, Paternoster and Simpson's findings suggest that offending intentions are constrained by certain and severe legal and/or informal sanctions (deterrent effects from these sanctions overlap), moral inhibitions and the sense of personal shame that would accompany the commission of the act. For the most part, these effects are most salient when directed at the individual, not the firm. Finally, conditional effects were noted. For instance, respondents who scored low on moral beliefs were more likely to take formal legal sanction threats into account. Additional analysis of these data by Elis and Simpson (1995), reveals the constancy of morality as an inhibitor of offending decisions. Respondent's perceptions that an act is immoral deters offending regardless of the type of social cost that may accompany the commitment of the act (e.g., commitment, attachment, and stigmatic costs) and how significant these costs are perceived to be for respondents. Morality effects are noted as well across equations in which informal sanction certainty and severity are treated as multiplicative with informal discovery.

One of the major limitations of the survey approach is that we know what respondents say they would do—but that is not necessarily the same as what they would actually do (or why) in a real circumstance. Economists generally dislike surveys for this reason, while sociologists and other social sciences often rely on surveys as though their results are identical to observing actions. Survey results should be taken with a considerable grain of salt. Respondents may not know how they would act in the scenario posed, or even if they do know, they might "lie" about their likely actions or true motivation. For example, convicted street offenders often blame drugs or alcohol for their criminal activities even though they are unrelated. This is a form of "deviance disavowal" that may reduce the personal guilt associated with the act. Similarly, individuals may respond that they are no more likely to commit a crime when they personally benefit—even if this is untrue. Even with these difficulties, in-depth interviews, study replications, and comparisons of self-reports with official statistics suggest that most respondents are remarkably open about discussing their own and their company's unethical and corporate misconduct (Braithwaite, 1984; Yeager & Kram, 1989; Simpson, 1992; Makkai & Braithwaite, 1994). Thus, while survey results should be viewed cautiously, they cannot be dismissed altogether.

POLICY IMPLICATIONS OF
THE RATIONAL ACTOR MODEL

This section considers the policy implications of the rational actor model of corporate crime. As described above, the rational actor model takes into account three main considerations: (1) Corporate crime is a consequence of an individual's "choice" to either violate the law or to take less than an adequate level of care to prevent an illegal act from occurring; (2) the parameters of the crime decision include individual and organizational constraints and benefits— pecuniary and nonpecuniary; (3) owner and manager/employee interests and constraints do not necessarily correspond.

As we see it, the key policy implications of the rational actor model involve the increased use of social norms, and the manipulation of rewards and sanctions at the corporate and governmental enforcement levels. With its focus on the relationships among informal legal sanctions, moral habituation, the negative consequences to conscience, to relations with significant others, and to future commitments (e.g., job, promotion, good reputation), the model suggests interventions to ensure compliance may need to include programs to socialize and train personnel (and students) about ethical issues. At the same time, compliance programs should identify organizational "hot spots" that motivate illegal activities (e.g., financial stresses, bottom-line performance evaluations, lack of top management commitment to ethical considerations) and incorporate mechanisms for discouraging, identifying, investigating, and responding to crime when it occurs.

Our rational actor model is consistent with policies that incorporate rewards and incentives into governmental regulatory action (along with more traditional punishments). Grabosky (1993) recommends pecuniary and nonpecuniary incentives brought to corporations and managers either directly (via subsidies and tax concessions, price preferences, or through awards and praise) or indirectly (through third party payoffs to whistle-blowers, recognition of good citizens). Grabosky's suggestions build on Ayers and Braithwaite's (1992) idea of "responsive regulation." Responsive regulation advocates building cooperation between regulators and corporations (such as those built into the U.S. Sentencing Commission Guidelines for Organizations) so that firms are rewarded for cooperation and punished when strategies of noncooperation are pursued. This approach assumes that corporate compliance is best achieved through an appropriate mix of cooperation and punitiveness—the exact proportion of which depends on company behaviors and characteristics. Say, for instance, a large publicly traded company discovers wrongdoing through an internal investigation and self-reports the violation to the appropriate agency. Under these circumstances, the firm will be rewarded for self-reporting and for having a reasonably efficient internal compliance program in place. Rewards are financial, in that the monetary sanction assigned to the illegal act will be lessened, and reputational (the firm is acknowledged as a good citizen—which will count positively in any future interactions with criminal justice agencies). However, if top management knew of the wrongdoing, failed to self-report, and chose not to cooperate with governmental investigators, the government retreats from a cooperative relationship with the firm and responds punitively.

Finally, the trend toward strict and/or vicarious liability is also consistent with our model. Specifically, to help ensure that the prosocial interests of owners correspond with those of management, laws that hold top managers accountable for the criminal conduct of lower-level managers and employees should encourage greater oversight and commitment to ethical standards of conduct, especially if, when wrongdoing occurs, all responsible parties are subject to sanction. An extension of liability to directors and/or owners is likely to further this type of oversight and internal control, but may be impractical. Even though criminal liability may not be extended, there is evidence that financial markets might already penalize owners through loss in firm reputation and market valuation.

The discussion above ignores an important limitation on any policy prescription designed to reduce corporate crime. Although society might employ these mechanisms to reduce the incidence of corporate crime, none of these mechanisms come without a "cost" themselves. Thus, as sanctions for antitrust violations become more punitive, for example, we may find that managers forego socially desirable pricing or marketing activities so that they will not risk being falsely accused of an antitrust violation.[10] As corporate officials are increasingly held personally liable and risk going to jail, we may see overly costly prevention programs or, as Bardach and Kagan (1982) caution, "cultures of resistance" developing as regulation is perceived to be unreasonable. In other words, the social cost of each proposed mechanism must be weighed against its social benefits. Since most corporate crime occurs in the context of other socially desirable activities, there will always be some risk of "overdeterrence." From a purely economic standpoint, whether we have "too much" or "too little" corporate crime is purely an empirical question. In contrast, sociologists may also consider the moral dimension of whether or not there is too much corporate crime.

CONCLUDING REMARKS

Both theoretical and empirical research support the notion that the origins of corporate crime can be traced to rational decisions made by individuals within an organization. Although these decisions may explicitly involve choices to commit a crime, they may also be choices that are not illegal in themselves, but instead affect the probability that a firm will commit an illegal act. As the theoretical framework makes clear, the mechanisms that affect criminal behavior are complex and involve more than one decisionmaker. Without necessarily assessing any "moral blame," we argue that whether a corporate crime occurs is jointly determined by such diverse decisionmakers as employees, managers, firm owners, government regulators (who decide on a level of enforcement/detection), legislators (who define illegal activities and set maximum penalties), judges or sentencing commissions (who put a "price" on committing a crime), and society (through social norms).

Although the literature is still very sparse, there is growing empirical evidence that the frequency of corporate crime is correlated with factors such as: (1) financial health of the firm, (2) perceived benefits to individuals who decide to commit a crime, (3) perceived risk and severity of punishment if a crime is detected, (4) moral climate or "culture" of the company, (5) industry or firm-specific factors that affect the opportunity to commit crime, and (6) degree of internal controls within a company. Despite this general knowledge, we know little about the exact relationship between these factors and the crime rate, or the interaction between factors. For example, although there is evidence that financial health affects the crime rate, there are not enough studies to decide whether this is primarily due to declining firms or declining industries, and whether firms with "abundant resources" are also more likely to commit crimes. Although some authors have detected more crime in larger firms, we are not able to separate out the "exposure" effect (i.e., larger firms have more opportunities to commit crimes) from the "monitoring" effect (i.e., larger firms might have less control over their employees). From a policy perspective, we know even less about the relative effectiveness (both costs and benefits) of measures that reduce the chance of firms committing crimes. In summary, although there is no lack of theories as to why corporate crime occurs, our empirical knowledge is still very limited. Over time, we can only hope that the quality of data and empirical analysis will substantially increase our knowledge in this area.

NOTES

[1]   The underlying economic theory of why individuals commit crime is generally attributed to Becker (1968), although the roots can be traced back much earlier to classical criminology. Cohen (1992:1063-1066) contains a brief review of subsequent refinements in the context of corporate crime. Classical criminologists (Bentham, 1789; Beccaria, 1963) philosophized about self-interested and "reasoned" offenders—a theme later developed and tested by deterrence scholars (see Paternoster, 1987 for a detailed review).

[2]   For a detailed discussion of how to incorporate moral behavior into the standard economic model, see Griffith and Goldfarb (1991).

[3]   For example, Lott (1992) contains some empirical evidence suggesting that higher-income individuals convicted of drug offenses have higher losses in subsequent earnings than lower-income individuals convicted of drug offenses.

[4]   Government enforcement levels and social norms have been "explained" by both the economics and criminology/sociology literatures. For example, Cohen (1987) provides a formal economic model in which the government chooses the level of enforcement and the firm decides on an oil spill prevention policy based on the government imposed constraints, and Cohen (1991) provides an economic explanation for social norms. In the sociological literature, government enforcement levels and social norms are often viewed as co-determined by external social forces (e.g., economic depression and/or political legitimation) which define normative standards and delimit the content, application, and support for enforcement efforts (see, e.g., Shover, Clelland & Lynxwiler, 1986; Yeager, 1991). Etzioni

(1989), on the other hand, asserts that individual choices, social norms, and public policy (e.g., government regulation) constitute both rational and moral dimensions—the latter of which is generally ignored by neoclassical economists.

5   In small, closely held firms, the owner and manager are the same and there is no such problem. However, there may be a principal-agent problem between the owner/manager and the employees.

6   Vaughan's recent work (1989, 1996) provides some direction here. Integrating the influences of the competitive environment, organizational characteristics, and the regulatory environment, she identifies the multiple sources of information, constraints, and incentives that lead to the decision to launch the Challenger. Yet, Vaughan and others (Jackall, 1988; Kram & Yeager, 1989) contend that organizations effectively neutralize moral issues so that agents' choices are devoid of ethical considerations. Our position is that morality constraints are variable. They depend on the organization, the strength of an individual's belief system, the degree to which individual's are integrated into intra and extra-organizational social networks, and so forth.

7   The U.S. Sentencing Commission Guidelines (1991) for corporate offenders have various provisions reducing the penalty when the firm had shown a good faith effort to comply. Cohen (1991:263-264) provides anecdotal evidence of pre-guideline judicial sentences that reduced the sanction for firms showing good faith either pre- or post-detection.

8   Alternatively, if employers want more corporate crime, then we would expect crime to be positively related to the "punishment" given to employees who do not commit crimes on behalf of their employers.

9   The single most significant limiting factor to our knowledge base in this area is the availability of data. The recent paper by Alexander and Cohen analyzed financial data for 7,500 firms over a period of 11 years. Data availability and computing power limitations made such a project virtually impossible until recently. However, we are still a long way from obtaining the type of data needed to fully analyze these issues. One reason for this lack of data is the reluctance of U.S. government agencies to make information on individual firm compliance records available to researchers. The U.S. Sentencing Commission has even denied access to researchers who request the names of companies convicted of felonies. Thus, researchers are forced to piece together data from public sources—a painstaking and often incomplete task.

10   For example, in a survey of 188 Fortune 500 companies, Beckenstein, Gabel, and Roberts (1983) reported that over one-half had explicit antitrust compliance strategies that included the avoidance of legal activities that might result in a government investigation or private litigation. See Cohen and Scheffman (1989:352-357) for other examples of the possible effects of imposing sanctions that are "too punitive."

3

Organizational Processes (Not Rational Choices) Produce Most Corporate Crimes

M. David Ermann
University of Delaware

Gary A. Rabe[1]
Minot State University

INTRODUCTION

When Diane Vaughan (1996) began her research on the *Challenger* launch decision, she assumed along with almost everyone else that pressures on participants caused them to rationally weigh risks against organizational benefits, approving the launch despite warnings that unusually cold weather could put the flight at risk. Among the pressures were NASA's need for a better on-time launch record to assure future funding, and the belief that President Reagan, in his State of the Union address that night, would salute schoolteacher Christa McAuliffe, who was to be the first civilian in space.

As her extensive research into the accident progressed, however, Vaughan became increasingly doubtful about that explanation. She eventually conceptualized the *Challenger* launch decision "as one decision in a decision stream begun many years before" (1996:278) which had produced a scientific paradigm that the risk was acceptable. This was a case where non-rational rule-based routines within NASA and its contractors had developed over time to produce a disaster. Vaughan thus moved from a "rational choice" model to an "organizational process" model, from an agency model to a structure model.

Applied to corporate crime, agency models argue that crimes result from proactive decisions made to maximize some desired end (usually profit), while of course trying to minimize risks of punishment. Corporate crimes result when maximizing people and organizations decide to commit crimes after calculating that doing so will optimize their benefits. Decisionmakers faced with constellations of expected costs and benefits analyze the odds of these costs and benefits for available options—some of which are criminal—and choose the illegal one if it has the best overall chance of paying off.

These models are generally favored in law, economics, and management technologies. In its search for blameworthiness, the law focuses on intent. Given its successful history explaining macro-economic phenomena by assuming rational pursuit of self-interests, economics now tries to use the same assumptions for explaining crimes by organizations. And, with their goal of devising technologies to improve management, consultants advocate rationality. Thus, "within accounting research, rationality is often associated with the prescription of rational choice models of decisionmaking, rather than with empirical descriptions. . ." (Mouritsen, 1994:194).

Structure models, on the other hand, try to look at actual rather than assumed decisionmaking, so they focus on departmental specialization, organizational environments, organizational cultures, bounded rationality,[2] and other constraints on purposive organizational behavior. Structural explanations may emphasize that motives of offenders often conflict with the profit goals of their organizations,[3] or that opportunities for crime are limited because costs and benefits are difficult to foresee or calculate. Ordinary people make decisions that reflect limited rationality, because they have severely limited information about the present, and estimates of the future consequences of current actions that are wobbly at best. These models are embraced by most works on organizational functioning, and by sociology and related disciplines that look for "latent functions," the unintended and unobvious consequences of actions that are not seen by ordinary folks.

As will become abundantly clear, we subscribe to the latter view. Well-informed and rationally made decisions may be useful heuristics and admirable goals, but they offer poor explanations of most known cases of corporate crime. "Formal rationality is an ideal-type construction, a one-sided exaggeration of features of social interaction and a heuristic that is not intended to acknowledge fully all of the complexities of a particular empirical situation" (Mouritsen, 1994:193). These ideal-types fail the test of usefulness when studying corporation crime—their simplifications of motives and opportunities fail to add more than they subtract from our understanding of corporate crime.

We believe students of corporate crime must begin by recognizing Marshall Clinard and Peter Yeager's assertion that:

> the first step in understanding corporate illegality is to drop
> the analogy of the corporation as a person and analyze the
> behavior of the corporation in terms of what it really is: a
> complex organization (Clinard & Yeager, 1980:43).

These complex organizations include profit-dependent organizations (e.g., most major drug, auto, military equipment, and chemical producers), as well as organizations that are governmental or voluntary (e.g., Department of Defense, Atomic Energy Commission, and local hospitals). Hence, it does not assume *a priori* that corporate profit-seeking provides overriding deviant motives and opportunities. Corporate crime is ordinary behavior within and by organizations. It is not extraordinarily rational. No organizational goal, not even profit, could be pursued with anything resembling the rationality presumed by the agency model.

Consider what the following representative summaries of our present and past knowledge of decisionmaking have to say about rationality. Mary Zey's (1992) anthology on decisionmaking begins with four "critiques of rational choice models," followed by 14 current selections that offer "alternative perspectives." W. Richard Scott (1992:50) summarizes past writing about "Organizations as Rational Systems" thus:

> With the important exception of Weber, the early rational
> system theorists did not take much notice of the effect of
> the larger social, cultural, and technological context of orga-
> nizational structure or performance. . . . [They] virtually
> overlooked the behavior structure of organizations. We
> learn much from them about plans and programs and
> premises, about roles and rules and regulations, but very lit-
> tle about actual behavior of organizational participants.
> Structure is celebrated; action is ignored.

Rational choice, though appealingly parsimonious, is too simplistic to explain (or help prevent) corporate crime. Profit is necessary for corporations, of course, just as food is necessary for people. But only in emergency conditions (impending bankruptcy or famine) does either overwhelm other goals. Most American corporations go about their business balancing short-term profit against long-term profit, security, or growth, just as most Americans see acquisition of food as only one of many goals.

AGENCY EXPLANATIONS

Economists' Agency Models. Rational actor/agency models advocated by many prominent economists conceptualize the organization and its agents as rational and calculating actors (see generally Becker, 1968, 1985; Posner, 1980). The profit goal is paramount and guides all organizational actors. Possible conflicts between the goals of managers versus those of stockholders are problems to be overcome with "compensation rules or incentive compatibility constraints" (Ryan, 1994:208). Such conflicts are not important impediments to what is essentially a rational pursuit of profit.

Gary Becker (1985), for instance, writes that "executives *contemplating* [emphasis added] whether to commit a crime take into consideration not only the punishment they face if caught but also their chances of being apprehended" (1985:20). Explaining the Ford Pinto case, Jack Anderson and Les Whitten assert that "Buried in the secret files of the Ford Motor Co. lies evidence that big automakers have put profits ahead of lives" (1976:B7). This assumed rational, effective pursuit of clear illegitimate goals seems surprising to us, since observers generally do not stand in awe of the rationality and foresight with which large corporate and governmental bureaucracies pursue their legitimate goals. Nonetheless, many commentators assume great organizational rationality and clarity of purpose when trying to explain antisocial organizational behavior.

Of course, they focus on the attempted rationality of the process, not on the actual rationality of the outcome. This approach is criticized by some economists, most notably Herbert Simon (1986:211):

> The rational person of neoclassical economics always reaches the decision that is objectively, or substantively, best in terms of the given [array of preferences]. The rational person of cognitive psychology goes about making his or her decisions in a way that is procedurally reasonable in light of the available knowledge and means of computation.

Similarly, Barry Staw (1980:69) asserts that "although organizations are intendedly rational their ability to achieve any measure of rationality is quite limited. Only very imperfectly does the organization input and process information, and it has difficulty with even the most primitive learning mechanisms."

Criminologists' Agency Models. Edwin Sutherland's (1949) landmark book that coined the term "white-collar crime" made assumptions not much different from those economists make. Following the understanding of organizations prevalent at the time he wrote, Sutherland assumed that corporations are "purposefully designed for the pursuit of explicit objectives" with clear goals and procedures producing rationality of action (Scott, 1981:408). Since Sutherland's time, however, the study of organizations has come a long way, now recognizing that organizations are coalitions with multiple goals and limited rationality.

Through the 1960s, criminological theories had moved away from perspectives which relied on criminal behavior as the product of some calculated choice. Most of these perspectives originated from the work produced by the Chicago School scholars which examined the influence of macro level social factors on crime rates. This work influenced Sutherland's concept of differential social organization, Merton's notion of strain, and many of the perspectives which examined the impact of social factors and power relations on crime (e.g., labeling, conflict, Marxist and feminists perspectives). More recently these macro level perspectives have been reexamined with the work of Messner and Rosenfeld (1994) and their reconceptualization of strain.

However, in the 1970s, agency models began to experience a renaissance. Most of the new choice models emphasized opportunity, cost and benefits, and offender decisions to commit crime. They were variously named "routine activities theory" (Cohen & Felson, 1979), "lifestyle theory" (Hindelang, Gottfredson & Garofalo, 1978), and "the rational choice model" (Cornish & Clark, 1986). A recent introductory sociology text unequivocally asserts that sundry corporate crimes, ranging from bribery, price-fixing, sale of unsafe products, and environmental pollution, "result from deliberate decisions made by corporate personnel to increase or maintain organizational resources or profits" (Farley, 1990:212). All of these works purport to describe the decisionmaking process that offenders actually engage in prior to offending. Like classical perspectives, the embrace the notion that crime results from a rational calculating process.

RATIONAL MOTIVES AND OPPORTUNITIES

Criminologists (and television scriptwriters) generally consider that all crimes must have motives and opportunities. In the following section, we will summarize briefly the motives and opportunities that agency models must assume. First, agency models assume a single overwhelming goal—profit maximization. Actually, motives compete. There are many levels of rationality. What is rational for the long-term health of the company may not serve the primary interests of institutional investors (who buy 70% of stock sold now), nor may it be rational in terms of the short-run interests of corporate managers or divisions. Corporate employees at Johns-Manville had clear rational motives to hide the hazards of asbestos, since the resulting lawsuits that bankrupted their employer came years after they had retired from the company. Similarly, department managers never volunteer to reduce the number of personnel in their department, even if doing so would increase the long-term profitability of the firm. Clinard and Yeager (1980:47) note that:

> especially for the very large corporations, which dominate
> the American economy, the role of profit consideration in
> illegal behavior needs to be qualified. . . . [F]irms may be
> possessed of multiple goals rather than simply high profits,
> and these other goals may also be important in the genesis
> of corporate crime. . . . [And they] may not seek to maxi-

mize profits and endure the business risk that strategy often entails but may instead seek satisfactory levels of profit rate and growth, which in turn will enable corporations to achieve their other goals.

Second, agency model commentators and social scientists assume that, if there is motive there will be crime. Organizational motives make organizational crime inevitable. They come to this conclusion by assuming that corporations are essentially identical to greedy or pressured persons, except that organizations are better able to see their needs fulfilled because they have fewer distractions and greater rationality (Gross, 1978).

This perspective makes too many questionable assumptions. Most importantly, it assumes that stockholder motives (e.g., profit) equate with the motives of people who actually run companies. In reality, of course, the best interests of employees are not necessarily consistent with the best interests of their employers. Interests of the principal (in this case, a corporation) and those of the agent (employee) may diverge. The problem is long-standing. The Dutch United East Indies Company declined because "a seismic shift in opportunity structure opened the way for heightened principal/agent problems and undermined group discipline, contributing to the demise of Dutch hegemony and the rise of the English empire in the eighteenth century" (Adams, 1996:12). From Berle and Means' (1932) classic work on the American economy to the present with the work of agency theorists, it has become increasingly apparent that this assumption violates much of what we know about motives in organizations.

Some new criminological perspectives recognize that rationality is bounded. It is limited by participants' perceptions. In essence, rationality is constructed by, and limited to, an individual's understanding of realities. Organizational agents merely engage in a systematic process calculating the *perceived* costs and benefits of engaging in criminal behavior.

Paternoster and Simpson, for instance, argue that "threats to profitability alone are not sufficient to cause managers across firms, or even the majority of managers within a firm, to violate the law" (1993:46). However, if the organizational agent perceives that the benefits of the criminal behavior exceed the costs, a criminal event will occur. Therefore an individual must rationally and sufficiently contemplate the following information prior to acting: (1) Perceived certainty/severity of formal legal sanctions; (2) Perceived certainty/severity of informal sanctions; (3) Perceived certainty/severity of loss of self-respect; (4) Perceived cost of rule compliance; (5) Perceived cost of noncompliance; (6) Moral inhibitions; and (7) Perceived sense of legitimacy/fairness. These considerations are tempered by the characteristics of the criminal event and prior offending by the person (1993:47).

Like motives, opportunities in the agency model are plentiful and clear. The most telling criticism of these assumed opportunities emphasizes how limited are organizational abilities to have, share, and act on useful information. No person can have the information needed for a decision, so organizations need meetings to coordinate, share authority, and diffuse responsibility and accountability. Even then, the quality of information and its use are bounded.

The image of the one-shot rational choice by single well-informed individuals comes from assuming that the prescriptive discussions of how managers should make decisions are also descriptive of how they actually do make decisions. In fact, so much is written about how to make rational choices exactly because managers so seldom can act in these ways. The ability of stockholders to serve their own interests is also limited. Criminal decisionmaking frequently harms their *long-term* interests, while enriching managers or just protecting their jobs and short-term interests. But stockholders have virtually no input into corporate decisionmaking. Hence, the prescription embedded in what is commonly dubbed the "Wall Street Rule" to sell stock when dissatisfied, not try to reform the company.

THE STRUCTURE MODEL

Opposing agency models are "organizational process" or structure models which argue that organizational crimes flow from organizational contexts rather than conscious motives. Kriesberg's (1976) adaptation of Graham Allison's (1971) analysis of the Cuban Missile Crisis is the earliest, and one of the most influential, uses of this perspective. Kriesberg portrays "the corporation as a constellation of loosely allied decision-making units (e.g., a marketing group, a manufacturing division, a research and development staff), each with primary responsibility for a narrow range of problems" (1976:1101). Because of organizational complexity, each unit has considerable autonomy in making decisions and setting goals.

The structural model permits rationality, but it starts from different observations about how corporations cope with the worlds in which they operate. They attempt, sometimes successfully, to balance incompatible goals. For instance, crime may be the product of a set of non-criminal decisions, which ultimately gives later decisionmakers the motives and opportunities to commit crimes. Consider Kermit Vandivier's experiences at B.F. Goodrich:

> Vandivier was working for B.F. Goodrich when his company won a brake contract for the Air Force's A7D light attack aircraft. One of Goodrich's most qualified and arrogant engineers prepared the design, which won because it minimized weight by using four brake disks instead of the usual five. It also won because Goodrich submitted an unusually low bid to overcome resistance due to a past company failure with the same purchaser. Parts for the new

brake were ordered, and work progressed on completing the design. Word around the plant was: "We can't bungle it this time. We've got to give them a good brake, regardless of the cost" (Vandivier, 1972:200).

Unfortunately, in the first of a series of government-mandated simulated braking tests using the plant's dynamometer, the brake "glowed a bright cherry-red and threw off incandescent particles of metal and lining material" (Vandivier, 1972:200). Employees running the test assumed that defective parts or unsuitable brake lining material caused this failure, and the next few, so they made adjustments. Only then did they begin to realize, in stages, that the four-disk brake design itself had insufficient surface area to do its job.

By then, however, time was running out as ordered parts began arriving and deadlines for delivering the assembled brake loomed. "Panic set in." But they plowed on, endangering lives and company profits until the dangers could no longer be hidden.

Instead of telling the purchaser that the four disk design was inadequate, key decisionmakers started to use large room fans to cool the brake during testing, as well as other more creative ways to "nurse" it to pass. Even these violations of the military's carefully-specified testing methods were insufficient. So Goodrich personnel used "engineering license" to alter actual test data. "Intelligent, law-abiding officials of B.F. Goodrich, one of the oldest and most respected of American corporations, were actually going to deliver to a customer a product that was known to be defective and dangerous and which could very possibly cause death or serious injury" (Vandivier, 1972:201). Several near crashes during flight tests began the process of exposing the brake design's inadequacies and the company's concealment of its hazards (Ermann, in preparation).

These acts were not irrational, but their rationality was limited in the three ways that Simon (1986:169) suggested that rationality may be limited:

1. uncertainty about the consequences of actions chosen from among alternatives;

2. incomplete information about the alternatives actually available; and

3. complexity of the world that makes calculation of the consequences of action impossible.

Rather than seeking the optimum solution, Simon suggests that it is rational to satisfice: to settle "for a satisfactory, rather than an approximate-best, decision" (1986:170). The most sophisticated of management techniques therefore simplify the real world so that the models can use optimizing models to generate approximations. It is therefore rational to plan by gradually building, step-by-step, decision-by-decision, rather than to preplan an entire series of steps to a given final forced decision.

Simon (1986:164) argues that rationality can be limited by the complexity and cost of even trying to calculate the best course of action. He draws an analogy to the game of chess, for which winning would be made trivial given the closed system and limited types of moves, were it not for the fact that an average game of, say, 40 moves could be played in 10 possible ways. Rationality is theoretically possible, but practically impossible. Thus, it is rational to limit the number of factors considered. Rules of thumb and approximate values are used to try to reach the most satisfactory solutions under the limits on getting full information of future outcomes.

In a world filled with uncertainty and the high cost of gathering information, muddling through on the basis of limited information and limited planning is rational and unavoidable. As part of this muddling through is an optimism that things will work out—as they often do. This can lead to overconfidence (Jemison & Sitkin, 1986), as in the Goodrich case summarized above. Often we act first and explain later.

In the processes that actually occur in organizations, rules do not always govern actions, individual goals and intentions are weakly linked to individual actions, and units are not closely coordinated with other units. Decisions seem to flow from shifting coalitions of interest groups within the organization. "[A]ll large organizations are not teams, but coalitions. A team is a group of persons working together who have identical goals. A coalition is a group of persons working together who have some but not all goals in common" (Downes, 1967:76). These are empirical, not normative, statements. And they do not suggest that loosely coupled organizations are poorly managed or ineffective.

More recently, James Coleman (1987) began his analysis by recognizing that organizations are divided into specialized sub-units, each with its own sub-goals. These departments do not have profit as their primary goals. Instead, they strive to meet diverse sub-unit goals (product development, manufacturing, distribution and sales, etc.) which are only indirectly related to profit. This perspective assumes that organizational structure loosely translates profit and other goals of the organization into a variety of behavior patterns by its sub-units.

These researchers assume that organizations have inherent irrationalities, limitations, and failures that produce crimes regardless of the moral or immoral motives of the organization's people. Organizations are limited tools for satisfying their own needs or the preferences of their stockholders and leaders. Organizations encourage outcomes regardless of the motives and needs of the participants. For example, the organization neutralizes the sense of personal responsibility by diffusing responsibility. Because responsibility and information are fragmented, prospective criminals can act in ways that would be unthinkable in their private lives. Organizational size, delegation, and specialization, for example, are said to:

> combine to produce an organizational climate that allows the abdication of a degree of personal responsibility. . . . Under these conditions, almost any type of corporate criminality . . . is possible. Executives at higher levels can absolve themselves of responsibility. . . . (Clinard & Yeager, 1980:44)

People in these cases can distance themselves from victims, since they are separated by social and geographical distance. Gone are the days when the factory owner or decisionmaker probably went to school with the person who died in an accident in his or her factory. With a national and international market, decisionmakers and victims often live thousands of miles apart. "For example, workers engaged in producing dioxin never witnessed the effects of the chemical on the residents of Love Canal in Niagara Falls. Similarly, pilots serving in the Vietnam War convinced themselves that they were bombing geographical targets on maps, not killing civilians in their homes" (Simon & Eitzen, 1990:299). Both the events and the people are ordinary. The events are small steps made now in the context of small steps made earlier, either by the current role occupant or his/her predecessor. Decisions are constrained by past decisions and subunit interest. There was no blueprint.

STRUCTURAL MOTIVES AND OPPORTUNITIES

An example of how organizational processes generate motives is "escalating commitment." Commitment escalates at both the individual and the organizational level. Human behavior at auctions illustrates escalating individual commitment. People attending auctions may calculate beforehand what they can afford to spend, but once bidding begins, they often continue to bid beyond their original intentions, and beyond levels that are prospectively and retrospectively rational. Escalating commitment at the organizational level is illustrated vividly by the following description of British Columbia's decision to host the Expo 86 world's fair in Vancouver:

> Despite rapidly increasing deficit projections (from a $6 million projected loss in 1978 to a $300+ million projected loss in 1985), the provincial government remained steadfast

> in its plans to hold the fair. Expo is therefore a visible and prototypical example of the escalation of commitment, a phenomenon subject to extensive laboratory research in recent years. . . . It is proposed the escalation starts with project and psychological forces but can evolve over time into a more structurally determined phenomenon (Ross & Staw, 1986:274).

Similarly, we have argued (Rabe & Ermann, 1995) that tobacco companies' motives and opportunities to hide tobacco hazards were organizational and cultural. Profit was just one of many organizational goals. Consequently, rational explanations of tobacco companies' actions lead to an incomplete analysis. Because of tobacco company reliance on tobacco, in part, they reacted to allegations of product hazards in two ways: with "smoke" screen research and with diversification. The companies were committed to tobacco well before scientific knowledge about the hazards began to emerge. It is not surprising that once confronted with their own research which supported the hazard allegation, they began an intense effort to limit commitment to tobacco by diversifying.

Commitments escalate for many reasons. First, motives change. Brockner (1985:224-238), for instance, describes three forms of entrapment over time. Individual entrapment occurs as organizational members escalate their personal commitments to failing projects because pay, promotion, and other rewards depend on the project's success. Group/role entrapment results from pressures to conform, diffusion of responsibility, and an unwillingness to be the bearer of bad news (even if the bad news results from decisions by a previous occupant of the bearer's role). Decisionmakers interpret signals from their colleagues. "Groupthink" (Janis, 1988) causes people who are deeply involved in cohesive groups to strive for unanimity and modify their beliefs. Finally, organizational entrapment occurs because a project has become irrevocable. Thus, decisionmakers act in the context of past decisions made by others as well as themselves.

Second, the structure model argues strongly that organizational motives compete with one another. This is well-illustrated in Arthur Haley's (1984:162) sociologically insightful novel, *Strong Medicine*, when a main character observes that:

> in any drug company a perpetual tug-of-war existed between sales and manufacturing on the one hand and research on the other. As the sales people expressed it, "Research always wants to be a hundred and ten percent sure of every goddam detail before they'll say, 'Okay, let's go!'" Manufacturing, similarly, was eager to gear up for production and not be caught out by sudden demands

> when a new drug was required in quantity. But on the other side of the equation, researchers accused the merchandising arm of "wanting to rush madly into the market with a product that's only twenty percent proven, just to beat competitors and have an early lead in sales."

Profit was never mentioned in this or most comparable scenarios, though it is a motive. Profit goals compete with and limit other organizational goals. The profit goals of owners compete (often unsuccessfully) with the security, prestige, income, and other goals of managers. Furthermore, as Clinard and Yeager (1980:46-48) have explained, profit maximization goals inevitably must be balanced against other goals such as the minimizing risk, since the most profitable courses of action in a competitive market also tend to be the most financially risky. Hence, behaviors with regard to profit-seeking goals appear best described as the result of management seeking profit levels sufficient to keep stockholders content and loyal while also protecting the long-term viability of the firm (Galbraith, 1967).

Opportunities for committing corporate crime require that *usable* knowledge of possible opportunities and risks be available, and then that the organization be capable of mobilization based on this knowledge. However, knowledge about corporate crime opportunities resists collection, interpretation, and dissemination. This is a much greater problem for white-collar than for street crime, and much more difficult than rational choice models assume. Knowledge about corporate crime opportunities must somehow be collected about a world outside the immediate personal experience of participants. Even more difficult is probabilistically estimating competing risks, communicating criminal risks and opportunities within the organization, and converting the resulting information into concerted action.

Collecting and interpreting information is slow and difficult. Even the best intentioned and most highly informed analysts will find the information available to them to be "messy," and their policy alternatives "ill-structured" (Mitroff & Manson, 1980:331). These analysts must therefore "frame" safety problems (Tversky & Kahneman, 1981), even though they lack the clear understanding of cause/effect relationships needed to make their framing valid. Thus, their evaluation process is inexact because their information is not particularly informative.

Problems of interpreting information are illustrated by the lack of governmental and public concerns about important chemical risks. In 1990, after years of focusing on chemicals as carcinogens, the federal government for the first time directed attention to a chemical hazard previously ignored—injury to the nervous system. The Office of Technology Assessment found that "Concerns about carcinogenicity have dominated discussions about the risks posed by toxic substances. However, the adverse effects on organs and organ systems, particularly the nervous system, may pose an equal or greater threat to public health" (Office of Technology Assessment, 1990:13).

During the coming decade, we may learn more about previously ignored neurological hazards of chemicals. Or, we may learn that corporate and governmental elites were correct all along to ignore these hazards. The search for these hazards, like the search for all hazards, is akin to looking for needles in a haystack without knowing whether a particular haystack even contains needles. Even if a new needle is found (e.g., even if a newly recognized risk from industrial chemicals is discovered), distribution and use of this knowledge within the organization is slow. Information travels slowly and unpredictably in organizations. We recognize information exchanges in our universities or offices are slow, unpredictable, and often inaccurate. We should likewise recognize that one person or group in an organization suspecting a hazard is not equivalent to the organization "knowing" the information.

Furthermore, information probably will not be fully or accurately transmitted. Information enters at specialized organizational positions with titles like medical researcher, pharmaceutical salesperson, or product safety supervisor. The people who occupy these positions, working in the privacy of their own offices, each labor on a small part of a large problem. They often lack opportunities or motives to observe or influence one another, or to exchange tentative information. Because they are specialized, they will get only partial pictures, despite attending a profusion of meetings to try to share their information. These people have details, but they have difficulty gaining the broad authority needed to correct a problem or kill a project (Anderson, 1980; Jackall, 1988). Perversely, those who enjoy broad authority are necessarily removed from needed detail.

IMPLICATIONS FOR CONTROL

Ermann and Lundman (1982) suggested that attempts to control corporate crime are either penetrating or nonpenetrating. Nonpenetrating controls, they suggest:

> assume that corporate actions can be influenced from the outside by selectively rewarding and punishing the corporation. . . . They avoid mandating specific changes in corporate structures, procedures, or personnel. Instead, these mechanisms seek levers outside the corporation that may cause it to make necessary changes itself (1982:132).

Agency models suggest nonpenetrating controls. Applying these models to crime control strategy involves a simple equation. Make the cost of crime exceed the benefit perceived or achieved. Fine the organization to the point that would make corporate crime unprofitable. In Becker's words, "Fines . . . would force companies to think longer and harder before committing white-collar crimes" (Becker, 1985:20). Posner (1980) and Parker (1989) have also proposed that fining is not only the best, but should be the only, form of corporate sanctioning. Like most economists, they assume that when organizational agents realize the cost of crime exceeds the benefit, they will be deterred.

However, Coffee (1977, 1979-1980, 1980, 1981), Stone (1975, 1977, 1981), Gruner (1988), and Coffee, Gruner, and Stone (1988) argue against over-reliance on fines as sanctions for organizational crime. Fines are not paid by the guilty parties. Organizational agents responsible for the criminal behavior are not harmed by an organizational fine. Instead payment of the fine falls on those who are not culpable—stockholders, creditors, the work force, and consumers. Coffee (1981:408) summarized what he believed to be the inherent flaw of the economic model:

> The Chicago School may therefore show mercy to the cor-
> porate executive. . . but it imposes a harsh penalty on the
> less privileged classes [such as employees, consumers and
> other dependents on the organization] who bear the indirect
> burden of corporate penalties.

Furthermore, if judges try to order fines in the amounts proposed by econo-mists, they would confront what Coffee calls a "deterrence trap." Fines would have to be so large that organizations would not have the resources to pay them. Fining would lead to bankruptcy and possible dissolution of the corporation. Repercussions for the criminal behavior would fall upon guiltless third parties.

Structure models, on the other hand, lead us to advocate "penetrating con-trols" which assume that:

> there are features of a corporation's structure and personnel
> . . . that increase the likelihood of deviance. They assume
> also that these aspects can be changed. In the case of the
> corporation, changes might include the way members of the
> Board of Directors are elected, how lower level managers
> are promoted, . . . the way top management is informed of
> the behavior of subordinates, and how it is accountable to
> the Board of Directors (Ermann & Lundman, 1982:133).

For the most part, Coffee (1977, 1979-1980, 1980, 1981), Stone (1975, 1977, 1981), Gruner (1988), and Coffee, Gruner, and Stone (1988) advocate pene-trating controls. They believe that sanctions other than fines should be directed at culpable parties. Examples of what they proposed as appropriate sanctions include equity fines, probation, publicity, community service, corrective adver-tising, private enforcement (civil suits), and criminal actions against culpable organizational agents. Disagreeing slightly, Geis (1972) suggested that penalties imposed at the organizational level will be ineffective. Instead, he argued, the best way to control corporate crime is to impose criminal penalties on corpo-rate agents who commit criminal behavior.

SUMMARY AND CONCLUSIONS

Organizational crime is multicausal. In the real world, motives and opportunities to *rationally* plan and execute corporate crimes seldom exist simultaneously. Our image of the organization thus is not of a tool to get profits, but rather:

> a constellation of loosely allied decision-making units (e.g., a marketing group, a manufacturing division, a research and development staff), each with primary responsibility for a narrow range of problems. Each unit operates under general corporate guidelines, but due to the complexity and breadth of its operations, the unit possesses some autonomy in setting priorities, processing information, defining problems, and initiating action (Metzger, 1984:23).

Each decision and non-decision must be understood in light of what has happened up to that point in the company, not in terms of the presumed guiding star of profit maximization. Corporate people are solving immediate problems, putting out fires, dealing with rival departments, and so forth. We advocate focusing on this corporate crime process rather than looking for a single decision or a single motive.

NOTES

[1]   This work represents the joint and equal contribution of the authors. The order of the authors is merely alphabetical.

[2]   This concept contributed to economist Herbert Simon's winning the Nobel Prize in Economics.

[3]   Economists, too, deal with this "agency" problem, but for them it tends to be a constraint on their model rather than the basis for it.

Section II

CORPORATE CRIMINAL LIABILITY

Corporate criminal liability, by which corporations are held legally responsible for the criminal actions of their agents, is the least discussed of the issues in this book. Despite several notable challenges (see, in particular, Mueller, 1957), corporate criminal liability is well established in American law and throughout the common law tradition, having evolved through the application of individual criminal liability to organizations via the juristic person standard (see Brickey, 1984).

However, its existence is not without controversy, from both agency and structure theorists. Among agency theorists, there is considerable debate about the economic utility and legal and moral propriety of assigning liability to corporations for the actions of their agents. Does such a legal regime provide incentives for law abiding behavior? Are these incentives gained at a reasonable price? Does it make sense to legally conceptualize organizations as actors? Among structure theorists, corporate criminal liability is more hospitably regarded, though an important strain of critique has emerged related to the rationalistic underpinnings of this form of liability (see Fisse, 1978 for an early statement of this position). In placing the organization at the causal center of corporate crime, the organization is in theory and in practice the appropriate location of liability for structure theorists. The one question that is sometimes raised, and the one potential shortcoming of this legal regime, is whether the individualistic origins of corporate criminal liability limit its effectiveness by placing undue burdens of identifying individual agency in imposing criminal liability on corporations. Thus, one of the most controversial issues in the corporate crime literature is whether a corporation can commit a crime even though no single person within that organization commits a criminal act.

In Chapter 4, Jeffrey Parker, a legal scholar centrally involved in the development of the federal organizational sentencing guidelines as counsel to the Sentencing Commission, provides a provocative and relentless critique of corporate criminal liability. Arguing from the classical economic agency perspective, Parker strongly opposes corporate criminal liability, asserting that its existence violates fundamental legal and moral requirements that intent precede punishment. Ignoring this exposes organizations to sanctions best reserved for individuals and best imposed by markets or the civil law. Moreover, he argues, not only is corporate crime a legal and behavioral fiction, it is very uncommon and not particularly harmful when compared to the potential harm to society from expanding criminal liability to vicarious and strict liability offenses.

In Chapter 5, Dutch judge Nico Jörg presents a tightly argued critique of corporate criminal liability. Rejecting Parker's insistence that we view the criminal justice system as concerned and capable of dealing with only the actions of natural persons, Jörg argues for a broadening of criminal justice so that it can more adequately encounter the corporation. Corporate entities have an existence independent of their agents and must therefore be legally accessible independent of these agents. Developing an adequate conception of corporate criminal liability does not require the suspension of long-standing criminal procedure, but rather a recognition that organizations have the capacities that the criminal law requires of responsible and therefore legally liable actors. Building on the Dutch model, Jörg spells out a more expansive, organization-specific, corporate criminal liability rooted in structure theory.

4

The Blunt Instrument

Jeffrey S. Parker[1]
George Mason University School of Law

Punishment is an ugly, brutal thing. By definition, punishment involves the deliberate infliction of pain and suffering on another.[2] It is the intentional creation of harm. Though we ordinarily think of punishment as a response to crime, we should be ever mindful of the fact that—by any known society's definition—punishment *is* crime, unless it is fully justified by some other and higher end. Worse yet, punishment is organized crime, and it is highly open and notorious crime, as it is usually associated with a regularized, state-sponsored public spectacle.

For these reasons, it has long been acknowledged that the wanton brutality that is punishment must be strictly and completely justified as serving some worthwhile aim—indeed, that ultimately the infliction of punishment does more good than its obvious and immediate harm,[3] and that both the manner and the degree of punishment are, in fact, strictly *necessary* to the achievement of that good.[4] Thus, the structure of the justification for punishment is precisely the same as the justification for the commission of an act that otherwise would be a crime: that the deliberately injurious act is the "lesser evil," as its commission is necessary to avoid an even greater harm.[5]

The justification of punishment is necessary to avoid an even greater evil than the punishment itself has had important implications for the development of legal policy towards crime and punishment. First, and most importantly, it has relegated criminal punishment to the role of society's sanction of last resort, to be invoked only when lesser responses have proved ineffective. As a result, the criminal sanction has been reserved for the most serious of offenses against the social order, to be imposed only after other options have been exhausted.[6] Second, even when invoked, criminal punishment is not inflicted until after extensive procedural protections have been afforded to the accused, including proof of guilt beyond a reasonable doubt, the privilege against self-incrimination, and the like.[7] Taken together, the extensive protections of criminal procedure make a deliberate trade-off of enforcement efficiency against minimizing the chances that the brutalities of punishment will be inflicted upon the innocent, even at the expense of allowing some of the guilty to go free.[8] Third, even when invoked as a last resort and preceded by extensive procedural protections, criminal punishment has been limited by a principle of proportionality requiring that the severity of the sanction be strictly related to the severity of the offense being punished, and to be distributed fairly across offenses (see generally Walker, 1991; Fletcher, 1978; von Hirsch, 1976).[9]

Even with these limitations of legal policy—which are virtually universal among the legal systems of advanced nations—punishment remains a public exercise in brutality that invokes widespread moral revulsion. To take only the most dramatic example, the imposition of the death penalty, even when fully justified by the offense and imposed only after very extensive procedural protections, is widely criticized as demeaning to a civilized society.[10] But the same reaction applies to many lesser forms of punishment—such as mutilation, torture, ridicule, whipping, or the like—and so we observe constitutional prohibitions against "cruel and unusual" punishments[11] and extensive efforts at penal reform to humanize the conditions under which even accepted forms of punishment are imposed.

Especially during the twentieth century, we have witnessed ambitious undertakings to tame the brutality of punishment by recharacterizing it as "correction" or "treatment" aimed at "reforming" or "rehabilitating" the offender rather than inflicting pain for its own sake, or even to deter other potential offenders by the example. At the same time, others have tried to replace the primal rationale of vengeance as the justification for punishment with the more civilized-sounding "desert," and have sought to suggest that the offender is thereby benefitted by his or her pain (see von Hirsch, 1976). But the institution of punishment has tended to resist these efforts to soften its brutal consequences, not least because of society's limited knowledge about how to turn punishment to benign ends. In the United States, perhaps the most dramatic acknowledgment of this failure came with the enactment of the federal Sentencing Reform Act of 1984, in which the Congress declared, in statutory text, that the new federal system of "determinate" sentencing without any provision for parole would "reflect the inappropriateness of imposing a sentence to a term of imprisonment for the purpose of rehabilitating the defendant or providing the defendant with needed educational or vocational training, medical care, or other correctional treatment" (28 U.S.C. §994(k), enacted by Pub. L. No. 98-473, Title II, §217, 98 Stat., 1976, 1987, 2017, 2022, October 12, 1984) which had been precisely the purposes of federal "corrections" for the preceding 50 years.

The accompanying report of the Senate Judiciary Committee elaborated on the rejection of the rehabilitative ideal:

> At present, the concepts of indeterminate sentencing and parole release depend for their justification exclusively upon this model of 'coercive' rehabilitation—the theory of correction that ties prison release dates to the successful completion of certain vocational, educational, and counseling programs within the prisons.
>
> Recent studies suggest that this approach has failed, and most sentencing judges as well as the Parole Commission agree that the rehabilitation model is not an appropriate basis for sentencing decisions. We know too little about human behavior to be able to rehabilitate individuals on a routine basis or even to determine accurately whether a particular prisoner has been rehabilitated (Senate Report No. 98-225, 98th Cong., 1st Session 40, 1983).

This rejection at the federal level was accompanied by similar rejections in several states, and had been prompted, as the Senate committee report noted, by findings in the literature that the rehabilitative model of punishment for individuals had failed. Prior to this recognition, enormous and well-intended efforts had been devoted for decades to reforming prisons into "correctional institutions" that would rehabilitate rather than simply punish (see von Hirsch, 1976; Morris, 1974). But in the end, all that came of it was punishment, meaning the infliction of pain, and the only justifications remaining were retribution, deterrence, or restraint—all of which recognize that the act of punishment in itself is inherently destructive, and can only be justified by reference to prevention of greater harms, either by the primary crimes themselves, or by acts of private vengeance motivated by the human passion for revenge.

So far, I have said nothing about "corporate crime," which is supposed to be the concern of this book, and the reader may well wonder what any of this has to do with the subject at hand. My answer is that these considerations strictly *define* the subject at hand, and that this condition may not be obvious to all or even most readers of this book. As I understand the object of the overall work from Professor Lofquist's introductory chapter, one of the editors' purposes is to stimulate an interdisciplinary dialogue on the issues presented by social responses to corporate misconduct. As I am a lawyer with some interest in economic analysis, I see my role as providing a legal and economic perspective on the subject. While an economic perspective may be familiar to sociologists and others, the legal perspective may be less familiar but certainly is more fundamental, because crime and punishment—at least insofar as they relate to public policy and debate—are strictly legal concepts, and they may not be well understood by the social scientists.

The best illustration of this fact is the famous 1949 book by the sociologist Edwin Sutherland entitled *White Collar Crime*, which presented a study of violations of law by the largest United States corporations. Despite the book's title, most of the cases examined by Sutherland—some 84 percent of the violations studied—did not involve "crime" at all, by any legal definition (see Sutherland, 1983:45).[12] Rather, they were instances of *civil* violations of law. Of course, this fact was known to Sutherland, who included a chapter in his book that presents arguments as to why the civil violations ought to be considered "crimes"—in essence, because most of them involved legal duties owed to a large group of the public, and, in most cases, were or could have been enforced by public officials (Sutherland, 1949). It has never been clear to me whether Sutherland was addressing his arguments to only his fellow sociologists, or to a larger audience.[13] His arguments are interesting, and may form relevant terms of debate within sociology. But they have very little to do with the legal institutions of crime and punishment in anything like their current forms.[14]

We may wish to have a more general normative debate on whether the prevailing legal conception of crime ought to be revised altogether. Such a debate could even have some policy significance, because, as a lawyer, I would be the first to acknowledge that, given sufficiently powerful influences over legislators, it is possible to have virtually anything enacted into legislation. But that would be a very different debate from the one now extant about the use of the criminal sanction against corporations. If we are to use the current institutional forms of the criminal law against corporations, we must all understand the nature of those institutions as a prerequisite to informed debate.

From this perspective, it is beneficial to recognize that the most general legal definition of "crime" is simply "that which is punished" (see LaFave & Scott, 1986:§ 1.2). Therefore, under current institutional forms, any discussion of crime is, by definition, a discussion of the application of punishment. As I have indicated, punishment is recognized to be an inherently destructive and evil thing, to be applied only under the principle of necessity, when all else has failed. Thus, punishment, and its necessary correlate of criminalization, is not an exercise in social fine-tuning; instead, it is an act of social desperation, a last resort to brutality, when all other means of social control have proved unavailing. It is, as the title of this chapter implies, a blunt instrument—an almost mindless act of violence in itself, strictly analogous, for example, to a killing in self-defense, which may be justified in the circumstances, but is not thereby something to be desired or extolled; it is something to be avoided whenever possible.

Furthermore, as illustrated by the experience with "enlightened" forms of "correctional treatment" applied to individuals, Herculean efforts to sharpen the blunt instrument have met with very little success. Lamentable though it may be, we are left largely with bludgeoning as the vastly predominant mode of the criminal sanction, and all of the features of the criminal process have been shaped in recognition of that reality. Mostly for this reason, the criminal process appears—especially to outside observers—to be abysmally inefficient as a mechanism of law enforcement.[15] But that feature is by design and long tradition, for if all one has to use is a blunt instrument that doubtlessly will create untoward collateral damage, there is a bias against its use unless absolutely necessary.

These features of the criminal process do not magically disappear simply by shifting our attention from individuals to corporations. To invoke the criminal sanction against corporate "misconduct" is to place such matters within an existing legal system that knows it is wielding a blunt instrument, and whose traditions, procedures, and personnel are profoundly influenced by that fact. Corporate criminal liability introduces a concept that is completely alien to the moral values embodied in the criminal justice system, and therefore will force its functionaries into an uncomfortable moral duality between the individual and corporate "departments" of the system. How well will they cope with that conflict? Will the introduction of such an abstract concept of "guilt" dilute the moral motivations—or the efficiency—of the system as applied to individuals? Even if the duality can be sustained, do we have any reason to believe that the blunt instrument can be sharpened in the corporate context, or the occasions for its application specified with any rigor? Can collateral damage be minimized? How can abuses be prevented? And overarching all of these questions is the fundamental criterion: is all of this necessary to some important social end, especially considering the available alternatives?

The remainder of this chapter will seek to address each of these questions, or at least to open the interdisciplinary debate on them. As may be obvious from the introduction, however, I do not believe that the crime of punishment can be justified as necessary in the case of corporations. Although there are several reasons, the principal one is that, under the current state of knowledge, we have not reached the point of desperation required to justify the criminal sanction in this context. There are many other options that not only are available, but in fact are now in place and operating, to address the problem of law violations within corporations and other business organizations. There is no evidence of which I am aware that these existing alternatives to the criminal sanction—including regulatory supervision of corporations by expert agencies, public enforcement of legal standards by various means, civil penalty proceedings, and the vigorous civil tort system, which in many if not most cases may all be applied simultaneously—are seriously inadequate to the task of sanctioning violations of law by corporations. To the contrary, these options seem in many ways superior, if what is desired is law enforcement. Moreover, extending the criminal sanction to corporate entities may already have had an adverse spillover effect on the efficacy of the criminal process as against individuals, and a further expansion may further impair the criminal justice system's ability to perform that primary role. In sum, the excursion into corporate criminal sanctions is a trip that is not necessary, and, as necessity—not desire—is the proper standard to apply, the trip should not be taken.

CORPORATE CRIMINAL LIABILITY
AND "STRUCTURALISM"

Professor Lofquist's introductory chapter frames much of the debate over corporate crime and punishment as a dialogue between two models of the problem, which he terms the "agency model" and the "structure model." This theme is picked up in the chapter on the structure model's implications for corporate criminal liability doctrine. I see from Professor Lofquist's chapter that I am classified as an "agency" theorist, and therefore I surmise that the spirit of the undertaking is that I provide an alternative to structuralist views. In fact, I am critical of some of the views expressed by structural theorists. Indeed, I am troubled by the structuralist chapter, for it provides some evidence that Continental European law may be following Anglo-American law down what I believe is the wrong path toward acceptance of corporate criminal liability. Up until very recently, the continental system wisely had stayed away from corporate criminal liability, except in emergencies such as wars (Mueller, 1957).

I have developed my own views on the corporate criminal liability doctrine at length elsewhere (Parker, 1996)[16] and I will not repeat that detailed discussion here. In summary, the historical evidence indicates that, with the exception of the recent developments in Europe, the idea of "corporate" criminal liability—that is, the liability of the business entity or organization, as distinct from its members, owners, officers, or employees—essentially is rejected by all developed legal systems outside of the United States and the few other countries whose legal system is based on English law. I believe that the acceptance of the doctrine in American law was an historical expedient of the nineteenth century that became ensconced by a combination of inertia and pressure groups' realization of its usefulness in social competition (Parker, 1996).

Concepts of corporate or collective responsibility had been accepted in primitive and Medieval legal systems. However, as societies developed more respect for the autonomy and responsibility of the individual, the corporate or collective forms of liability were abandoned, and that was true in England and the United States as well as other countries. However, corporate criminal liability later re-emerged in mid-nineteenth century Britain and America, but not in Continental Europe. There is no general agreement as to why this differential development occurred. My hypothesis is that it was attributable to a unique confluence of economic and legal conditions in Britain and America at that time. In the nineteenth century, Britain and America had almost no public law enforcement apparatus other than criminal prosecution. However, at the same time, they faced economic conditions of rapid industrialization, which created a demand for public law enforcement. As there were no other public law enforcement institutions then available, they turned to the criminal system merely as a practical expedient. Continental Europe did not do the same because its code-based legal systems already had provisions for non-criminal public enforcement, and because its slower pace of industrialization at that time did not place as much pressure on the law enforcement system.

In the 150 years since corporate criminal liability was first recognized, the American law enforcement system has changed very dramatically. Among other things, the system now embodies a wide array of public law enforcement options—regulatory agencies, civil penalties, and the like—that were not available in the mid-nineteenth century. For this reason, it is no longer necessary to look to the criminal system simply for public law enforcement, as it may have been in the nineteenth century. And yet, corporate criminal liability persists. This can be attributed to the fact that corporate criminal sanctions have a political constituency that puts together a number of different groups: anti-corporate or anti-business forces; anti-free market forces; public regulatory officials, who want to assure themselves the full range of legal sanctions; and, ironically, corporate managers, who may prefer entity-level sanctions to deflect or at least weaken the impact of the obvious alternative of individual sanctions (Parker, 1993).

Thus, in my view of the evidence, corporate criminal liability is a historical artifact of nineteenth century law enforcement conditions that no longer prevail. Its original justification as a law enforcement stopgap no longer has any basis in the public interest, though the doctrine apparently has political support from sufficiently strong private interests to avoid abolition. Part of its attraction to some or all of those private interest groups is the connotation of moral blame that ordinarily accompanies the imposition of the criminal sanction. Although empirical evidence raises substantial doubt whether the strategy of "blaming" corporations through the criminal process actually has its intended effect,[17] the question remains whether such corporate "blaming" is justified, morally or otherwise.

Under general standards of criminal law prevailing in all developed legal systems, corporate criminal liability is unjustified. The general standard is that only morally "blameworthy" conduct will be subject to the criminal sanction, and this is operationalized in Anglo-American law in the doctrine of *mens rea*—the "guilty mind," which essentially means conscious awareness of the conditions that make the conduct wrongful (Parker, 1996). The traditional analysis is that since corporations do not have "minds" at all, they could not have the "guilty mind," and therefore could not have criminal responsibility. While that analysis may sound simplistic, it is doubtful whether it can be improved.

Of course, there have been many previous attempts to anthropomorphize the corporation by inventing a fictitious "mind" in the firm's senior management or the like.[18] But from a moral point of view, they all falter on the problem that an abstract and purely instrumental construct such as a corporation cannot qualify as a moral actor. Apparently, this is where the "structure model" plays a role.

Although I do not pretend to have mastered all of the literature cited on the structure model, I am familiar with the works of Braithwaite, Fisse, Coffee, and French, and Judge Jörg appears to rely most heavily, in his theoretical discussion, on French (French, 1984). Writing from the perspective of moral philosophy, and motivated by what he characterizes as the "anthropological bigotry" of Western moral tradition (French, 1984:x)—apparently meaning the same thing as Judge Jörg's (Chapter 5, this publication) criticism of British legal doctrine as "anthropocentric"—French proposes to invest corporations with moral competence by constructing a corporate "mind" in what he calls the "CID" structure, standing for Corporate Internal Decision structure. Apparently, CID is to be located not only in the explicit policies of the corporation, but is the amalgam of those sources plus the organizational reporting responsibilities, implicit decision rules or circumstances, and the general atmosphere of corporate objectives, operations, and norms of behavior, all interpreted after the fact (French, 1984). In short, CID is what others have referred to as "corporate culture" or "ethos" (see Bucy, 1991).

Judge Jörg applies CID aggressively to the problem of corporate intent, ultimately arguing that, because corporate behavior generally is "avoidable," then anything that occurs within the scope of corporate operations must thereby be deemed "intentional," as it is the product of CID, the corporate "mind," even if no one individual or group of individuals willed the event or were even aware of it. As Judge Jörg writes, "there is very little light between a positive answer to the question of perpetration"—meaning merely whether the event occurred within the scope of corporate operations—"and the answer to the question of intent" (Jörg, Chapter 5, this publication).[19] In other words, if it happened, it was intentional and the corporation is "guilty."

It may be that this view of things could suffice as a theory of moral responsibility in some unknown context. I am extremely doubtful that any such context exists, but a full treatment of that question would unduly extend my contribution here,[20] and it would be somewhat beside the point. As an academic, I am quite willing to engage in a discussion of life on Mars, whether or not any such thing exists; I might even criticize the views of French and Jörg as "terracentric," for having failed to account for possible moral standards of hypothetical Martian lifeforms. However, as a lawyer and policy analyst, I feel compelled to refocus our attention on the question at hand, which is whether such a view of responsibility can live within the moral world of our existing criminal justice system. To this question, the answer plainly is no.

The structuralist basis for corporate criminal liability essentially eliminates the central doctrine of criminal responsibility, which is the requirement of *mens rea*, the "guilty mind" (see Hall, 1960). What Jörg describes is a standard of *civil*, not criminal, liability, of the strict-liability type, which has never been accepted as a generally sufficient moral basis for criminal punishment.[21] Moreover, the logic of the proposal is in no way unique or inherently limited to the corporate context, and it therefore threatens to undermine the entire moral foundation for criminal responsibility.

To take a concrete example, suppose that you purchased a new and highly-touted software product for your personal computer, but that the new program did not work as advertised. Judge Jörg's theory implies not only that you might "blame" a corporate entity that marketed the software—though perhaps not its individual developers, if there were several of them—but also that you could "blame" the program itself. After all, the program has an "ID" structure—not a CID, but an SID, a Software Internal Decision structure. Like a corporation's CID, the program's SID ultimately is based upon and derived from the judgments of individuals, it has the capacity to gather information, to analyze and react in accordance with its predetermined norms and values, and its own internal logic for decisionmaking. According to Judge Jörg's analysis, the program therefore has moral competence and can be held morally, and criminally, responsible. Under this moral theory, there is no distinction between the corporation's CID and the computer program's SID. Nor need we stop there, as the same analysis could be applied to virtually any contract,[22] or, for that matter, any product, all of which embody information in an organized form and therefore could be described as having an "ID" structure. A defective toaster that started a fire in your kitchen could be described in exactly the same terms.

Troubling as it is to have a moral theory that fails to distinguish between a corporation and a computer program, it is all the more troubling to have a moral theory that fails to distinguish between a computer program and a human being, for that is the import of the theory. If a corporation can be elevated to the same status as a human moral actor by its CID, and, by a parity of reasoning, a computer program becomes the moral equivalent of a human actor, then how is a human being to be distinguished morally from a computer program, or, for that matter, a toaster? I realize that this is "anthropocentric" thinking, but then, so are the moral foundations of our criminal law.

As I have pointed out elsewhere (Parker, 1996), the entire edifice of criminal responsibility is predicated upon an "anthropocentric"—or more conventionally termed, a humanistic—ethic as the foundation for our society. Furthermore, that ethic is individualistic. "Corporate" criminal liability, in terms of its moral foundations, is anti-individualistic and collectivist. I believe that both French and Jörg would acknowledge this point.[23] As Judge Jörg himself sums up his critique of British legal doctrine, "the individualist British criteria do not reflect this collective corporate responsibility" (Jörg, Chapter 5, this publication). It is not my purpose here to join issue on the merits of the debate between individualism and collectivism as social theories, but only to point out that they are, in fact, conflicting theories, that our existing criminal justice system is based entirely in the individualistic ethic, and that collectivist theories of liability—such as corporate criminal liability—are completely alien to that system.[24]

Two practical points follow from these observations. First, corporate criminal liability—or, for that matter, any form of criminal liability—is not an appropriate arena for the much broader clash between individualist and collectivist ethics. We might have such a debate, or even my fanciful debate on "anthropocentrism" versus "terracentrism," in an entirely abstract context, and presumably everyone would have some fun with it, and no one would get hurt. But a debate about criminal liability in the real world of our criminal justice system is, by definition, a debate about punishment; and punishment is about hurting people—it is about a destructive act. Society's last desperate response to a social problem is not the place to introduce innovative notions of moral responsibility. I understand that corporations, as abstractions, seem initially to be attractive targets for innovative theories of punishment, but that is only until someone realizes that corporations also are productive instrumentalities that can and have benefitted a number of natural persons as well, notwithstanding that they also can create external harms. From this perspective, applying destructive forces to corporations also passes through the destruction to those natural persons, including not only shareholders and managers, but also employees and consumers, which is everyone.[25] And if the forces applied are to be non-destructive, then we are no longer discussing punishment, and therefore we should no longer be discussing criminal liability.

Second, by introducing the moral dissonance of corporate criminal liability into a system that is very predominately concerned with the different problem of individual criminal liability, we run a grave risk of impairing both the efficiency and the moral authority of the criminal justice system more generally. If a structuralist theory such as Judge Jörg's was accepted as a morally sufficient basis for "blaming" corporations, then the likely result would be to dilute the standards of moral responsibility for individuals, both by deflecting blame from culpable individuals acting within the corporate structure and, more generally, by undermining the idea that the criminal sanction is reserved for seriously blameworthy individuals. The narrower effect is recognized—and apparently endorsed—by Judge Jörg, whose concluding paragraph asserts that, while his theory "does not necessarily absolve human beings from individual liability . . . often the only fully and really blameworthy entity is the corporation" (Jörg, Chapter 5, this publication).

Even more troubling is the possible extension of the theory to other individuals, either by similarly absolving them, or, by extension from the CID theory, attenuating the relationship between individual moral culpability and criminal responsibility. For individuals also may have an "ID" structure—call it the IID, for Individual Internal Decision structure—under which they could be found not culpable in the usual sense, but perhaps suffering from same sort of "disease of sloppiness" that Judge Jörg believes should be sufficient for criminal liability. That would introduce an element of strict liability—or at the very most negligence—into a system that heretofore has required a much higher level of culpability. The criminal sanction could then lose all of its moral authority—which is based upon a very general acceptance of its standards of moral responsibility, and not on moral innovations—and its imposition could be widely perceived as a random and unjustified act of state violence. In that case, the blunt instrument would become still more blunt.

CORPORATE "CORRECTIONS"?

Professor Lofquist's introductory chapter seems to present a somewhat different view from Judge Jörg of the structure model's implications, at least insofar as the application of sanctions is concerned. Instead of focusing on a conflictual blame-and-punishment model of corporate sanctions, as I take Judge Jörg to do, Professor Lofquist suggests that the structure model implies a more cooperative relationship between corporations and the government, especially in what he refers to as "regulatory relations in corporate crime control." In this regard, he (Lofquist, Chapter 1, this publication) writes that:

> [S]tructure theorists assert that because corporate structures and cultures, rather than rational actors, are the source of corporate crime, regulation is improved to the extent that regulators take a negotiative, educative, and reformist posture . . . [which] allows regulators to steer corporations toward compliance, minimizing the antagonism that accompanies adversarial relations, while maintaining a viable state presence in the case of corporate recalcitrance. This distinction parallels the larger distinction between corporatism, which is characterized by cooperative, planning-oriented relations between business, labor, and the state . . . and free market capitalism or state-centered socialism, which presume more adversarial relations between business and state actors.

Similarly, in discussing the sanctioning process itself from the structure perspective, Professor Lofquist refers, *inter alia*, to the works of Coffee, Gruner, and Stone, in describing proposals for "remedial interventionist sanctions" (Lofquist, Chapter 1, this publication) primarily supervisory organizational probation.

Obviously, these proposals bear a strong kinship to the massive effort undertaken during this century to transform individual punishment into a more benign form of "correctional" or "rehabilitative" treatment—an effort that now is widely regarded as a failure. We should learn a lesson from that history. If anything, undertaking a similar experiment with respect to corporations has even less prospect for success—and vastly more potential for a broadly destructive social impact—than the failed efforts with respect to individuals.

Of course, in its broadest terms, this idea simply is to replace the market with central planning by the state. At this level of generality, the idea has nothing to do with corporate violations of law. Like the concept of collectivized responsibility, this is a much broader attack on the fundamental tenets of our social organization, and is out of all proportion to a discussion of law enforcement; it is the tail wagging the dog. If collectivization is the agenda, why bother to discuss law enforcement policy, or organizational theory? Why not simply outlaw the corporate form, and all other forms of organization or affiliation among individuals? If private property is a social pathology, why not simply seize or (what is the same thing) destroy it and declare all markets unlawful? These things have been done elsewhere, with results that are known to be disastrous to human freedoms and economic well-being, and to make even human subsistence difficult. If this is the proposal, it cannot be taken seriously.

Even at the somewhat more muted level of the so-called "mixed" economies of some Western European countries, proposals for a more "cooperative" relationship between business and government have little relevance to social conditions in the United States, and almost no relevance to the problem of law enforcement against corporations. Here again, the proposal would be something akin to the government either buying or seizing equity interests in private firms, and then managing them toward more "socially responsible" activity. That question also is uninteresting under anything like the current social or political conditions in the United States.[26]

Now narrowing the focus to something like the current social and political conditions in the United States, where free enterprise is the rule and state intervention a limited exception, and further narrowing the focus to law violations by private corporations, for which a proposed solution is the sort of interventionist remedy suggested by Coffee, Gruner, and Stone,[27] and partially adopted in the U.S. Sentencing Commission's sentencing guidelines for organizations,[28] I still have two major objections:

> First, there is no reason to believe that society as a whole, particularly as it acts through government, has anything like the amount of knowledge required to "correct" organizational problems, and there are strong reasons to believe that government will never be able to generate the requisite information. Second, even if—contrary to all economic logic—such information could be generated, it would not provide a justification for invoking the blunt instrument of criminal punishment, especially as there are much sharper instruments at hand for that purpose, supplied by non-criminal law.

The Limits of Social Knowledge

Our poor experience with attempts to rehabilitate individual offenders should give us pause before embarking upon a similar experiment with corporations, even if we had a sound basis in theory and empirical evidence for doing so. But in fact there are no such bases. Indeed, the most that is claimed for such measures is that "[t]he extent to which organizations can be manipulated, particularly when viewed from a structural perspective, suggests that these measures may have a better chance of success than individual rehabilitation" (Lofquist, Chapter 1, this publication). There "may" also be life on Mars, but I am unwilling to stake a substantial amount of money, much less our nation's economic health and to some extent our private freedoms, on that prospect. To make that gamble on the similarly speculative prospect that corporation "rehabilitation" can succeed where the more tractable project of individual rehabilitation failed strikes me as an irresponsibly risky undertaking. Certainly the fact that organizations can be "manipulated" tells us nothing about the prospects of success. Individuals can be "manipulated" too, but it did not follow that they could be rehabilitated reliably, or that attempting to do so was worth the social costs of wielding the blunt instrument for that purpose.

In characterizing the prospect as merely speculative, I may err too far in favor of corporate "rehabilitation" proposals. We actually know more than that. Although the current state of our knowledge is primitive, unless the several studies to date are seriously in error, the actual incidence of "corporate crime" in our society is vanishingly small. In the federal system, which is the most focused on corporate violations and follows the most expansive notion of corporate criminal liability yet proposed—though without any moral overtones—corporate defendants account for less than one percent of criminal defendants, at the rate of approximately 300-400 firms per year, as compared with over 50,000 individuals.[29] Furthermore, at least 80 percent of those firms are too small to have the sorts of organizational problems that could be remedied by the interventionist sanctions. Therefore, at most we have something less than 100 firms per year that could benefit from corporate "rehabilitation," even assuming that the government knew how to accomplish that task.

On the other side of the balance, we have millions of firms in the United States that account for a healthy percentage of our gross national product, and supply most of our material needs and productive employment. They are the principal productive nexus of our economy, and they are overwhelmingly law-abiding. Judging from relative prosecution rates, firms are about *twice* as law-abiding as individuals,[30] before even considering the fact that government in its various forms watches them more closely for law violations and before considering the vastly broader scope of activity engaged in by many corporations. There is no indication that there are huge amounts of undetected "corporate crime," and even if there were, a revision of theories of liability or sanctioning—as opposed to enforcement efforts—would have little or no effect on detection and prosecution rates. In short, the entire "corporate crime problem," as compared with other public issues and problems, appears to be quite trivial. Therefore, even if corporate rehabilitation worked, it would not be worth much investment on a national basis.

But what if corporate rehabilitation did not work? What if, in fact, the mere threat of corporate rehabilitation—now affecting the vast majority of law-abiding firms—induced organizational changes that actually reduced the efficiency of business firms, even by a minuscule percentage? Obviously, there would not have to be much of an effect to overwhelm whatever positive effects corporate rehabilitation might have for some firms, leaving us all worse off, and perhaps with more corporate crime, if prescribed forms of compliance programs and the like were less efficient at preventing offenses, as they may be (Block, 1991). We certainly have no evidence to suggest otherwise. From the standpoint of a public policy analyst, this is a very poor risk to take.

But I may still be far too optimistic about the prospects for corporate rehabilitation as a successful social policy in the United States, because of a basic insight from economics, which is that those in the best position to implement corporate compliance measures and organizational changes, and with the strongest incentive and the most expertise in doing so, are the firms themselves. I concede that there is a vast literature on organizational theory identifying various forms of organizational dysfunction, by reason of information stoppages, inappropriate "culture," or any number of other reasons, structural or otherwise. Much of that literature has been financed, directly or indirectly, by business firms, for the obvious reason that they have powerful incentives to refine their organizational structures. I am aware of no literature suggesting that the problem of internal control over law compliance is fundamentally different in nature from any of the myriad of other internal control problems faced by business firms.[31] Moreover, I am aware of no literature suggesting that government has a magic bullet for corporate internal control problems. Indeed, governmental organizations, no less than private ones, are subject to all of the same problems identified by organizational theory; some would suggest that government's problems are even worse, as it lacks the profit motive as a control mechanism.

Therefore, from a public policy perspective, we must somehow be convinced that the government is in a better position than the firms to solve the firms' own internal control problems. Moreover, even though that was so in some circumstances, we would have to explain why the firms do not simply go to the government and seek to engage its services, without the need for a threat from the government against the firm. In fact, I think that we do observe such behaviors by firms in some circumstances, for which the best example is the punishment of individuals who commit crimes within organizations. This is a context in which the government actually may have some advantage, given the government's monopolization of the use of force. As private firms are denied the lawful use of certain sanctioning forms, such as imprisonment, firms may and do seek out the government's assistance. But apart from that context, we have no reason to believe that adding a layer of governmental bureaucracy to a corporation's private bureaucracy will solve problems created by the failures of bureaucratic control.

As I conceive the problem—as an "agency theorist"—the entire public policy objective is to provide the firm with appropriate external incentives to solve its internal control problem, or if it cannot do so, to seek out the government's assistance by assuring that offending employees are identified. This in itself can be a delicate and sophisticated problem of establishing an optimal incentive structure (see Cohen & Simpson, 1997), but it does not require any form of sanction other than a monetary fine, supplemented by more directive sanctions only in cases where an appropriate monetary sanction encounters an insolvency limitation (see Block, 1991). With that exception, non-monetary sanctioning forms will, as a matter of economics, always produce inefficiencies.

The main reason for this conclusion is relatively straightforward, which is that business corporations seek to maximize profits. If they do not seek to maximize profits, then, in a competitive market structure, they do not stay in business very long, and so we need not worry about their law violations. In that context, firms that fail to maximize profits will make none at all, and will exit. If government policy has imposed the appropriate external sanction by a monetary fine—and, by "appropriate," I mean an expected sanction that fully internalizes the external harmful effects of law violations—then corporations will maximize profits by being efficiently law-abiding. By "efficiently" law-abiding, I mean that they will spend the *socially* optimal amount on crime prevention, which is the same amount that the government itself would spend to prevent the violation in question. Contrary to some of the rhetoric one hears occasionally from politicians, this is always a finite amount, for any crime, including murder.

The fact that some individuals within the firm, or even entire firm structures, will not always behave "rationally" in this manner is neither an objection nor even a qualification to the economic theory. In a competitive market, even an "imperfectly" competitive one, such "irrational" behaviors will be "punished" automatically through the operation of the profit mechanism. It is important to bear in mind that only the organization will ever seek to maximize profits. Almost no individual within the firm will do so. Economic theory recognizes this phenomenon, which is referred to as the "agency" problem, and gives rise to "agency costs." In any actual organization, agency costs are never zero; they are always positive.

What has been referred to previously as the "structure model" is essentially the same thing as the economic theory's recognition of non-zero agency costs. Given the appropriate external monetary sanction on the corporation, the entire debate between "agency theorists" and "structure theorists" comes down to a single issue: who is in a better position to minimize the agency costs of law violation—the corporation itself, driven by the profit motive; or a governmental agent or bureaucracy, driven by motives that are far more difficult to characterize other than to say that they are in some sense "political"? Notice that, given the condition of a socially optimal external monetary sanction, this is strictly an issue of economic efficiency. It is not an issue of social responsibility, because that factor already is reflected in the socially optimal fine. The simple issue is whether governments can run firms—or re-specify their organizational structure—in a more *economically* efficient manner than the firms' own management. On this point, I believe that we have a high degree of confidence that firms are relatively more efficient at maximizing their own profits than are governments. Among many other reasons, firms have a strong incentive to do so—as their survival in the marketplace depends upon it—whereas government does not.

Therefore, unless one believes that governments are better *business* managers—not better social managers—of firms than are the firm's own business managers, then the case for *any* possible benefit from "structural" sanctions has not been made. And that case is further weakened by the risks of error and inefficiency that governmental intervention poses, as well as the relatively insignificant incidence of corporate violations of any kind. Adding the organizational problems of governmental agencies themselves—which parallel those of private corporations, and in some ways are even more severe, given the absence of the profit motive and possible corruption through external influence by interest groups—makes the prospect for effective governmental intervention all the more bleak.

Why the Blunt Instrument?

My second major objection to even a benign form of "structural" criminal sanction is that, even if "structural" remedies by governmental intervention were demonstrably more efficient than internal corporate control motivated by a socially optimal external sanction—and I stress that such an assumption is entirely contrary to virtually all of our experience with governments and markets—it still would not justify the involvement of the criminal justice system. To the contrary, if such efficient structural remedies existed, then it would be demonstrably more efficient to apply such remedies through one of the many non-criminal enforcement options. The main reasons for this conclusion are the several features of the criminal process that have been shaped in direct response to the bluntness of the criminal sanction, precisely in order to limit its imposition and thereby its collateral damage, even at the expense of its law enforcement efficiency. In other words, if these structural remedies were sharp rather than blunt, why limit their application as if they were blunt?

The most obvious example is the higher burden of proof—beyond a reasonable doubt—imposed in criminal proceedings. This burden is an explicit trade-off of law enforcement efficiency that tolerates a higher incidence of false negative liability findings in order to minimize false positives. If in fact the structural remedies can be precisely tailored to eliminate collateral damage to the productive structures of an organization, this seems an unnecessary sacrifice of efficiency in law enforcement. The same is true of many other features of the criminal process, not least of which is the remedial stage itself. As compared with civil and administrative procedures and institutions, the criminal process lacks sophistication in terms of information gathering and expertise in organizational matters. Again, why sacrifice those efficiencies?

There is some indication that the advocates of structural sanctions recognize this problem, and indeed they propose what is essentially a separate "department" of the criminal justice system for organizations, not only with its own separate liability structure but also with its own specialized procedures and expert personnel. But this explanation also is unconvincing, because it seeks to re-invent the wheel: our legal system already has such procedures and personnel in its civil and administrative branches, which now carry out very similar if not identical functions. The federal Department of Justice, and many U.S. Attorneys' offices, already have specialized departments dealing with virtually all categories of corporate violations of law. Moreover, most such categories already involve regulatory supervision and civil or administrative enforcement, including "structural" sanctions, carried out by specialized regulatory agencies staffed by experts in the fields in question, such as the SEC, FTC, EPA, OSHA, and FDA. Certainly, the use of these existing resources makes more sense, if law enforcement efficiency is the objective.

The conclusion seems inescapable that something other than law enforcement efficiency is the desired end. Two possibilities come to mind. First, perhaps the "structural" remedies are not so sharp at all, but in fact are the blunt instrument of punishment, which undermines the entire case for their application as "rehabilitative" measures. Second, the entire point of the "structural" remedies is to destroy or at least disable, in which case the "structural" remedies are neither "correction" nor punishment, but in fact are crime. In neither case is the invocation of the criminal process justified, and both cases are examples of the abusive potential of "structural" remedies and of the "structural" theory of corporate criminal liability.

POLITICS, RECONCILIATION, AND ABUSE

Professor Lofquist's introductory chapter refers to the structure model in the alternative as a "politics-based" theory of control over corporate behavior, as distinguished from the agency model's "market-based" theory. As he points out, these perspectives are not entirely distinct in actual policy formulation, although they are generally opposed theoretically (Lofquist, Chapter 1, this publication).

Here again, there is both a broader and a narrower interpretation of this dichotomy. If understood as merely one battleground in the epic struggle between the individualist and collectivist ethics as a normative matter, then I very seriously doubt whether the dialogue between the structure and agency models of corporate criminal liability and punishment can lead to constructive results. But there may be an even deeper point. Framing the debate as one between politics and markets—as if these were fully substitutable methods of social control, to be selected by some supreme governmental authority in much the same manner as one would decide whether to have apples or oranges for lunch—runs afoul of an even more fundamental mistake of indulging in the unwarranted assumption of a statist society. This is not only a normative point—and is not mentioned here as such—but also a positive one.

As I have indicated above, using the corporate crime debate as a vehicle for advancing a collectivist vision of society as against our individualist tradition strikes me as a singularly inappropriate approach under current social conditions. If collectivism is the agenda, then it should be advanced openly, and not smuggled in through the back door of "corporate crime." The same considerations apply with even greater force to the assumption of statism, which is demonstrably counter-factual in our society. Because it is counter-factual, it is positively inappropriate to the debate. Simply as a historical matter, the United States arose in a revolt against a statist system, at that time in the form of monarchy. It was not the object of the American Revolution to replace one sort of monarchy with another. As a legal matter, the fundamental organic law of the United States is not the Constitution, but rather is the Declaration of Independence, which recognizes the transience of any particular form of government, including the one later established by the Constitution.[32] According to the Declaration of Independence, governments are established to secure the rights of the people, and "whenever any Form of Government becomes destructive of these Ends, it is the Right of the People to alter or abolish it, and to institute new Government, laying its Foundation on such Principles, and organizing its Powers in such Form, as to them shall seem the most likely to effect their Safety and Happiness."

For these reasons, simply as a matter of our organic law and political existence, the choice between politics (in the sense of legislative enactment) and markets as social organizing criteria is not simply a policy choice made by an all-powerful state. I do not deny that the state has intervened—increasingly so in recent decades—in the operation of markets, nor do I deny that markets have an impact on politics. But the entire existence of the United States is predicated on the idea that government—however broad its delegated powers— is the servant and not the master. At least until the next revolution comes along, I believe that we all have to live with that fact. And that fact of our political, social, and legal life is very different from the social conditions obtaining in even the most liberal of the Western European nations—at least those on the continent—whose legal traditions follow from the more nearly statist premise of the French Revolution (Merryman, 1985).

In practical terms more narrowly focused on the current subject, these considerations counsel us to concentrate our debate on corporate crime more closely on what all would concede are legitimate functions of government. Law enforcement is one of those, so long as law is understood as something approximately coinciding with the foundations of our polity. The "structure" model overreaches itself when it requires us to rip apart the foundations of our political and legal systems merely to address a social problem that has not been shown to be of more than routine concern from the standpoint of national policy. In that sense, the "structure" model itself becomes the "blunt instrument" of destruction. If the debate can be re-focused on a more routine level of policy, then a constructive dialogue can ensue. Having now examined the theoretical underpinnings of the "structure" model, I am not convinced that it has a large potential for that purpose, unless it can be reconciled with a more generally accepted social conception.

Of course, certain aspects of the structure model have entered our social dialogue, and in some instances our positive law. One prominent example is the current federal doctrine of corporate criminal liability, which closely approximates in result even a fairly expansive interpretation of "structural" liability, though it does so without all of the trappings of moral responsibility. So, too, the current federal criminal sentencing guidelines for organizations embody some elements of "structural" sanctions—too many, in my opinion (Parker, 1993)[33]—but again without a wholehearted endorsement of the underlying theory, and without very much in the way of moralization. As the courts and the sentencing commission appear to have taken a rather pragmatic, utilitarian approach, I might suggest that this is the appropriate one for the academic debate and further empirical investigation.

In the meantime, the Congress has been relatively quiescent on the entire subject. Though it continues its seemingly endless march toward more and more criminalization in general, it has not intervened in any of the debates. It has never endorsed nor rejected the general doctrine of corporate criminal liability, and it stood by passively while the Sentencing Commission promulgated the organizational sentencing guidelines in 1991. That may have been a deliberate act, or simply attributable to a generalized legislative paralysis when confronted with issues of law reform.

In the states, neither expansive corporate liability nor structural sanctions appear to have gained much support from either courts or legislatures. The generally prevailing view of corporate liability follows the Model Penal Code's "superior agent" rule, which is firmly grounded in the individualist tradition. Although there are no comprehensive empirical studies of which I am aware, my guess is that the frequency of corporate criminal prosecution in the states is even smaller than the tiny incidence found at the federal level. As the principal enforcers against the core of "index" crime by individuals—murder, rape, robbery, arson, burglary, assault, and theft—I believe that the states are far too busy with the serious business of applying the blunt instrument in cases of social necessity to divert their attention to the marginal case of "corporate crime." I would suggest that we leave them to that important business.

In any case, the involvement of legislatures (or quasi-legislative agencies) at either the federal or state level introduces new dimensions of potential abuse that are particularly troubling in the case of the "structure" model. From a utilitarian perspective, corporate crime and punishment have absolutely no justification as a mechanism of law enforcement: virtually everything that could be done in terms of law enforcement under the structure model for corporate criminal sanctions already can be done—and, in many cases, now is being done—under existing civil and administrative law; and that includes "blaming" corporations. From a moral perspective, "blaming" corporations within the criminal system makes no sense in terms of the shared concept of "blame" that now permeates that system; if anything, "blaming" corporations dilutes the moral authority of our criminal justice system.

Given these conditions, what is the point? I can think of only two possibilities, both of them abusive: (1) blame-shifting (and sanction-shifting) by responsible individuals; and (2) use of the criminal process for purely destructive purposes, to damage or discredit political rivals. As I have suggested previously, a coalition between these two interests may well account for the current state of federal liability law and corporate sentencing guidelines (Parker, 1993). Unless we can safely exclude these possibilities of political abuse, then we should back away from wielding the blunt instrument in this context, which in any event is unnecessary.

IS THIS TRIP NECESSARY?

In concluding, I return to the concept of necessity as the only justification available for invoking the blunt instrument of criminal punishment. Because of its recognized destructive potential, punishment is never invoked unless forced on society as its last resort. Even then, the infliction of punishment is not a happy occasion. Only a society based on sadism would find happiness in the intentional infliction of harm. At best, punishment is a grim necessity.

The standard of necessity is not met in the case of corporate criminal punishment. There is no moral imperative to punishment, because the moral basis for corporate criminal liability—if it exists at all—is too far removed from the shared values embodied in our criminal justice system, which focuses on individual moral responsibility based on personal guilt. As society's last desperate response, the criminal sanction must be limited to widely shared visions of moral responsibility in order to be effective and accepted. Injecting a rarified vision of abstract culpability into that system would undermine its moral authority.

Furthermore, that compromise with the moral values of our criminal justice system cannot be justified on utilitarian grounds, and this remains true whether or not corporate "corrections" are feasible. If corporate "corrections" are constructive, then they can be applied more efficiently and precisely through the non-criminal alternatives of civil and administrative law, without paying the price of diluting individual criminal responsibility, and perhaps with the bonus of encouraging more cooperative efforts from the corporations themselves. They can also be implemented in a more plentiful informational environment supplied by regulatory law and institutions, and without the costs of false negatives implied by the criminal process. But if corporate "corrections" turn out to be destructive after all—as economics indicates that they are—then we would be doubly foolish to impose them through the blunt instrument of criminal punishment. Without either a moral imperative in the shared values of our criminal justice system or a utilitarian justification in efficient law enforcement, corporate criminal liability and punishment threatens to degenerate into either a mechanism for political predation, or a mindless exercise in destruction. In either of those cases, corporate criminal punishment is no longer punishment at all, but in fact is crime.

NOTES

[1] Professor of Law, George Mason University School of Law; formerly Deputy Chief Counsel (1987-1988) and Consulting Counsel (1988-1989) to the United States Sentencing Commission.

[2] Any ordinary dictionary will confirm this fact: the word "punish" is derived from the same Latin root as "pain"—poena. Even in general contemporary usage, to "punish" is synonymous with "hurt." See *Merriam-Webster's Collegiate Dictionary* (9th ed., 1991:955).

[3] Though most strongly associated with utilitarian justifications, this principle is not so limited; even non-consequentialist theories of punishment, such as retribution or "desert," are based upon a moral justification for the infliction of pain upon the offender (see Walker, 1991).

[4] A clear embodiment of this principle in positive law is the current federal criminal code, which, in its sentencing provision, requires in every case that an offender's sentence be "sufficient, but not greater than *necessary* to comply with the purposes [of punishment]" 18 U.S.C. §3553(a) (emphasis added).

[5] Most criminal codes include a general defense to liability of justification by what is called the "necessity" or "choice of evils" defense. As generally formulated by the *Model Penal Code* (a publication of the private American Law Institute, which has widely influenced both state and federal criminal codes in the United States, such that a majority of states now have criminal codes largely based on it), the "choice of evils" defense will justify otherwise criminal conduct—up to and including the

intentional killing of a human being—which "the actor believes to be necessary to avoid a harm or evil to himself or another," when "the harm or evil sought to be avoided by such conduct is greater than that sought to be prevented by the law defining the offense charged" *Model Penal Code* §3.02 (American Law Institute, 1985). More familiar forms of justification defenses—such as self-defense or defense of another—are simply more specific applications of this same principle, which is distinguished from another class of "excuse" defenses—such as insanity or duress. In the case of "excuse," the plea is that the actor did the wrong thing but could not help it, given the circumstances, whereas, in justification, the plea is that, notwithstanding the evil result, the actor did the "right" thing, on balance (see generally LaFave & Scott, 1986). As LaFave & Scott point out, this very same principle of justification is what provides a defense to public officer—such as an executioner or a prison warden—engaged in the infliction of state-sanctioned punishment. See *id.* §5.5(a).

[6]   Writing in 1881, Oliver Wendell Holmes, Jr. (then a law professor at Harvard, and later one of the most famous of Supreme Court Justices), observed that "a law which punished conduct which would not be blameworthy in the average member of the community would be too severe for that community to bear" (Holmes, 1963). In other words, criminal prohibitions traditionally have been limited to minimal standards of behavior that have significant harmful effects on society, and not extended to aspirational norms or to purely private activity, even if considered reprehensible by some or most members of society. One of the major debates in criminal law over the past generation has been whether our current criminal codes already go too far toward "overcriminalization," by including prohibitions against "victimless" crimes such as homosexuality, prostitution, or drug use (see Packer, 1968, presenting an argument against criminalization of consenting behaviors; and *Bowers v. Hardwick,* 478 U.S. 186 [1986], a Supreme Court decision ruling that the state may criminalize private consensual homosexual acts between adults) and hypertechnical "regulatory" crimes that arguably are better relegated to private tort or public civil law (see Coffee, 1991, discussing recent federal cases; and *Liparota v. United States,* 471 U.S. 419 [1985], a Supreme Court decision requiring proof that a defendant knew of the regulatory prohibition before conviction of a criminal violation of regulations restricting the use of federal food stamps).

[7]   For an overview of American criminal procedure, see generally LaFave and Israel (1992), especially Chapter 1, which summarizes the constituents and values embodied in the criminal process.

[8]   In explaining the constitutional standard of proof beyond a reasonable doubt, the Supreme Court has stated that "a fundamental value of our system is that it is far worse to convict an innocent person that to let a guilty man go free" (*In re Winship,* 397 U.S. 358 [1970]).

[9]   These principles also are embodied in current federal sentencing statutes. Sentencing courts are required to consider both "the need for the sentence imposed . . . to reflect the seriousness of the offense," 18 U.S.C. §3553(a)(2)(A), and "the need to avoid unwarranted sentence disparities among defendants with similar records who have been found guilty of similar conduct" 18 U.S.C. §3553(a)(6). Similarly, the

United States Sentencing Commission is directed to formulate guidelines and policy statements for the federal criminal justice system that "provide certainty and fairness in meeting the purposes of sentencing, avoiding unwarranted disparities among defendants" 28 U.S.C. §991(b)(1)(B).

[10]   The literature on the death penalty is vast. A standard reference work is Bedau (1982). For a brief summary of the arguments, *see* American Law Institute, *Model Penal Code and Commentaries* §210.6, at 111-17 (ALI, 1980).

[11]   The Eighth Amendment to the U.S. Constitution provides that "Excessive bail shall not be required, nor excessive fines imposed, nor cruel and unusual punishments inflicted." Most U.S. State constitutions have similar provisions. At either or both of those levels, many variations on these forms of punishment have been declared unconstitutional (see LaFave & Scott, 1986).

[12]   Later sociological studies followed the same pattern. In the post-Sutherland era, the most extensive study was Clinard, et al., (1979), which formed the basis for Clinard and Yeager (1980). As with Sutherland, the Clinard study focused only on large corporations, and did not distinguish civil from criminal violations.

[13]   As it first appeared, *White Collar Crime* omitted the names of the corporations involved, and these were not restored until an "uncut version" of the work appeared in 1983 (Sutherland, 1983). This recent edition includes an introduction explaining why the original version was edited—Sutherland and his publisher realized that characterizing the civil violations as "crimes" was actionably libelous (Sutherland, 1983:x-xi). The description of the thought process by one of Sutherland's colleagues at the time provides an excellent example of the economic concept of "revealed" as opposed to "expressed" preference:

> Sutherland agonized over the question whether to make the excisions. He often invited students and colleagues into his office to discuss the issue. Donald Cressey, one of those advisers and later Sutherland's collaborator, has recalled his reaction to Sutherland's dilemma:
>
>> Had the original manuscript been published, and had a libel suit been filed, then Sutherland's contention that the listed offenses are in fact crimes might have been tested in a court of law—a corporation might have argued that the statement is libelous because its behavior is not a crime, with Sutherland giving the arguments presented in his book. I was one of Sutherland's research assistants at the time, and I urged that the original manuscript be published for this reason, if no other. However, my idealistic desire to see a scientific principle tested in a court of law was not tempered by any practical consideration such as having money riding on the legal validity of the scientific principle. This was not the case with either the publisher or Professor Sutherland (Sutherland, 1983:x-xi).
>>
>> I believe that Professor Sutherland's "revealed preference" as to the law of crime—and of defamation—reflected very good judgment.

[14]   Among other things, Sutherland's arguments failed to appreciate that criminal and civil violations of the same statute have different proof requirements. See, *e.g.*, *United States v. United States Gypsum Co.*, 438 U.S. 422 (1978)(so holding as to criminal versus civil violations of the antitrust laws, one of Sutherland's principal examples). However, as indicated in the previous note, Sutherland seemed to have been well aware of the deficiencies of his arguments as a matter of law.

[15]   This is not to say that such a perception would be accurate. To the contrary—and notwithstanding a constant drumbeat of criticism in the popular media and by politicians running for office—it appears that our criminal justice system is on the right track, at least in terms of the traditional category of what the FBI calls "index" crime—murder, rape, robbery, arson, assault, burglary, and theft. According to the Department of Justice's annual National Crime Victimization Survey, estimated underlying crime rates (including reported and unreported crimes) have been declining on a per capita basis virtually every year since 1981, resulting in a cumulative decrease of 19 percent through 1992 (U.S. Department of Justice, 1994a). Due to fluctuations in reporting rates, the rate of reported crimes has fluctuated. But even that figure peaked, on a per capita basis, in 1980. It has been variable since that time, falling through 1984, then rising until 1991, and then falling again in 1992-1993 (U.S. Department of Justice, 1994b:Table 3.94). Of course, these data exclude the "victimless" crimes such as drug sales and use (though any drug-related violence or property crime is included), which have come to dominate much of our criminal justice effort in recent years. For example, in the federal courts, drug offenses accounted for 36 percent of all convictions, and nearly 50 percent of all imprisonment sentences imposed, in the United States District Courts in 1992 (U.S. Department of Justice, 1994b:Tables 5.19 & 5.23).

[16]   This article is a revised and updated version of a paper I first presented in October 1991, at the Cato Institute's conference on the then-new federal corporate sentencing guidelines.

[17]   Recent empirical studies on publicly-traded firms indicate that there is no differential "stigma" effect from criminal as opposed to civil enforcement as against corporations (Block, 1991; Karpoff & Lott, 1993). What this implies is that "blaming" corporations works equally well (or equally badly) with or without the "criminal" label, which itself is an argument for not using the label, as its use is more expensive in terms of law enforcement effort, and ultimately may dilute the association between the "criminal" label and moral blameworthiness, even for individuals.

[18]   The prevailing pattern in American states follows the Model Penal Code's concept of locating the corporate "mind" in a "high managerial agent" (see American Law Institute, 1985), which is also referred to as the "superior agent" rule (LaFave & Scott, 1986:§3.10). A similar rule prevails in English law, as the "organ" or "alter ego" doctrine (G. Williams, 1961:§§279-280). However, American federal law has given up on the fiction of the corporate "mind." It plainly acknowledges the rationale of strict liability at the corporate liability level, without any moral overtones (Parker, 1989).

[19]   I should note in passing that here Jörg may be extending the concept far beyond what French himself claims. French's main concern is not with legal doctrine, and his brief treatment of that subject indicates his belief that the Model Penal Code's version of the "superior agent" rule would be consistent with an operationalized version of French's theory of the CID Structure (see French, 1984). But the Model Penal Code's scope of liability is far narrower than Jörg's argument.

[20]   Those interested in a full development of my views will have to await the appearance of my monograph now in progress, tentatively titled *The Criminalization of the Corporation*, which is expected to appear later in 1997.

[21]   As Judge Jörg recognizes, the scope of liability he describes does approximate that of current American federal law, though "the route is different." American federal law does not purport to find the corporate entity "blameworthy" at all, but explicitly acknowledges that it is a theory of strict and vicarious liability, without any moral connotations, that ordinarily would be insufficient to hold an individual criminally responsible (see Parker, 1989).

[22]   It is good to remember that corporations are not the only form of business organization. Proprietorships and partnerships are more numerous, and new forms, such as the Limited Liability Company—which is neither a corporation nor a partnership—arise all the time. All of these forms, to the extent that they represent a plurality of actors, essentially are contracts, not "persons" in any economic or other sense. In some cases, such as partnerships in most American states, they do not have any legal "personality"—they cannot sue or be sued as distinct from their members. The legal "personality" of corporations is a mere artifact of legislative convention, of varying legal significance depending upon the issue at hand (see Ribstein & Letsou, 1995).

[23]   The title of French's monograph, and its contents, make the point repeatedly.

[24]   This point is clearly recognized by what I consider to be the most important early work arguing for the sort of governmental interventionism that seems to be the aim of the "structure" model—Christopher Stone's 1975 book titled *Where the Law Ends: The Social Control of Corporate Behavior*. Stone's book was not especially concerned with the civil/criminal distinction, but he recognized clearly that the impediment to interventionist measures was Anglo-American law's almost exclusive concern with the individual over the group as the locus of moral responsibility.

[25]   Legal policy tends to be driven by more practical and common-sense considerations, stated in terms similar to those that I used in my 1990 Congressional statement, in which I explained the basis for a monetary sanctions policy for organizations to a Congressional subcommittee (see U.S. House of Representatives, 1990b).

[26]   Nationalization of private corporations is never far below the surface of the "corporate crime" critique (see Clinard & Yeager, 1980). A variation on that theme, of "federal chartering" for large corporations, was proposed by Ralph Nader in the 1970s (Nader & Seligman, 1976), but went nowhere politically even then, when "big government" was at its peak. Under current conditions, when our President

recently has declared, in his 1996 State of the Union address, that "the era of big government is over," such proposals are even farther away from the political mainstream.

27   Coffee, Gruner, and Stone had developed an alternative proposal on corporate probation, which was published, together with other proposals and papers, in the United States Sentencing Commission's 1988 *Discussion Materials on Organizational Sanctions*. Except for my own policy paper, those *Discussion Materials* were published as a special issue of the *Whittier Law Review* in 1988 (volume 10, number 1), with an introduction written by Professor Gruner. My own policy paper from the *Discussion Materials* was published separately (Parker, 1989), together with an extensive empirical study by Professor Mark Cohen (Cohen, 1989), which was an expanded version of the empirical work that had appeared in the *Discussion Materials*. The corporate probation proposal by Coffee, Gruner, and Stone had drawn upon their prior published work (Coffee, 1981; Gruner, 1988; Stone, 1975, 1980).

28   The Commission did not promulgate final corporate sentencing guidelines until late 1991. Both the process leading to their promulgation, and their ultimate contents, were controversial, and I have been one of the principal critics. However, as Professor Lofquist notes, the Commission's action was not intended as an adoption of a structure-based standard of corporate liability, as indeed the Commission has no authority over liability standards, which in the federal system are based upon a strict and vicarious liability in the corporation.

29   This was one of the principal findings of the U.S. Sentencing Commission's study of federal prosecution activity in the mid- to late-1980s, and, so far as I am aware, has been confirmed by all subsequent studies.

30   In round numbers, there are about four million business corporations in the United States, of which about 400 are charged annually in the federal courts, for a prosecution rate of one in 10,000. Taking the individual population as about 250 million, and individual federal prosecutions at 50,000 annually, yields a prosecution rate of two in 10,000. Thus, the randomly selected individual citizen is twice as likely to be charged with a federal crime as the randomly selected business corporation.

31   Both of these points are illustrated by an interesting contribution to this literature by Baysinger (1991). Baysinger's paper was solicited and published in connection with a conference sponsored by the Law and Economics Center at George Mason University School of Law, and the conference was financed in large part by corporate contributions. I am sure that the firms valued Professor Baysinger's contribution to the literature on their organizational problems.

However, in terms of the substance of Professor Baysinger's critique of external sanctions, his comments are misplaced. He analogizes the external sanction to the assumption of "a closed hydraulic system" (Baysinger, 1991:343-345), that translates the impact through the organization, and then argues that interventionist measures are justified by the fact that there are some leaks in the figurative hydraulic cylinders. Although the simile is useful, the argument is incorrect: economics does not assume "perfect" hydraulics. In fact, economics recognizes that many firms' hydraulic systems are quite leaky—this is what is meant in economics by "agency costs."

The issue between "agency" and "structure" theories is not whether firms' hydraulic systems are leaky, but rather is how anyone could believe that the government is better at finding and plugging the leaks under a diffuse set of bureaucratic incentives than are the firm's own mangers, when supplied with the external incentive of a socially optimal fine, in the monetary terms that the firms' managers can directly translate into business incentives.

[32]   For those who doubt my statement of the law, I suggest that they go to the library and look at the first volume of the current official *United States Code*. In that volume, they will find a section entitled "Organic Laws of the United States of America," which precedes the ordinary statutes enacted by the Congress over the years, which begin in that volume in Title 1 and go on for another 50 titles or so, in many volumes. The "Organic Laws" section includes the Constitution, but the first document printed there is the Declaration of Independence.

[33]   One central point of that critique is that the current organizational sentencing guidelines go too far toward the statist vision.

5

The Promise and Limitations of Corporate Criminal Liability†

Nico Jörg[1]
Court of Appeals—Arnhem, The Netherlands

INTRODUCTION: CORPORATE CRIMINAL LIABILITY IN THEORY AND PRACTICE

It has been demonstrated that legal entities existed during the Middle Ages (churches, towns) and in many respects have been dealt with on an equal legal footing as individuals (Coleman, 1974). Gierke (1887) has found that in the Middle Ages municipal communities could act as separate entities towards the citizens making up those communities. The civil corporation has long been accepted as a competent legal entity and participant of legal life. We could hardly envisage our daily life without the prevalence of corporations. The same applies to the public corporation in public and private law. Numerous issues in commercial law have been dealt with by legislators and the judiciary. Coleman (1974:49) is right in saying:

> It is the corporate actors, the organizations that draw their power from persons and employ that power to corporate ends, that are the primary actors in the social structure of modern society.

Yet, according to Friedrich von Savigny, the nineteenth-century German philosopher, the criminal law is directed to beings who are able to think, to

---

† The author expresses his regrets not to have been enabled to comment on the original contribution of Mr. Parker, which could have led to a congruent exchange of ideas during the materialization of this book or afterwards.

intend and to feel. Only human beings have these capacities. The so called intent or crime of a legal entity, even the legal entity itself is pure fiction (von Savigny, 1840). This forms the classical approach to the question of corporate criminal liability: the principle of culpability prohibits the extension of human criminal liability to corporate criminal liability. It is the major problem to be solved if legal entities are to be punishable. Many regard this as an insurmountable obstacle.

There are a few minor problems too. One is the attribution of acts to others than the person who acted. In this respect, solutions can be and have been borrowed from civil doctrine: vicarious liability and agency. Another problem is criminal liability without fault, generally to be found as corollary to mere regulatory offenses. This problem has also been addressed in legal doctrine. There the culpability principle plays a far less dominant role, because the violation of regulatory law ordinarily does not stigmatize individuals as criminals. A third problem is how to proceed against legal entities. A fourth one, what are appropriate sentences for corporations? The basic question remains: is it possible to blame a corporation in the same criminal sense as human beings can be blamed? Practical as they are, American courts did not see theoretical, dogmatic objections in accepting criminal liability of corporations.[2]

What then do we mean by the principle of culpability? It is generally seen as a prerequisite to punishment. Punishment has at least these two aspects: retribution and deterrence. Punishment as retribution requires someone to understand why retribution has to be made; punishment as deterrence requires someone to be free and able to change future actions in acceptable directions. It is common thinking that only human beings have these capacities at their disposal. Culpability can be defined as the capacity to hold someone responsible for an illegal act which he or she could have avoided. Culpability encompasses unlawfulness which could be avoided and for which the individual can be blamed.

The ability to be blamed requires that the actor has moral competence, that he or she is a moral actor (Spit, 1986). Moral competence means that the actor has the ability to discriminate wrong from right and to act accordingly; to practise this to (the interests of) others, and finally to render reasoned account of his or her own judgment and acts. To cite H.L.A. Hart in shorthand, the capacities as central to moral responsibility are reasoning, understanding and the capacity to modify conduct (Hart, 1968). In this perspective an animal is not morally competent; a child is a developing moral actor; and the moral competence of a senile person is in decline. It is not asserted that a moral actor knows what is wrong or right; only that he or she knows that those categories exist.

Jurisprudence does not use the term moral competence. But when it uses the terms will, knowledge, and freedom to act, it basically expresses the same requirements for culpability. From the statement that a corporation is incapable of being culpable, it follows that a corporation is not a moral person. It implies that corporations cannot form part of the moral community and contribute to its development (French, 1984). Some go further and deny that corporations are social actors or even actors at all. An alternative to this agency line of reasoning is the structural approach: a corporation is an entity, a *sui generis* unity, distinct as to time and place. A corporation is in real existence, albeit not tangible, but metaphysical. For instance: a university does not exist any less than its students and faculty do, but differently. We are transported by United Airlines, although a human pilot flies the plane. We shop at Safeway, but pay the cashier.

Compared to an animal, a corporation takes part only in the social reality, while an animal takes part only in the natural reality. Social reality means a reality governed by rules. An animal may be subjected to rules and "punished"—disciplining in order to reach automatic behavior—but it does not create rules, does not construe them nor contemplate compliance. In contrast, a corporation exists thanks to rules; rules define its structure. It can create rules, construe them, and decide whether to comply with them. Contemplation is of course human activity, but the decision is a corporate one, like its execution, although human beings perform the physical side of the execution of decisions. It will be clear that human beings combine belonging both to the natural and the social reality.

One further question needs clarification in pursuing the structural approach. Have corporations the ability to *act*? Or is it preferable to regard corporate behavior as *conduct*? Conduct has a wider meaning than acts or omissions, the classical legal categories of human behavior. Acts or omissions relate to (the absence of) physical movements; they relate to the natural reality, to which corporations do not belong. Conduct means acts or omissions in the social reality. As corporations belong only to the social reality, it is preferable to speak of conduct by corporations. Of course corporations conduct themselves only by physical acts or omissions of human beings, but theoretically there is no need to look for human behavior as a prerequisite to corporate liability. It is the corporation itself which has to respond to legal obligations, i.e., to obligations existing in the social reality. If a company fails to return tax, it is the failure of the company, which is the addressee of the norm. Apart from this, it may be individuals who neglect their corporate duty in this respect, but this is not the first concern for the structural approach of corporate liability.

Speaking of conduct clarifies immediately one culpability issue—the avoidability of unlawful behavior. Corporations do not physically act or omit; they make no movements. Their conduct is rational—albeit not always right. Their conduct is not impaired by fatigue, rage, anger, alcohol, etc. Corporate conduct is the result of consultation and decisionmaking whether on the spot or by anticipation. As soon as unlawful corporate conduct has been proved, the question of avoidability will be answered in the positive. But the essence is, whether it can be said that the corporation conducted itself. Summarizing the external aspect of corporations, the structural approach of corporate criminal liability takes the view that a corporation is a social entity, with the capacity of conduct; it is a social actor.

Apart from the previous, external, aspect, there is the internal aspect, with the essential terms: will, knowledge, and freedom to act. Can it be said that legal entities may possess those culpability elements? It is asserted that they may as a result of the corporate structure, corporate decisionmaking, and corporate objectives. The corporate structure encompasses the arrangements of the internal decisionmaking process. They may be called rules of recognition. There are the rules which facilitate a judgment by outsiders, whether they are confronted with valid (i.e., binding) corporate decisions. The corporate structure is also expressed by the way tasks are distributed among positions. Tasks are accompanied by formal powers, the execution of which may have external effects, and may be regarded as conduct of the corporation.

Nevertheless reality rules over formal structure. The internal decision-making process may deviate from the formal structure. It is important to understand that corporate reality in decisionmaking often circles around the formal structure, instead of coinciding with it. The crucial question is to determine corporate policy. One element is the objectives formulated in the charter of the corporation; another, the goals that emerge unmistakably from corporate documents and actual action taking by functionaries, whether formally authorized or not, provided that the action is de facto tolerated.

According to French (1984), three elements—corporate structure, decisionmaking, and objectives—form the Corporate Internal Decision structure (CID). Here is where the corporate will is located, one of the elements of moral competence. In other words, if determined that persons in the formally right positions and according to the right procedures take or execute decisions in conformity with formal objectives or corporate policy, one may conclude that at least these actions are intentional and deliberate conduct by the corporation. There may be more intentional corporate conduct than follows from the corporate charter, hence the words "at least."

Once determined that corporate conduct is intentional conduct, it is immaterial whether the individuals making decisions or taking action acted in bad faith—bribed, exploited, dealing as an insider, etc. Equally, if the objection of a leading functionary did not prevent the decision being made or the action being taken, the corporate intention may be there, depending on the wider decision preparing and making process. Day-to-day routine by lower functionaries may give a much clearer picture of corporate policy than the formal accounts by leading persons. This is especially true regarding large enterprises; corporate policy is in certain ways independent from ruling functionaries, there is more continuity than chance. It may be less applicable to small enterprises in which corporate policy may be essentially the expression of the director's policy. Under those circumstances the corporation may be seen as the *alter ego* of the director.

Corporate intentionality is an element that can be determined irrespective of, even contrary to, the directors' will. A competing theory, adhering to the identification doctrine, locates corporate intention and corporate knowledge at the very top of the corporation or at a competent superior functionary.[3] Whether a corporation can be attributed will and knowledge depends essentially on the question of whether corporate management possesses will and knowledge. This line of thinking is prevalent in Anglo-Saxon law; it has been abandoned in the neighbouring country of the Netherlands. The reasoning behind abandoning the identification doctrine is that, in reality, corporations vary enormously as to intensity of leadership. Some aim at omniscient and censorious management, others at maximum independence of corporate (sub)divisions.[4] It follows that it is more realistic to locate the corporation's will at the Corporate Internal Decision structure.

What has been said of the corporate will applies equally to the corporate knowledge. It develops in the Corporate Internal Decision structure, there is no need to restrict it to management. From the formal corporate objectives and the actual corporate policy, acts may result by executive personnel which are—within the given structure and decision-making process—not necessarily known to the management. Because of the significance of the corporate internal decision structure lack of knowledge by the management does not impede knowledge by the corporation. Of course corporate will and knowledge is different from the human will; a human being who deliberately acts has knowledge, immediately and in an undivided consciousness (Spit, 1986), of what he is doing. Corporate consciousness is a result of the decision-making process.

It has already been noted that corporate conduct is essentially avoidable. It means that the corporation has the freedom of choice, to take a certain decision or not, and to implement and execute it or not. It is not the case that once a corporation has a legal duty of conduct, it has no freedom of choice anymore (Nichols & Buono, 1986). The corporation has the freedom to conduct itself contrary to legal norms, yet has no right to do so. It has to vouch for the consequences. This is not different from a driver who refuses to take a breath test.

Summarizing thus far, one may say that will, combined with knowledge and freedom of action, results in the power of the corporation to conduct itself in a certain way. From the elements forming the internal decision structure follows the possibility to reformulate policy, give new orders, restructure tasks and powers, take measures, precautions, guidance, and to improve personal good behavior and prevent and terminate undesirable conduct by instruction, training, and other forms of communication. In other words, to influence acts and omissions of staff and subordinates resulting in conduct of the corporation. French (1984:145) calls this corporate effort "responsive adjustment;" Fisse (1983) calls corporate neglect to react "reactive fault."

CORPORATE MORAL COMPETENCE

In the previous text a legal entity is regarded as a social entity competent of conduct, having an internal decision structure, where the will and the knowledge of the corporation are formed in a setting of freedom of action. The question remains whether a corporation is a moral actor. Three conditions of moral competence have also been identified. The first, has a corporation the ability to discriminate wrong from right and to conduct itself accordingly? Knowledge of the corporation originates at the internal decision structure based on judgments of individuals. This knowledge encompasses what is, and is not, in the best interest of the corporation. It stems from a process of balancing pros and cons which may travel through various levels of the corporation. Each level may have contributed to it by the gathering and exchange of data and the presentation of eventual corporate policy. In the balancing process, not only corporate norms and values (employment, job satisfaction, profit) will play a role, so will norms and values of individuals employed by the corporation, derived from society at large and the philosophy of life. Thus external norms and values penetrate the corporation. They can and will play a role in the decision-making process, disengaged from the individuals importing them (see R. Williams, 1961). They form part of corporate knowledge. A specific corporate culture develops. It follows that a legal entity can discriminate between wrong and right. The corporate internal decision structure also accommodates the will of the corporation to conduct itself according or contrary to the understanding of wrong and right.

The second condition of moral competence is, has the corporation the ability to practice this distinction of wrong and right to others? When the corporation by means of the internal decision structure has a rational understanding of wrong and right, it can have understanding of the interests of others, too. One may say that a legal entity is in a better position than individuals to identify others and their interests. The ability to generate such knowledge by cooperative effort is much greater than by individual effort.

The third condition of moral competence is whether the corporation has the ability to render a reasoned account of its own judgment of wrong and right and its own acts. Corporations are able to do this. The internal decision structure enables it to dig into the finesses of the corporate conduct and to reason how and why the corporation balanced pros and cons, and which information has been used. This account can be required to satisfy the requirements of maximum rationality, including the balancing of general social norms and values. The conclusion is that a legal entity has moral competency, it is a moral actor. Hence criminal liability of corporations cannot be opposed on principle.

Before turning to applications of the structure theory of criminal liability of corporations, it is preferable to apply it first to disasters. French demonstrated the usefulness of this approach of moral competency because causes of disasters are ordinarily intensely researched by independent committees, the reports of which tend to touch on all aspects that may have contributed to the occurrence of the disaster. Many examples could be discussed; we will focus on just one because it has a special bearing on the subject of this contribution as a criminal liability battle followed in the wake of the inquiry: the shipping disaster of the Herald of Free Enterprise at the port of Zeebrugge, Belgium, in 1987; 193 persons on board drowned because the P&O-ship set sail before the bow door had been closed.

The Herald of Free Enterprise was a roll-on-roll-off ship, a construction with large movable bow and stern parts by which cars and lorries may enter and leave the ship. The car decks are not divided into watertight compartments. This means that waves entering the deck(s) can move all the way up and down the ship and to one side, which is particularly risky as the ship may become unstable by the weight of the water at one side. As cars are not secured to the deck, they may start sliding to the lower side, reinforcing the off-balance. The dangers are inherent to this type of ship and well-known. In this particular case, the ship capsized within 60 seconds of the water entering the ship.

The inquiry resulted in a report (*M.V. Herald of the Free Enterprise*, 1987) of the following facts. The assistant bosun was responsible for closing the bow doors. He was asleep in his cabin at the time of departure. The instruction for the loading officer contained the duty to check personally that the doors were closed at the time of setting sail. A second instruction required him to be present on the bridge at the same moment. From the bridge the position of the doors could not be observed. The first instruction had been neglected by him. The ship's captain was required before setting sail to inquire whether the ship was ready for departure. This had been neglected, too.

The report did not restrict itself to enumeration of these individual shortcomings. It stated (*M.V. Herald of the Free Enterprise*, 1987:Sec. 14.1):

> [A] full investigation into the circumstances of the disaster leads inexorably to the conclusion that the underlying or cardinal faults lay higher up in the Company. The Board of Directors did not appreciate their responsibility for the safe management of their ships. They did not apply their minds to the question: What orders should be given for the safety of our ships? The Directors did not have any proper comprehension of what their duties were. There appears to have been a lack of thought about the way in which the HERALD ought to have been organized for the Dover/Zeebrugge run. All concerned in management, from the members of the board down to the junior superintendents, were guilty of fault in that all must be regarded as sharing responsibility for the failure of management. From top to bottom the body corporate was infected with the disease of

sloppiness. The failure on the part of the shore management to give proper and clear directions was a contributory cause of the disaster. This is a serious finding which must be explained in some detail.

The shipping company had been criticized heavily by the commission for three circumstances in particular. First, the deriding rejection of the suggestion to install bow door warning lights on the bridge. Second, the lack of gathering of information on similar previous incidents (5 or 6 in the last 3½ years), although those incidents were known to various persons employed. Third, the failure to develop a sound system for safeguarding the highest safety norms on board. If an unsafe system has the potential of such grave consequences, the ship owner has a comparable onus to provide a safe system, said the commission of inquiry.

What does this example mean for our subject? First of all, a shipping company is not a natural, but a social entity; it cannot move, but it can conduct itself. It transports passengers, freight, competes with other ship owners, pays taxes. It has a structure, a certain way of decisionmaking, and it has objectives and goals. These three elements form the corporate internal decision structure in which the will, the knowledge, and the freedom to act are located. As explained, these are conditions for being allowed to reproach somebody in a criminal sense. Moreover, culpability requires moral competence of the perpetrator. Had the shipping company the ability to distinguish wrong from right, and act accordingly? Had the company the ability to practice this in the interests of others, the passengers? And finally, had the company the ability to render a reasoned account of its own judgment and its own conduct? The answer is three times yes, and the company was reproached by the committee for not properly exercising its abilities.

From a structural point of view, there are no objections to holding corporations morally competent. From this flows that there are no objections against the concept of criminal liability of corporations. From a policy point of view, it is even often preferable to apply that concept to corporations, "the law, long oriented toward the behavior of individuals, is frequently a clumsy tool for penetrating organizational boundaries" (Vaughan, 1983:94). It does not follow that individuals inside corporations are immune from prosecution if the corporation gets the blame for violation of the law. Often there are sufficient reasons for lifting the corporate veil, but that is a different subject.

CORPORATE CRIMINAL LIABILITY

Once the concept of corporate criminal liability is accepted because of agreement on the fundamental issue of moral competence, the theoretical possibility of such liability starts. What is needed more is a legal concept of conditions to be met in order to find a corporation guilty, and hence liable *in concreto*. This requires the development of criteria according to which traditional legal questions can be answered as regards corporations. Those questions are fourfold. First, when can it be said that a corporation has committed a criminal offense? In other words, what are the limits of perpetration regarding corporations? Second, can a corporation have criminal intent or be criminally negligent? Third, to what extent was the corporate conduct unlawful? Finally, to what extent can the corporation be blamed for its conduct? These are traditional questions to be answered in every concrete case. They are practical questions following the theoretical acceptance of the moral competence of corporations. Even moral competence *in concreto* does not prejudge criminal liability *in concreto*. But criminal liability without moral competence is an impossible case.

As to the first criterion of the limits of perpetration, it is clear that a physical approach to perpetration is inappropriate. However, the physical approach of perpetration is the traditional way of thinking about crime. Corporations do not move like burglars do. They conduct their affairs by acts of human beings. But often the link to human beings is totally irrelevant, as is the case with vicarious liability in general. Priority is given to the investigation of the conduct of the addressee of the legal prohibition or command. This concept of vicarious liability is an established one, starting in the past with cases of nuisance and the selling of liquor to minors. The acts by an employee are functionally attributed to the employer. Legal norms like these have expanded in the wake of the welfare state. We would prefer to call this phenomenon the concept of "functional perpetration" (van Woensel, 1993) which starts from a point of view slightly different from the concept of vicarious liability. Vicarious liability is the end result after several factual and legal questions have been answered to the detriment of the defendant, while functional perpetration is only a prerequisite to liability. One can be a functional perpetrator of an offense without being liable for it. The functional perpetrator may have an affirmative defense as to preclude liability. It is clear that, if corporations can be perpetrators of criminal acts, they can do so only functionally.

As no physical evidence of perpetration by a corporation can be observed, one has to invent criteria to determine perpetration by some body which did not act itself. One could borrow the criteria from vicarious liability which would mean that liability results from a criminal offense occurring during the course of employment of a corporation's agent within the scope of the agent's authority. Generally an additional element is required regarding corporations, to wit, acting for the benefit of the organization.[5] American case law has made clear that neither the criterion of the course of employment,[6] nor that of the scope of authority,[7] nor the (intent to) benefit criterion[8] are strictly applied.

The same applies to the Netherlands, where criminal liability of corporations emerged after World War II. In one of the first cases in which a determination under Dutch law had to be made whether the defendant corporation

was the (functional) perpetrator, the same criteria were used. In the *Vroom &
Dreesmann* case,[9] a chain of department stores was prosecuted for selling furniture for a price in excess of the relevant statutory maximum, which was a
strict liability offense. The corporation was convicted, despite the fact that the
manager of the furniture department of the store had been forbidden to sell in
excess of the statutory maximum by corporate management. The company
claimed that this prevented the corporation from being liable, but the Supreme
Court ruled that this was irrelevant, the department manager was authorized to
sell goods and he had testified that he acted for the benefit of the company.

If applied strictly, agency criteria readily prevent the determination of corporate perpetration. Hence the tendency to apply them loosely, and especially
to ignore the *ultra vires* defense. In the corporate world, this seems less hard,
as offending against strict liability prohibitions is often regarded as a risk of
doing business. But if the agency criteria are being applied rather loosely, one
may wonder whether they restrict arbitrary application of the law at all. Is it
not preferable to develop criteria that structure and limit liability in a more or
less foreseeable way? Those criteria should fit the organizational reality regarding criminal acts. Such reality has two main aspects. First, what are/were the
possibilities for the corporation to prevent the criminal acts from being committed? Second, are/were the criminal acts accepted or usually accepted by the
corporation? It will be clear that corporate criminal liability flows easily from
involvement of management with the illegal corporate act. For this reason we
shall limit the discussion to subordinate involvement.

As to the first aspect, one may presume that functional acts by corporate
personnel is corporate conduct. It is within the sphere of the corporation to see
that employees do not transgress their authority, do not transgress the limits of
the criminal law in the first place. Organizations employ various means of monitoring subordinate activity—financial controls especially are used extensively—
and it does not seem unreasonable to require organizations to check the
lawfulness of employees' conduct. So the question arises, if a corporation is
accused of criminal conduct, what efforts does the corporation take in general
to keep its personnel law abiding, and what did it do in particular in this case?
What kind of personnel were/are hired? Were/are they being trained, instructed,
and supervised effectively? It is unnecessary to go into detail as to the nature
and size of corporations in order to determine a reasonable corporate effort in
this respect. There may be disagreement as to whether due diligence in this
respect, or only absolute impossibility to prevent the employee's act from being
done, precludes the corporation's criminal liability. But it is clear that what can
be called the *power criterion* forms the entrance for discovering corporate
behavior aimed at prevention and redress of wrongdoing by subordinates.

As to the second aspect, it is equally important to investigate eventual
acceptance of illegal acts by the corporation. Lack of adequate monitoring, and
tolerance of illegal behavior will often go hand-in-hand. A corporate warning

that illegal subordinate behavior will not be tolerated is only in theory, not in practice, contrary to the existence of an informal corporate policy to accept the proceeds of illegal activity. The investigation should reveal whether the corporation checked the legality of the revenues. Thoroughness in controls prevents assertions of a corporation taking chances as to the source of the earnings. Yet, what can be called *acceptance criterion* has broader consequences than the agency theory's benefit criterion; the receipt of illegal benefits activity is only one pointer in a certain direction. Formal and informal corporate policy are subject to investigation as to the question of eventual, actual, or moral acceptance of illegal acts by the corporation.

These two criteria are typically organizational criteria in that power and acceptance point not to the judgment of isolated acts by individuals, but to continuing collective processes. Both suggest more than just a generalized value judgment. Should this have been allowed to happen? They require concrete examination of the relationships between individuals and corporate groups and a focussing on corporate decision-making processes.

In Dutch case law these power and acceptance criteria emerged in the wake of the *Vroom & Dreesmann* case. The first case (*IJzerdraad*[10]) in which the Supreme Court expressed liability along these lines concerned an unincorporated firm, owned by a sole proprietor. The export manager had deliberately filled in a false export return in relation to the export of some steel wire in violation of exchange control rules. A court of appeal adopted the broad criteria of the *Vroom & Dreesmann* case. The defendant was declared liable for those violations performed by his subordinate in the course of his employment and within the scope of the business. The employee's acts were clearly intended to benefit the firm, and so it came within the scope of the criteria.

The Supreme Court reversed. Its opinion was that the employee's act could only be regarded as the employer's if:

1. it was within the defendant's power to determine whether the employee acted in this way, and

2. the employee's act belonged to a category of acts "accepted" by the firm as being in the course of normal business operations.

These "power" and "acceptance" criteria created a more restricted yet more typical organizational approach toward liability than previously was the case. As the defendant was a human being, it is possible that the Supreme Court was unhappy with the loose agency criteria and looked for more restricted ones.

Although the *IJzerdraad* case referred to a sole proprietorship and to a strict liability offense, academic commentators also began to advocate the adoption of these more restricted criteria for corporate liability for *mens rea* offenses, which became a legal possibility after a 1976 amendment to the Dutch Criminal Code (article 51). These were seen as more appropriate in limiting liability to situations in which the corporation could be plausibly seen as culpable.

The Supreme Court decided accordingly in the *Kabeljouw* case.[11] The court of appeal had acquitted the corporate defendant, the shipowner, for operating a ship in contravention of fishing regulations. It regarded the following facts as decisive: the corporation had equipped the ship with nets especially designed for fishing for permitted species and had ordered the ship's captain to fish only for such permitted species. On appeal to the Supreme Court, the Advocate-General[12] argued that the court below had taken too restrictive a view, arguing that the traditional *Vroom & Dreesmann* criteria should be applied. The Supreme Court however, adopted the criteria developed in the *IJzerdraad* case and confirmed the acquittal. Thus the court did not accept that liability flowed simply from corporate benefit or the master/servant relationship.

The concepts of "power" and "acceptance" seem to have led in the *Kabeljouw* case to criteria arguably more suited to the evaluation of collective enterprise. The stress was upon the institutional practices of the corporation— what kind of nets were supplied and what instructions were given by the corporation? This reflects French's argument that corporate intentions can be traced in constitutionally determined (and thus authoritative) corporate policy. "Power" and "acceptance" are general terms that have to be operationalized in concrete cases. A good example can be found in the *Hospital* case,[13] the first Dutch conviction of a corporation for manslaughter. The hospital was charged with gross negligence in failing to properly ensure that old, redundant anaesthetic equipment was removed from the hospital or made unusable. The equipment was no longer listed as in-service and maintenance of it had ceased. Further, the hospital was charged with failing to establish a well-balanced safety system for checking the work of the technicians entrusted with the service, repair and replacement of such equipment. As a result, equipment was used in an operation that had been jettisoned as obsolete and lacking up-to-date safety attachments. A further error by the hospital's technicians led to tubes being wrongly connected. A patient died because the lack of up-to-date safety monitoring systems on the machines meant that the error in connecting the tubes was not discovered.

In sentencing the hospital trust, the district court emphasized the fact that the organization and procedures of the technical department had not been subject to appropriate monitoring in relation to maintenance and repairs. All records of the anaesthetic trolley had disappeared from the hospital's files and therefore safety procedures, especially in repairs, showed the sloppiness of the hospital's supervision.

The court did not explicitly rationalize its decision in terms of power and acceptance. However, the facts are indicative of the meaning of the "power" and "acceptance" criteria. It seems likely that acceptance involves judgment on corporate monitoring of risky or illegal behavior, and power is a judgment on corporate response to those risks. It is also clear that there is a normative element in these criteria, that cumulatively they demand an overall judgment on the quality of corporate diligence in establishing, monitoring, and enforcing appropriate standards. In the *Hospital* case, the management claimed that they could not prevent the unsafe practices because they did not know what was going on. The court's response was, that liability was founded on the fact that the management was totally unaware of the routine practices of the hospital and they ought to have been aware of them.

It has to be stressed that the normative content of the criteria create no automatic criminal liability as soon as some shocking, at least criminally intolerable, act occurs. Neither is there any presumption that if a corporation brings about such a result, the internal decision-making process has failed. The focus is on the corporate policy and practice parallel to French's thoughts about the moral competence of corporations. From the investigation of this policy and practice flows the corporation's culpability or not. By exploring the power and acceptance criteria we have set limits to our first, the perpetration issue.

Our second issue was whether a corporation can have criminal intent or be criminally negligent. If one follows the concepts of French about moral competency, no objections can be made against implanting in the corporate internal decision structure the three elements required for criminal intent: knowledge, will, and freedom to act. This means a clear rejection of the Anglo-Saxon identification doctrine. This doctrine requires knowledge at the level of the directors of a corporation in order to possibly find a corporation guilty of a *mens rea* offense. It makes a division between the hands and the brains of the organization, in essence an anthropocentric approach. The same applies *mutatis mutandis* to negligence.

According to the organizational approach to corporate crime such a division is immaterial. Most corporate acts will be intentional acts, and the question of corporate intent apart from subordinate's intent can be answered by investigation of the corporate policy, practice, and decision-making processes. It is not necessary that at least one director is informed of the details of a criminal offence, or the risks that it be committed, as long as the criminal act belongs to the category of acts of which the corporation is or should be aware. In essence there is very little light between a positive answer to the question of perpetration according to the power and acceptance criteria, and the answer to the question of intent, c.q. negligence.

One could argue that the end result does not differ essentially from the American aggregation doctrine as applied in cases like *Inland Freight Lines v. United States,*[14] *United States v. Sawyer Transport, Inc.,*[15] and *United States v. Bank of New England.*[16] The route is different as is demonstrated in the *Rijksuniversiteit Groningen* case.[17] The university claimed that its criminal liability could not extend to cover the acts of individual researchers within the organization. This was rejected by the Supreme Court. It said that the power to determine the activities of those within the organization was not limited to those at the highest organizational levels. As the excavation was a deliberate act, no objections can be made against holding the corporation liable for an intentional offense. The *Hospital* case shows the same with regard to negligence—the technicians had made mistakes which did not constitute criminal negligence in themselves. But the sloppy organization of the technical affairs contributed essentially to criminal negligence as a whole of organizational and human failure. The third question put above was to what extent was the corporate conduct unlawful? This question does not pose particular organizational problems. It requires the usual skills of lawyers to determine whether the corporate conduct violated statutory or common law prohibitions.

Finally, to what extent can the corporation be blamed for its conduct? The criteria for perpetration by the corporation (i.e., power and acceptance) have some normative contents, so that some defenses tend to bar determination of perpetration by the corporation. For instance, if a plant has to emit an ordinarily unacceptable quantity of a dangerous gas as part of an emergency stop because of an imminent natural catastrophe, a defense of necessity will bar fulfillment of the acceptance criterion. Or if a train driver fails to see a red light and the railroad company has issued all the proper instructions, given the proper training and located the signal correctly, it may be said that in practice the railroad company lacked the power to prevent the consequences of individual failure. It is evident that a powerlessness defense negates the power criterion.

We would like to conclude this chapter by a comparison of the actual British and the possible Dutch answer to the above mentioned Zeebrugge disaster. Because of the identification doctrine, the British had to find one or more directors responsible for the mismanagement of safety affairs of the company. The problems of the identification doctrine are exacerbated by the rejection of aggregation of fault. It was submitted in *R. v. H.M. Coroner for East Kent, ex parte Spooner*[18] that is was not necessary to find someone identified with the corporation who was individually liable in order to make that corporation liable. It was argued that is was possible or ought to be possible to aggregate together the fault of several of the directing minds so that various acts of minor negligence or recklessness could be seen *in toto* as involving more serious fault on the part of the corporation itself. Bingham, L.J. responded to this argument:

> I do not think the aggregation argument assists the applicants. A case against a personal defendant cannot be fortified by evidence against another defendant. The case against a corporation can only be made by evidence properly addressed to showing guilt on the part of the corporation as such.

It will be clear that this is a circular argument, one can only show guilt on the part of the corporation if one succeeds in identifying a guilty director. By a convenient division of labor inside the board individual directors may never get informed of the whole safety gap. By prohibiting aggregation of knowledge and fault or intent, a corporation will never be found guilty under such circumstances. What remains is the attribution of failure to individuals, the assistant bosun who failed to shut the bow door as the ship sailed, or the loading officer, formally entrusted by a general corporate instruction with a duty to ensure that bow doors were secure when leaving port. But as the Sheen report (*M.V. Herald of Free Enterprise*, 1987) recognized, the corporate management may also be regarded as morally responsible for allowing pressure to build on the crew to improve turn around time, for failure to scrutinize the enforcement of corporate instructions on bow doors, and for not properly considering alternative checks or properly defining responsibility for safety. The collapse of the P & O trial merely serves to demonstrate the way that the individualist British criteria do not reflect this collective corporate responsibility.

A judgment according to the criteria of power and acceptance would require an investigation of the corporate decisionmaking regarding the safety features of this, in some respects, dangerously designed type of ship. As the Sheen committee (*M.V. Herald of Free Enterprise*, 1987) reported:

> All concerned in management, from the members of the board down to the junior superintendents, were guilty of fault in that all must be regarded as sharing responsibility for the failure of management. From top to bottom the body corporate was infected with the disease of sloppiness.

Moreover, two circumstances in particular demonstrate how the power criterion has been met. First, the decision not to install bow door warning lights on the bridge, a rather easy modification. Second, the lack of gathering of information on known similar previous incidents (5 or 6 in the previous 3½ years). Finally, the committee's finding of the overall failure to develop a sound system for safeguarding the highest safety norms on board is a clear reply to the question whether the corporation took at least reasonable measures to prevent foreseeable accidents. Various negligent acts on the part of the subordinates can hardly be regarded as only individual shortcomings, as incidents over which the company had no power. If the assistant bosun is able to be absent while required to be on duty, and nevertheless the ship sets sail, there is clearly something wrong with the instructions and their compliance. The same applies to the loading officer and the contradictory instruction to be at two different places at the same time. Also, the captain's failure can hardly be regarded as personal aberration. There is every reason to aggregate their personal negligence—each of which might be too slight to meet the legally required degree of criminal negligence—with negligence on the part of the corporation.

An objection could be made that the corporation did not nor does usually accept these acts. The occurrence of previous failures to close the bow doors before setting sail is a strong counter-argument, as is the company's refusal to install warning lights. The sloppiness of the organization, as the Sheen commission concluded, demonstrates also a climate in which the risks of disobedience of instructions seemed to be taken routinely. The company will reject the allegation that it accepted this particular consequence, but for acceptance it would suffice if the style of management was a sloppy one, facilitating risks being taken that ought to have been outlawed.

CONCLUSION

As organizations play so dominant a role in everyday life, theories of corporate liability need maturing in every respect. The criminal law seems to be the last bastion of no complete acceptance of the phenomenon of corporate wrongdoing. The Anglo-Saxon approach shows serious flaws by adhering to the identification doctrine and the rejection of the aggregation theory. Elsewhere theories of liability are borrowed from civil law doctrine, basically the agency theory. In practice the agency theory has to be compromised in order to produce acceptable results.

This chapter suggests a structural approach towards corporate criminal liability, starting with the assumption of a corporation as an entity, a *sui generis* unity. Capable of being a social actor, and of being a moral actor, of being morally competent. As such, there is every reason to develop organizational criteria according to which criminal acts can be defined as criminal corporate conduct. It is essential to investigate the internal decision-making process—apart from the formal corporate structure and the corporate objectives—in order to discover the organizational reality. This facilitates the answer whether the organizational criteria of criminal corporate conduct have been met.

It is suggested that two criteria suffice—power and acceptance. Was it possible for the corporation to prevent the criminal act from being committed? And, was this particular criminal act actually, or were similar criminal acts usually accepted by the corporation? A mature criminal theory of corporate wrongdoing does not necessarily absolve human beings from individual liability. On the contrary, corporations may be the alter ego of human beings, generally there may be reason for lifting the corporate veil. But often the only fully and really blameworthy entity is the corporation. Criminal theory should address this reality adequately.

POSTSCRIPT

On March 5, 1996, the British Law Commission published its report on *Involuntary Manslaughter*, in which the Commission concluded that there should be a new offense of corporate killing. It would arise only where the body corporate's management failure is the cause (or one of the causes) of a person's death, and that failure is conduct which falls *far* below what could reasonably be expected of the corporation. A management failure would arise if the way in which the corporation's activities were managed or organized failed to ensure the health and safety of persons employed in or affected by those activities. In Recommendation 12 the Commission recommends that, for the purposes of the corporate offense, it should be possible for a management failure on the part of the corporation to be a cause of a person's death, even if the immediate cause is the act or omission of an individual. It remains to be seen whether the Commission's proposals will become part of the law. It is evident that they deviate considerably from the existing law, while the boundaries or corporate penetration are not at all clear.

NOTES

1   Judge at the Court of Appeals, Arnhem, The Netherlands; formerly associate professor of criminal law and procedure, Utrecht University.

2   *New York Central & Hudson Railroad Company v. United States,* 212 U.S. 52, 84 S. Ct. 1594, 12 L. Ed. 2d 678 (1909).

3   Supreme Court of the Netherlands: HR 22 April 1880, *Weekblad* 4516: "The will of a legal entity is revealed by the formally authorized act of a lawful organ." Proponents of the introduction of corporate criminal liability into the Dutch Criminal Code based their efforts on the same footing: M.A. van Rijn van Alkemade, Strafrechtelijke aansprakelijkheid voor feiten gepleegd door corporaties, *L Tijdschrift voor strafrecht* (1940:189-229); Commissie-Wijnveldt, De strafrechtelijke aansprakelijkheid voor feiten, begaan door corporaties, *Nederlands Juristenblad* (1941:412-415).

4   For a (not so) academic example see: HR 10 November 1987, *Nederlandse Jurisprudentie* (NJ) 1988, 303. A researcher of the school of archeology of the University of Groningen had unlawfully excavated a preserved tumulus. This was done in the course of executing a research and educational plan, drawn up by the school's elected council, on which the university board had no material, only financial influence. Nevertheless, the university got convicted and sentenced to a fine.

5   For instance, *Egan v. United States,* 137 F.2d 369 (CA8, 1943).

6   *United States v. American Radiator & Standard Sanitary Co.,* 433 F.2d 174 (CA3, 1970).

7   *Continental Baking Co. v. United States,* 281 F.2d 137 (CA6, 1960).

8   *United States v. Cadillac Overall Supply Co.,* 568 F.2d 1078 (CA5, 1978); *United States v. Automated Medical Laboratories,* 770 F.2d 399 (CA4, 1985).

9   HR 27 January 1948, NJ 1948, 197.

10   HR 23 Februari 1954, NJ 1954, 378.

[11]   HR 1 Juli 1981, NJ 1982, 80.

[12]   An independent member of the office of the public prosecution at the Supreme Court, producing a (scientific) opinion for the consideration of the court to assist in the decision-making process though the opinion has no binding authority.

[13]   Rechtbank Leeuwarden 23 December 1987, NJ 1988, 981.

[14]   191 F.2d 313 (CA10, 1951).

[15]   337 F. Supp 29 (DC Minn, 1971).

[16]   821 F.2d 844 (CA1, 1987).

[17]   See footnote 10.

[18]   (1989) 88 Cr. App. R. 10.

Section III

CORPORATE CRIMINAL SANCTIONING

The United States Sentencing Commission brought the issue of corporate criminal sentencing to the forefront of attention as a result of a deliberated, multi-year effort to draft and enact corporate sentencing guidelines. This culminated in the enactment of corporate sentencing guidelines on November 1, 1991. Relevant to the purposes of this book, these guidelines include extensive fine and organizational probation provisions, and draw from both agency and structure theories, as the following two chapters illustrate.

In Chapter 6, law and economics scholar Thomas Ulen presents an economic argument for reliance on fines in sanctioning corporations. This argument is rooted in the agency view of corporate crime as the product of rational self-interested actors subject to deterrence through fines in excess of benefits expected from criminal conduct; in fact, he argues, corporations are more rationally or more likely to be rational than are individuals. More specific calculation of the threshold of deterrence requires consideration of the likelihood of detection, arrest, and conviction. However, Ulen notes, economic efficiency lies in focusing more on setting high costs associated with crime rather than high likelihoods of detection due to the investments associated with expanding crime control resources.

In addition to this clear, well-detailed, and empirically grounded advocacy for market-based sanctions, Ulen argues in support of the economic efficiency of corporate criminal liability and the inadequacy of civil enforcement mechanisms. This contrasts with Jeffrey Parker's earlier argument (see Chapter 4) portraying corporate criminal liability as legally and theoretically unfounded, and civil enforcement as a legally defensible and adequate alternative. Considered together, the contributions of Ulen and Parker provide insights into the range of agency theory while also clearly illustrating shared assumptions of rationality, individual utility maximization, and market discipline. With regard to the views of Richard Gruner expressed in Chapter 7, Ulen takes the position that the inefficiencies associated with non-monetary sanctions, such as organizational probation, impose undue inefficiencies and lack theoretical justification.

Richard Gruner, a legal scholar actively involved in the development of the federal corporate sentencing guidelines, argues in support of structural sanctions by noting that even within agency logic there are reasons to doubt the efficacy of fines. The structural logic so clearly developed by Ermann and Rabe in Chapter 3 and Jörg in Chapter 5 provides further support for sanctions designed to penetrate and remediate organizational structures and policies. Gruner advances this argument by noting the extent to which the federal Organizational Sentencing Guidelines, particularly the organizational probation provisions and compliance planning specifications, promote "offender reform" through incentives for internally initiated structural organizational changes and provisions for state-based organizational interventions. Finally, Gruner notes the linkages between structural approaches to sanctioning and regulatory relations by linking the effectiveness of structural sanctions to negotiative regulatory relations.

6

The Economic Case for
Corporate Criminal Sanctioning

Thomas S. Ulen[1]
University of Illinois College of Law

INTRODUCTION

In 1984 the United States Congress created the United States Sentencing Commission to examine federal criminal sentencing practices and to recommend changes in those practices. The Sentencing Commission promulgated sentencing guidelines for federal crimes committed by individuals in 1987 and for those committed by business organizations in 1991.[2] With respect to the individual guidelines, the Commission's recommendations sought to increase the predictability and, therefore, the deterrent effect of federal criminal sentencing by standardizing those sentences and reducing their variance. With respect to criminal sentences for business organizations, the Commission's principal objective was to standardize and raise the level of punishment inflicted on corporations. In this it was successful, since 1991 there has been a significant increase in the average level of fines imposed for federal corporate crime (see Cohen, 1991).[3]

The argument for reform of individual criminal sentencing was well-known and widely shared. However, the argument for reform of criminal sentencing for business organizations was more obscure. Indeed, there was no clear consensus among students of the matter about the need for reform of criminal sentencing for corporations (for a notable exception, see Stone, 1975, 1980). While in the late 1970s and early 1980s everyone could tell that there were too many crimes being committed by individuals and that a failure to impose consistent sentences was a part of the cause, there was no parallel feeling with respect to crimes committed by corporate entities. A few contended that corporate crime was increasing secularly; some held that the level of corporate punishment was systematically low; and others purported to find a causal link between the low level of fines and an increase in corporate crime.

When the Sentencing Commission decided to pursue corporate criminal sentencing reform in the mid- and late 1980s, there was some controversy—within the Commission, its staff, and the academics whom the Commission consulted—about the theoretical basis for corporate criminal liability and about the appropriate form for that liability to take. For example, both before and since the passage of the corporate sentencing guidelines in 1991, some have criticized the underlying basis of corporate criminal liability laid out in the Act and the increase in the level of fines imposed (and in the way those fines are calculated) as being fundamentally flawed (see Arlen, 1994; Byam, 1982; Karpoff & Lott, 1993).

This book provides an opportunity to look again at the basis of corporate criminal liability and the appropriate corporate criminal sanctions. In this chapter I seek to place the 1991 Act on solid economic ground. I shall argue that the critics are wrong—that the Sentencing Commission's basis for imposing corporate criminal liability and the levels at which it established the sanctions for that liability make a great deal of practical economic sense. I begin with a very brief overview of the use of economic theory to examine legal rules and institutions—especially crime and punishment—and then turn to the economic case for imposing criminal liability on business organizations and, in more detail, a justification for relying on monetary fines.

LAW AND ECONOMICS AND THE ECONOMICS OF CRIME AND PUNISHMENT

The strongest case for the reform of corporate criminal liability and sanctioning comes from a legal innovation known as "law and economics" or the "economic analysis of law." Some of the readers of this volume may not be familiar with that innovation, so I begin this section of the chapter with a brief overview of law and economics. Then I shall show how this new field discusses criminal behavior and its punishment. Finally, I show how this economic analysis of crime and punishment applies to the issue of corporate criminal sanctioning.

AN OVERVIEW OF LAW AND ECONOMICS

Law and economics uses the insights of microeconomic theory to examine legal rules and institutions. To show how, I must first say a word about microeconomic theory and then explain how that theory of market behavior has come to be used to explain non-market behavior like that encompassed by the law.

Rational Choice Theory: Market and Non-Market Behavior

Microeconomic theory offers a model of human decisionmaking, principally but not exclusively of behavior in the marketplace. The theory is starkly simple: people are rationally self-interested decisionmakers. They are capable of computing the costs and benefits of the various alternatives open to them, and they seek to choose that alternative that is likely to give them the greatest happiness.[4] This theory of human decisionmaking is called "rational choice theory."

The great strength of the economic model lies in its ability to explain market behavior. For example, the model makes testable predictions about how consumers choose which goods and services to buy and in what amounts, and how consumers' choices are likely to respond to changes in market prices, to increases in consumer income, to the introduction of new, competing products, to the change in the price of a complementary good or service, and the like. In similar fashion, rational choice theory offers testable explanations and predictions of behavior by individuals in their roles as the suppliers of labor and other productive resources. It also offers an account of the market behavior of firms (their decisions about what to produce, how to produce it, how much of it to produce, what price to charge, and the like) and of governmental bodies (what services to provide, in what quantities, how much to charge for those services, etc.). There is widespread agreement among economists about the usefulness of microeconomic theory in explaining individual and corporate behavior in the marketplace.[5]

One of the important innovations of microeconomics in the last quarter-century has been its application to human decisionmaking in *non-market* settings. For example, there are insightful economic theories of the family (Becker, 1992, 1981), of sexual behavior (Posner, 1993), and of aging and old age (Posner, 1995). These theories purport to show how rationally self-interested actors choose, among other things, spouses and how many children to bear and raise, whether to purchase the services of prostitutes, whether to form new friendships, and whether to invest in new learning as one grows older. In addition, some scholars in such contiguous social science disciplines as political science and sociology now routinely use rational choice theory to examine the subject matter with which their disciplines are concerned (see Ordeshook, 1986).

There is not the same widespread consensus about the value of these applications of microeconomic theory to non-market behavior as there is about its application to market behavior. In part, this is due to the fact that these innovations are so novel that they have not had the time to develop theoretically, to receive empirical confirmation or refutation, and to command institutional and individual loyalty that scholarly innovations ultimately need, if they are to be accepted. It would be rash to suggest that all of these innovations will survive the next 50 years, but surely some of them will.

An Introduction to Law and Economics

One of the non-market applications of rational choice theory that seems most likely to survive is "law and economics" or the "economic analysis of law." Even within the last 20 years, its insights and explanatory power have been so valuable that it has already become a standard part of the legal curriculum and a routine part of the tools of most practicing lawyers.[6]

Until recently, law confined the use of economics to the areas of antitrust law, regulated industries, tax, and the determination of monetary damages. But this limited interaction changed dramatically in the early 1960s when the economic analysis of law expanded into the more traditional areas of the law, such as property, contracts, torts, criminal law and procedure, and constitutional law. This new use of economics in the law asked such questions as, "Will private ownership of the electro-magnetic spectrum encourage its efficient use?", "What remedy for breach of contract will cause efficient reliance upon promises?", "Do businesses take the right amount of precaution because the law holds them strictly liable for injuries to consumers?"

Why has this scholarly innovation succeeded so impressively?[7] Simply put, law and economics provide persuasive and useful new answers to old legal questions. Lawmakers and adjudicators often ask, "How will this law affect behavior?" For example, if punitive damages are imposed upon the maker of a defective product, what will happen to the safety and price of the product in the future? Lawyers answered such questions in 1960 in much the same way as they had in 60 B.C.—by consulting intuition and any available facts. There were, of course, better and worse intuition and more and less pertinent facts, but there was no scientific theory. Economics has provided a scientific theory to predict the effects of legal sanctions upon behavior. To economists, legal sanctions look like prices, and presumably, people respond to these sanctions much as they respond to prices. Thus, heavier sanctions are like higher prices, and because people respond to higher prices by consuming less of the more expensive good, they argue that people respond to heavier legal sanctions by doing less of the sanctioned activity.

Consider an example. Suppose that a manufacturer knows that his product will sometimes injure consumers. How safe will he make the product? The answer depends upon two costs: first, the actual cost of safety, which depends in turn upon facts about design and manufacture, and the "implicit price" of injuries to consumers imposed through the manufacturer's legal liability. The producer will compare the cost of more safety and the benefit that safety conveys in reducing the implicit price of accidents (namely, the compensatory damages for which the producer may be liable if there is an accident). A safer product costs more to produce, but it also reduces the likelihood and severity of accidents. Presumably, the profit-maximizing producer keeps building more safety into his product until the last unit of safety costs exactly as much as it reduces the implicit price of liability.

In addition to a scientific theory of behavior, economics provides a useful normative standard for evaluating law and policy. Laws are not just arcane technical arguments, they are instruments for achieving important social goals. In order to know the effects of laws on those goals, judges and other lawmakers must have a method of evaluating law's effects on important social values. One of those goals is economic efficiency. Efficiency is always relevant to policymaking, because it is always better to achieve any given policy at lower cost than at higher cost. To continue the price metaphor, the efficiency criterion in law and economics argues for setting the implicit price in a legal rule so as to induce efficient behavior. For example, setting the "price" for breach of contract correctly will induce contractual parties to breach a contractual promise only when it is more efficient to breach than to perform.[8]

Thus, law and economics has both positive and normative aspects. The positive aspect seeks to identify the implicit price contained in a legal rule and to make predictions about behavior in response to that implicit price. The normative aspect seeks to identify the "correct" implicit price—the one that induces efficient behavior.

AN ECONOMIC ANALYSIS OF CRIME AND PUNISHMENT GENERALLY

We have now seen the general outline of law and economics. Next, I shall briefly look at the economic analysis of crime and punishment and then turn specifically to the economics of corporate crime.

Distinguishing Crimes from Civil Wrongs

There are two fundamental questions that an economic theory (or any theory) of crime and punishment should answer. First, the theory should explain when and why we need something more than mere civil remedies for certain wrongs. That is, the theory must give an account of why private causes of action are inadequate to deterring what we call "criminal" wrongs. Second, the theory should be able to explain the kind and magnitude of criminal sanctions to impose for different sorts of crimes. How, for example, is the criminal sanction for murder to be calculated? How does that sanction compare to the sanction imposed for manslaughter? And how do both of these compare in magnitude to sanctions imposed for an inchoate crime such as conspiracy to commit murder?[9] I shall focus on the economic answer to the first question in this section and turn to the question regarding sanctions in the next section. As we shall see, it is difficult to put a wall between the two questions; I shall have to say a word or two about sanctions in this section, too.

Private causes of action are inadequate for dealing with the following situations:

1. Where there is a non-zero probability that wrongdoers will not be caught or that victims (who are entitled to a civil remedy) will not bring suit.

2. Where a wrongdoer *intends* to do harm, whether he or she succeeds. Inadvertent harms ought to be deterred (as by exposure to tort liability), but *intentional* harms should be prohibited.

3. Where the actions of the wrongdoer inflict costs not only on easily-identified victims but also on others who are not easily identified.

Let us briefly look at these points. If the only remedy available for injury was the payment of compensatory money damages, then there would be some wrongs for which the wrongdoer might derive a greater benefit from doing wrong than from doing right. To see why, suppose that the probability of being caught converting someone else's property is 0.5, or that only one-half of all those whose property is stolen bring an action against the person who took their property.[10] Suppose that if the thief is caught and sued by the rightful owner for the civil wrong of conversion, the thief can expect to be held liable either for returning the property intact or surrendering its monetary value to the plaintiff. Further suppose that the wrongdoer's options for acquiring a television are to purchase it legally for $500 or to steal one. The wrongdoer's expected cost of acquiring the television by theft is 0.5 x ($500) or $250. Because the net cost of acquisition by theft is less than that of acquisition by legitimate purchase, there is an incentive to steal.

Society prefers that resources move by voluntary agreement (rather than by theft). The consent of both parties creates a strong presumption that the transfer makes both parties better off and that the resources are moving to higher-valued uses.[11] Moreover, a general presumption in favor of voluntary exchange allows owners to economize on resources devoted to protecting their property from involuntary transfer. As a result, there is a social interest in deterring the involuntary transfer of resources. In the example of the previous paragraph, society favors reversing the wrongdoer's incentive to acquire a television set by theft rather than by legitimate purchase. The question is how to do that.

Economics suggests a means of reversing the incentive to steal created by the low probability of detection, arrest, and conviction or by the failure of victims to sue. First, recall that economics assumes that criminals (like all economic decisionmakers) are rational. They commit a crime if the expected benefit of the crime exceeds the expected cost. If the expected cost of crime exceeds the expected benefit, they refrain from committing the crime. It follows that a criminal may be deterred from criminal wrongdoing by setting criminal sanctions so that the expected cost for committing the crime is greater than the expected benefit.[12]

There are two general ways to increase the expected cost of crime. The first involves altering the rules and procedures of private causes of actions. The second consists of creating a distinct class of wrongs called "crimes." As we shall see, there are potential inefficiencies in trying to reform civil actions so as to adequately deter the particular wrongs with which we are concerned.

First, society could heighten the incentives for the victims of wrongdoing to bring private causes of actions for relief against those who they think have wronged them.[13] For example, victims could be allowed to recover punitive damages more easily or to recover their legal and other costs from a losing defendant. There are some predictable results of making these changes in civil liability. First, it may correct for the failure-to-sue problem, at least in part. If victims can more routinely recover punitive damages or their litigation expenses, then their incentive to bring actions against wrongdoers will increase. Second, while these increases in damages or in victims' ability to recover litigation expenses will obviously *not* address the likelihood of detection and apprehension, there may, nonetheless, be a decline in the amount of wrongdoing because these actions raise the cost to wrongdoers of being held liable. That is, these actions constitute an increase in the expected cost of wrongdoing and will, therefore, lead to a reduction in the amount of wrongdoing.

But there are also difficulties with this method of correcting civil liability so as to achieve the right amount of criminal deterrence. For instance, it may be difficult to confine society's use of this incentive just to those instances of wrongdoing where there is an inefficiency because of a low probability of detection and apprehension and the failure of other victims to sue. Punitive damages are typically available only for willful, wanton, or grossly negligent behavior on the part of the wrongdoer. It is not obvious that there is a clear connection between that behavior and the under-apprehension and failure-to-sue problems we are here addressing.[14] Indeed, it is possible that, on the theory we are currently considering, there is no moral culpability on the wrongdoer's part; rather, he or she is simply being made an object lesson for other potential wrongdoers who are not likely to be apprehended or sued. We rightly ought to be squeamish about treating some wrongdoers as object lessons. Finally, there is the possible inefficiency that the level of punitive damages or litigation expenses may not be calibrated correctly and may lead to *too much* deterrence.[15]

Second, we could entirely remove this wrong from the realm of civil wrongs and create a new class of wrongs that would more directly address the problems of under-apprehension and failure-to-sue. This is, in fact, the solution that society has by and large adopted: creating a class of statutory wrongs called "crimes." Society's method of optimally deterring these particular wrongs, consistent with other societal values—such as individual liberties, is to remove private plaintiffs from the picture, substitute the government as the complainant, raise the burden of proof to one of "beyond a reasonable doubt," and to impose punitive sanctions on those found guilty of these wrongs. In addition, society devotes real resources (police, prosecutors, registration systems, and the like) devoted to detecting, apprehending, and convicting wrongdoers. Doing so will raise the probability of being detected, arrested, and convicted for criminal wrongdoing. The difficulty with this latter part of the solution (by comparison to the alternatives, as we shall shortly see) is that it is expensive. The real resources necessary to raise the expected cost of crime significantly may be substantial—so substantial that the public balks at fully funding their purchase. Moreover, there may be substantial indirect costs of this method of deterring crime—namely, a significant loss of personal freedoms, as when more and more citizens are stopped and frisked in retail stores or on the public streets.[16]

Recall that there were three defining elements of a crime. We have been dealing with the first. The second reason—that the wrongdoer *intended* to do harm, rather than merely inadvertently or carelessly doing so—is related to, but distinguishable from, the first reason. Clearly, intending to do wrong is a much more serious and less tolerable wrong than unintentionally doing wrong, a distinction widely recognized in the law.[17] To fill out our economic theory of crime and punishment, we must explain why it is efficient for the law to recognize this distinction between intent and inadvertence and how it is that the law does so.

First, suppose that the law failed to make a distinction between intent and inadvertence so that causing harm (perhaps negligently, perhaps strictly) simply triggered liability for compensating the victim. Under that rule, the law would create a windfall for those who derive pleasure from harming others. Put starkly, they would perceive the "price" charged to them for causing harm (compensatory money damages) as being a bargain and would, therefore, not be deterred but would continue to derive pleasure from doing harm. This would not be socially desirable.[18]

Second, suppose that the failure to distinguish went the other way, in that causing harm, whether intentionally or inadvertently, triggered *criminal* sanctions, which would be far more burdensome than mere compensation. In that case we might be deterring those who take pleasure from harming others, but we would be *over*-deterring those who carelessly caused harm, with chilling inefficiencies. If inflicting harm on another car owner subjected the wrongdoer to incarceration, there would almost certainly be much less driving. Distinguishing between crimes and civil wrongs on the basis of intent avoids both of these inefficient outcomes.[19]

Recall that the third element of criminal wrongs is that, in addition to (or instead of) the particular victim, there is a diffuse group of victims—society. Criminal wrongs inflict costs on society beyond those imposed on any particular victims. For example, theft wrongs not only the rightful owner but also puts other owners in fear of losing their property. This fear may induce owners to expend resources in safeguarding their property (beyond mere prudence) from loss through theft. Society can minimize the waste from unnecessary protection by making certain that the sanctions imposed on a criminal wrongdoer capture these societal costs in addition to the costs imposed on the immediate victim.[20]

To summarize, the economic theory of crime holds that the three most important reasons for defining a separate class of wrongs beyond mere civil wrongs are (1) the under-apprehension of criminals and the failure of victims to bring an adequate number of actions, (2) the intentionality of the wrongdoer's harm, and (3) the social loss caused by the wrongdoer's actions. Attempts to achieve the social goal of criminal deterrence by altering the substantive rules and procedures of civil liability will be unavailing. Deterrence of crime requires, instead, a separate branch of law, with different rules and procedures (designed not only to achieve criminal deterrence but also to have due regard for constitutional rights). I do not want to make too much of this distinction between civil and criminal wrongs.[21] There are, as everyone knows, important similarities between crimes and intentional (civil) wrongs. Nonetheless, I am making the case for a distinction in order to show the logic of the economic analysis of crime and punishment, and to establish a foundation from which to discuss the central topic here—the criminal conduct of business organizations.

The Economics of Criminal Sanctions

Now I want to turn to an explicit discussion of the economics of criminal sanctions. The economic theory of crime holds, recall, that criminals are rationally self-interested—they commit a crime if the expected benefit of the crime exceeds the expected cost, and refrain from criminal activity if the expected cost exceeds the expected benefit. The clear implication for criminal justice policy is that society can achieve any level of deterrence it desires by altering the factors that make up the expected cost of crime.[22] In the previous section I briefly alluded to the fact that the expected cost of crime equals the probability of detection, arrest, and conviction times the value of the criminal sanction. I now want to elaborate briefly on the implications of this view.

Let us leave to one side for the moment the question, "At what level should we fix the expected cost of crime?"[23] Instead, let us concentrate here on the question of the most efficient means of setting the expected cost of crime. The literature has looked at this matter as a comparison between monetary and non-monetary sanctions.

As we have seen, the underlying elements of the expected cost of crime are two: the probabilities of detection, arrest, and conviction, and the value of the criminal sanctions. Society can increase the expected cost of crime by increasing one or both of these elements. Which should it do? The standard economic answer is that it is just as effective and more efficient to achieve any given level of deterrence by raising the level of sanctions, rather than by raising the probabilities of detection, arrest, and conviction (Becker, 1968). The reason for this is that raising the probabilities requires expending real resources (e.g., hiring more police and more prosecutors) with uncertain marginal results.[24]

By contrast, increasing the expected cost of crime (to exactly the same level) by raising the level of the criminal sanction is virtually costless and is extremely flexible. Take these characteristics in order. First, changing the level of sanctions may require statutory change, but even though that is sometimes not easy, it does not necessarily require a commitment of new funds. For example, raising the sanctions may involve nothing more than doubling the average incarceration time or tripling the monetary sanction for a particular crime. Someone might object that these changes are, in fact, very costly. For instance, doubling the prison sentence for a crime may require building more prisons. But that is only approximately correct. If the doubling achieves the desired result of deterring crime, then there will not be any more prisoners who need incarceration for the longer time sentences. Or if there is a transition period during which there *are* more prisoners (until the increased sanction has its desired effect of reducing crime), then they might be handled by letting the *quality* of existing incarceration facilities deteriorate, as through doubling up the carrying capacity of individual cells.[25] Raising the level of monetary sanctions does not even have these undesirable outcomes, they directly increase the expected cost of crime without any necessity of further expenditures or deterioration in criminal justice facilities.

Second, changing the level of criminal sanctions is, in principle, flexible—more flexible, at least, than is affecting the expected cost of crime by altering the probabilities of detection, arrest, and conviction through the commitment of real resources. If one round of changing the level of sanctions does not achieve the desired level of deterrence, then the level can be raised or lowered until it does. Or if the appropriate sanctions as between different crimes need adjusting (because, for example, the perceived social cost of one crime has changed vis-à-vis another crime), that, too, can be done easily. Note, by contrast, that if one were using changes in real resources to make these adjustments in the level of sanctions or in the relative level of sanctions between crimes, there would be costly adjustment problems. It is not so easy to hire more prosecutors or fire existing ones, nor is it easy to re-deploy criminal justice resources from, say, drug enforcement to child abuse to take account of a perceived need to adjust the relative social costs of those crimes. Real criminal justice resources can often be crime-specific and, therefore, inflexible, while the level of sanctions is a far more malleable tool.

Finally, as between monetary and non-monetary sanctions, the economic analysis argues for monetary over non-monetary sanctions. All of the arguments that I made in favor of altering the criminal's expected cost of crime by means of changes in the level of sanctions rather than in the form of changes in the relevant probabilities apply to the preferability of monetary sanctions. They are less expensive and just as deterring, and they are more flexible than are non-monetary sanctions.

Are there any costs of using monetary sanctions rather than non-monetary sanctions to defer crime? The most obvious exception to this general rule is the insolvent criminal (i.e., a criminal who has inflicted social losses greater than his total wealth); in fact it can be argued that non-monetary sanctions such as incarceration should be reserved for insolvent criminals.[26]

To the extent that criminals are rational decisionmakers, society can affect the amount of crime committed by altering the expected cost of crime. The components of that expected cost are the probabilities of detection, arrest, and conviction and the value of the criminal sanctions. Raising the cost by increasing the probabilities typically requires the expenditure of real resources. Equally effective, but much less expensive, is raising the expected cost by increasing the level of criminal sanctions. Therefore, an economic analysis of crime and punishment generally argues for achieving a given level of deterrence by raising the sanctions level. In addition, as between monetary and non-monetary sanctions, an economic analysis favors monetary sanctions as the principal method of deterring crime. They are less expensive and more flexible than the alternative non-monetary sanctions.[27]

AN ECONOMIC ANALYSIS OF CORPORATE CRIME

Thus far in the exposition of the economic theory of crime and punishment, I have made no distinction between individuals and business organizations who commit crime. For instance, our conclusions that any level of deterrence can be achieved by raising the expected costs of crime and that this is most efficiently done by raising the level of sanctions (particularly, monetary sanctions) seem, at first, to apply equally to individual and to corporate criminals. But will that impression survive further scrutiny? Can we extend the economic theory to probe the difference, if any, between business organizations and individuals as criminals? And, assuming that we can, does the conclusion that monetary sanctions are to be preferred to non-monetary sanctions carry over to the case of business organizations as criminals?

Corporations as Criminals

The extension of the previous section's general model to the issue of business organizations as criminals raises two particular issues. First, the economic theory assumes that criminals are rational decisionmakers. Does that assumption apply to business organizations? I shall argue that it does, but by an unconventional route. I seek to show that the empirical literature suggests that the economic theory of crime and punishment does not adequately explain the behavior of many *individual* criminals but that the same factors that make this theory inadequate as to individuals makes it likely to be applicable to corporations. Second, corporate criminal liability is a form of vicarious liability—the law seeks to punish the organization for the actions of some individuals in the organization. Does this central aspect of corporate criminal liability require any changes in our basic economic theory? I shall argue that it does not.

Rationality Among Individuals and Corporations[28]

Most people do not commit crime. Apparently, for them the expected benefit of crime is less than the expected punishment. But there are some people who *do* commit crimes; indeed, there are some who make a career of crime. Unlike the vast majority of us, these career criminals must believe that the expected benefits of crime exceed the expected punishments. Why do they reach a different conclusion from that of the vast majority of law-abiding citizens? If they are rational, then career criminals may differ from the rest of us in their preferences, attitudes towards risk, or valuations of time. However, they may not be fully rational. Career criminals may be mistaken in their belief that the expected benefits of crime exceed the expected costs. One cause of this mistaken belief would be *temporal inconsistency*—the view that immediate benefits (however small) count much more than deferred costs (however large).[29] If those who commit crime suffer from this mistaken belief, then they may overvalue the immediate payoff from crime and heavily discount the possibility of detection, arrest, and conviction.

Recently, James Q. Wilson and Allan Abrahamse (1992) attempted to estimate whether habitual criminals were rational or suffered from temporal inconsistency. They compared the gains from crime and from legitimate work for a group of state prison inmates in California, Michigan, and Texas, all of whom were career criminals. Wilson and Abrahamse divided the inmates into two groups—mid-rate offenders and high-rate offenders. Using data from the National Crime Survey's report of the average losses by victims in different sorts of crimes, the authors estimated the annual income from crime. For example, they estimated that the value of a stolen car was 20 percent of its market value. And following a study of drug dealing in Washington, DC, they estimated that the net income of the average drug dealer was $2,000 per month. They then compared these estimates of the income from crime with the prisoners' estimates of their income from legitimate sources.[30] The following excerpt gives the flavor of the investigators' conclusions:

> A mid-rate burglar free on the street will commit about nine burglaries, 10 thefts, and 85 drug sales, plus a smattering of miscellaneous offenses. The total estimated crime earnings for the year are $2,368, tax-free. If this offender spent the same amount of time working at a legitimate job that paid $5.78 per hour, he would have earned $9,914 before taxes or $7,931 after taxes. For him, crime pays less than working.

Wilson and Abrahamse found that for high-rate burglars crime produced roughly the same income as work. Crime was more lucrative than legitimate work for only one group of mid-rate offenders—auto thieves. But for high-rate offenders, crime paid more than legitimate work for *all* crimes except burglary, and for auto thieves it paid substantially more. The results are summarized in the following table:

Table 6.1
Criminal and Legitimate Earnings per Year (1988 Dollars)

Crime type	High-Rate		Mid-Rate	
	Crime	Work	Crime	Work
Burglary/Theft	$5,711	$5,540	$2,368	$7,931
Robbery	6,541	3,766	2,814	5,816
Swindling	14,801	6,245	6,816	8,113
Auto theft	26,043	2,308	15,008	5,457
Mixed	6,915	5,086	5,626	6,956

Source: J.Q. Wilson & A. Abrahamse (1992). "Does Crime Pay?" *Justice Quarterly*, 9:359.

These figures do not take into account the major cost of crime to criminals— time in prison. When the authors included those costs, the net income from crime fell below the income from legitimate work for both mid-rate and high-rate offenders.

Why, then, do career criminals commit crime? Wilson and Abrahamse consider and reject two explanations. First, the prisoners may have felt they had to commit crime because they had no meaningful opportunity for legitimate work. The authors doubt this view; two-thirds of the prisoners were employed in legitimate jobs for some length of time during the period examined. Second, the prisoners may have had such serious problems with alcohol and drugs that they could not hold a legitimate job. The authors argue that although two-thirds of the offenders had a drinking or drug problem, the evidence from other studies is that these problems do not preclude legitimate employment except in relatively rare circumstances. Wilson and Abrahamse conclude that career criminals are "temperamentally disposed to overvalue the benefits of crime and to undervalue its costs." They suffer from temporal inconsistency; they are "inordinately impulsive or present-oriented."[31]

How does this important conclusion apply to the issue of the economics of corporate criminal liability and sanctioning? Ideally, there would be a study of corporate criminal decision-making like the Wilson and Abrahamse study, designed to show how corporations make choices as between criminal and legitimate actions. There is, to my knowledge, no such study.[32] However, there are lots of intuitive reasons for believing that the imperfections that Wilson and Abrahamse found in the decisions of career criminals (and that others have found in the routine economic decisions of many people) will *not* be present in the decisions of business organizations. Corporations exist to make money. Not all of them are sophisticated in finance, investment, and managerial techniques, but most know something about those matters. Take, for example, the issue of comparing current values with future values, or comparing a current amount with a stream of future values. The economic theory of crime and punishment (and many other areas of law and economics, for that matter) assumes that decisionmakers can and do compare current and future values and current stocks with future flows. But as anyone who has ever taught the techniques of discounting to present value to a bright group of undergraduates or law students knows, most individuals do not know how to do that unless specifically trained.[33] The implication of this observation is that law and economics ought not to presume that individual decisionmakers are conversant with present discounted value; that is, that individuals may make mistakes in situations that call for them to compare current and future values. That is, of course, precisely what Wilson and Abrahamse found for career criminals. By contrast, it seems to me fitting to assume that every business organization knows how to make that comparison; they do it as a routine matter of course.

Discounting to present value is only one example of the calculations that the economic theory presumes wrongdoers make. What about computing the other elements of expected costs and expected benefits? Whatever doubts one may have about the comparison of expected benefit and expected cost as a description of individual criminal behavior, those doubts seem misplaced as a description of organizational behavior. Businesses compare costs and benefits all the time—with regard to employment decisions, decisions about incorporating safety and warnings into their products, decisions about the introduction of new product lines, and more.

The implication of these observations is that, whatever its shortcomings as a description of individual behavior, the economic theory of crime and punishment would seem to be an excellent starting point for looking at criminal behavior by business organizations. The computational requirements of the economic theory may be beyond the ken of the many individuals, but they are the routine in a wide range of business behaviors.

The Economics of Vicarious Liability

In private causes of action there are circumstances in which one person may be held responsible for the wrongs committed by another. Where this happens, the third party is said to be "vicariously liable" for the tortfeasor's acts. Vicarious liability may extend from an agent to his or her principal, or from a dependent child to a parent, but by far the most common instance is that of employers' responsibility for the tortious wrongs of their employees under the doctrine of *respondeat superior* ("let the master answer"). The bare bones of this doctrine are that an employer will be held to answer for the unintentional torts of his employee if the employee was "acting within the scope of [his] employment."

The economic argument regarding *respondeat superior* is that it induces efficient behavior by both employers and employees. If an employer can be held liable for the wrongs of his employees who are acting at his behest, then the employer has a heightened incentive to monitor his employees' behavior. The employer will select employees more carefully than in the absence of such a rule and will take extraordinary care in assigning them tasks and in deciding with which tools to equip them. Presumably the employee will find this state of affairs efficient, too.[34] Relieved of liability for work-related accidents, the employee will turn his or her attention to the tasks his employer wants done. In the absence of this liability shield, the employee might be timid about pursuing duties (to the employer's detriment), or might become fastidious about inquiring about who would bear liability for injuries in certain aspects of the job (again interfering with the progress of the work).[35] In addition to these clear efficiency reasons for vicarious liability in the workplace, there is the additional point that the employer is far more likely to have the resources to compensate a victim than is the employee.[36]

How do these considerations apply to the vicarious *criminal* liability of the corporation? The arguments are exactly the same as they were in the private law realm. Business organizations are in the best position to police the behavior of their employees against criminal actions through monitoring, hiring, and task-assignment. Moreover, there would be serious moral hazard problems if employers were *not* liable for their employees' crimes (when acting within their responsibilities). Some employers would have an incentive in those circumstances to announce, with a wink and a nod to the wise, a policy against criminal conduct with the understanding that they would turn a blind eye towards the criminal conduct of their employees. Employees might be willing to accept these conditions of employment; they might be individually criminally liable if caught, but if they were not caught, they would have performed valiant service for their employers and would hope to be rewarded in the future in terms of salary and promotion for taking on this risk for their employer. Assigning criminal liability to the employer removes the incentive on the part of both employers and employees to commit crimes on behalf of the corporation.

Federal and state law follow this economic logic by making business organizations vicariously liable for the crimes of their employees when acting within the scope of their responsibilities. Courts have interpreted this criminal liability very broadly, so that a business organization may be held liable for its agents' crimes even if there was an explicit corporate policy against the behavior—the theory apparently being that the business organization is responsible for enforcing the policy, not just for promulgating it.

The Efficient Sanctions for Corporate Crime

If there is professional disagreement about a subject having to do with the corporate criminal sentencing guidelines, it is the appropriate level of sanctions. In this section I shall very briefly summarize the application of the economic theory of crime and punishment to the issue of sanctions, then summarize the actual guidelines, and, finally, discuss several important caveats from the recent literature that is critical of the guidelines.

Monetary v. Non-Monetary Sanctions

Recall that the economic theory of crime clearly came out in favor of using alterations in the level of sanctions as the principal means of affecting the expected cost of crime and thereby deterring crime. Moreover, as to the form of the sanctions, monetary sanctions are generally more efficient than are non-monetary sanctions. These conclusions hold whether the criminal is an individual or an organization. And just as the earlier part of the economic theory of crime seemed to apply more clearly to organizations than to individuals, so, too, with the economic theory of sanctions. When a business organization commits a crime, the argument in favor of monetary sanctions over non- monetary sanctions is even more persuasive than in the case of an individual. There are several reasons for this. First, the usual alternative to monetary sanctions—incarceration—simply is not available for the business organization (although it is available for the individuals within the organization). There are other non-monetary sanctions against the corporation that might be possible— such as management for a period of time by a court-appointed trustee. But that seems to be an inappropriate and inefficient means of getting the business organization to quit committing crime. With more force than in the case of individuals, it seems safe to say that corporations commit crimes if they perceive the expected benefit to exceed the expected cost, and that they will refrain from crime if the expected cost exceeds the expected benefit. This leads to the second point in favor of monetary sanctions—business organizations exist to make a profit and understand the concept of expected cost. Third, unlike the individual, the business organization is, in general, not judgment-proof, and, therefore, one need not overly worry about the possibility that the deterring monetary fine will exceed the criminal's ability to pay.

The Level of Monetary Sanctions

I said at the beginning of this chapter that while there was a general consensus about what was wrong with individual crime in the 1970s and early 1980s, there was no such consensus about corporate crime. There are several explanations for this lack of consensus. One is that the argument for corporate vicarious liability was not yet widely shared; rather, individuals, not organizations, were the principal perpetrators of crime. Another is that there was no observable secular increase in corporate crime. A third is that while there were problems with corporate crimes, they were generally hidden from view. While there may be some truth in all three of these possibilities, there is some evidence that the third view should take pride of place. One indication of this lies in the relatively recent discovery that the median corporate criminal fine imposed by federal courts before the imposition of the U.S. Sentencing Guidelines was equal to 13 percent of the actual harm.[37] According to the economic theory (and to non-economic theories of crime) this is ludicrously low and clearly inefficiently deterring. As we have seen, criminal monetary sanctions should be a multiple of the actual harm caused, with the multiple depending on the probability of detection and arrest and on the extent of the social losses from the criminal act. The actual losses suffered are a floor from which to build. Indeed, if those actual losses were completely compensatory, there would be no need for a crime beyond the civil wrong.

There is some controversy about the actual level that the corporate fines should take. The economic theory argues for a multiple of the actual losses, designed to approximate the *social* losses, but there is some uncertainty about how, precisely, to measure the appropriate multiple. The problems are perhaps best seen in the context of an example, to which we shall shortly turn. Before we turn to that example, let me briefly describe the actual sentencing guidelines and indicate how they embody the economic principles we have just discussed.

The U.S. Sentencing Guidelines

The United States Sentencing Commission promulgated its organizational sentencing guidelines in late 1991 (U.S. Sentencing Commission, 1991a). The guidelines call for federal courts to assess monetary fines for corporate crime, with the court to begin the calculation by taking as its base the greatest of the following possibilities:

1. the monetary gain that the business organization realized from the criminal act;

2. the monetary loss suffered by others because of the criminal wrongdoing of the business organization;

3. a monetary fine presented in a matrix in the guidelines with the extent of the fine to be determined, in part, by the seriousness of the crime.

The figure resulting from this inquiry was then to be multiplied by a factor of between one and four, depending on the degree of culpability of the business organization. Culpability could vary according, for example, to whether or not senior management of the firm was involved in the criminal wrongdoing.

Finally, the guidelines allowed for the mitigation of the monetary fines if the corporation had an effective monitoring program, promptly reported any criminal wrongdoing to the federal authorities, and aided the authorities in their inquiries.

Note that the guidelines are consistent with—indeed, informed by—the economic theory of crime and punishment. Allowing for difficulties in measuring the appropriate amount of social harm done by the corporation, the guidelines ensure that the loss to victims or the gain to the firm are the floor from which the monetary sanction is to be calculated. The multiple can be as high as four, in the case of egregious criminal conduct, but will in no case be below the actual loss suffered by victims or the gain enjoyed by the firm. And the mitigation principle makes economic sense, too. It clearly creates an incentive for the business organization to be vigilant in looking for, terminating, and correcting criminal wrongdoing. Failure to have provided that mitigation might have reduced the firm's incentive to take these socially beneficial actions.

Some Recent Literature

Several authors have recently argued that the sentencing guidelines are flawed. For instance, Professors John Karpoff and John Lott have argued that the guidelines' monetary sanctions are too high because they ignore the reputational loss suffered by a business organization convicted of a crime (see Karpoff & Lott, 1993). The guidelines ignore that element of expected cost and instead calculate the monetary sanctions so as to set the expected cost greater than any expected benefit from criminal wrongdoing. But a rational business organization will count the loss in reputation as being a substantial cost of committing crime and will figure that cost as part of the expected cost of committing a crime. When combined with the expected monetary sanctions of the guidelines, the reputational loss may make the expected cost of crime so substantial that firms are over-deterred from committing crime.[38] This is, no doubt, a real possibility, but so far there is no clear confirming or refuting empirical evidence on this matter.

In a recent article, Professor Jennifer Arlen (1994) argues that the guidelines contain a fundamental inefficiency, that they are not, as I argued in the previous section, economically sound. The flaw, she argues, lies in the fact that vicarious corporate criminal liability induces enforcement expenditures by the firm and that these expenditures may be inefficient. The potential inefficiency results from her contention that the enforcement efforts of the firm induced by vicarious corporate criminal liability are a double-edged sword. They may make criminal actions by the firm's employees less likely but may also heighten the likelihood of discovering criminal actions that its employees commit and, thereby, increase the probability that the firm will be found criminally liable. "If corporate enforcement expenditures increase a corporation's expected criminal liability by more than they reduce it, then imposing strict vicarious liability on a corporation will not cause it to increase its enforcement expenditures—no matter how large the fine" (Arlen, 1994:843). Indeed, exposure to criminal liability may induce the corporation to take *less* enforcement effort than it would in the absence of vicarious liability.[39]

This is a sophisticated and potentially troubling discovery. However, as with the possibility of reputational losses leading to over-deterrence, the empirical evidence is not yet in on the fundamental issue to which Professor Arlen draws attention—namely, whether vicarious corporate criminal liability induces too much or too little enforcement activity by comparison to the social optimum.

CONCLUSION

In this chapter I have sought to provide an economic grounding for corporate criminal liability and sanctioning. We have seen that society defines criminal wrongs to correct for some of the shortcomings of private causes of action. Some civil wrongs go undetected, and some victims do not bring actions against their injurers; some people intend to cause harm to others; and some wrongs impose costs on society, beyond the immediate victims of the wrongdoing. In the economic theory crime results when rationally self-interested actors perceive the expected benefits of crime to be greater than the expected cost. Society can deter crime by raising the expected cost, principally through altering the level of sanctions imposed on convicted criminals. While there may be doubts about the descriptive power of the economic model when applied to individuals, there can be little doubt about its applicability to the criminal behavior of business organizations. Two of the important conclusions that have come from the economic analysis of corporate crime are that (1) criminal sanctions against business organizations should take the form of monetary fines, and (2) the level of those fines should be systematically greater than the actual losses resulting from the criminal wrongdoing. Finally, we saw that the U.S. Sentencing Commission's Guidelines for corporate sentencing follow the prescriptions of the economic theory of crime and punishment, while taking due regard for the practical difficulties of implementing the theoretical insights.

NOTES

[1]   Professor of Law and of Economics, College of Law and Institute of Government and Public Affairs, University of Illinois at Urbana-Champaign.

[2]   Congress had increased federal fines imposed on business organizations (or made them more certain) in the Criminal Fine Enforcement Act of 1984, Pub. L. No. 98-596, 98 Stat. 3134; and Criminal Fines Improvement Act of 1987, Pub. L. No. 100-185, 101 Stat. 1279.

3   Professor Cohen reports that prior to the 1984 and 1987 Acts mentioned in the previous footnote, 60 percent of the (real) fines imposed by federal courts on corporations for criminal conduct were below $10,000, with the average (real) corporate fine imposed before 1984 being $45,790. After the passage of the 1987 Act, Professor Cohen found that 60 percent of the (real) fines imposed on corporations by federal courts exceeded $100,000, with the average (real) corporate fine after 1987 being $825,636.

4   Some critics of rational choice theory contend that the simplifications that rational choice theory makes of the extremely complex process of human decisionmaking are so seriously misleading that one should be extremely cautious about premising accounts of human behavior on rational choice theory. For a brief summary of some of these criticisms, see Ulen (1994). Later in this section I shall look at these criticisms as they apply to criminal behavior.

5   There are, of course, controversies among economists about aspects of the theory, but there is far less controversy than popular jibes would have one believe ("If all the economists in the world were laid end to end, they wouldn't reach a conclusion.").

6   For an introduction to the field, see Cooter & Ulen (1996), from which some of this section derives.

7   Recently, an exhaustive study found that articles using the economic approach are more frequently cited in the major American law journals than articles using any other approach (Landes & Posner, 1994). Professor Bruce Ackerman of the Yale Law School described law and economics as "the most important development in legal scholarship of the twentieth century."

8   The traditional goal of the law is, of course, justice. There is extensive literature and vigorous debate about the suitability of using efficiency as a legal norm (see, generally, Posner, 1990).

9   I should also note that there are other important aspects of criminal law that any comprehensive theory ought to explain—namely, the fact that the burden of proof for the complainant in criminal actions is "beyond a reasonable doubt," rather than the "preponderance of the evidence" standard that characterizes civil actions, and that the complainant in a criminal action is the government, not a private party. While there is an economic explanation for these aspects of criminal law, our task of explaining corporate criminal liability does not require us to focus on either the burden-of-proof issue or the fact that the complainant is the government.

10   In actuality, both possibilities are far less than 0.5.

11   Put in the negative, the law adopts a presumption *against* the involuntary transfer of resources. For example, one generally cannot make use of another's property without that owner's consent. Failure to do so triggers liability for damages. There are, however, exceptions to this general presumption. Private individuals may make involuntary use of another's property in dire emergencies, and the government may (through its "taking" power) compel private owners to sell their property for public use. Contract law has the same general presumption in favor of voluntary exchange but also recognizes exceptions.

[12]   The expected cost of crime is equal to the probability of detection, arrest, and conviction multiplied by the value of the sanction imposed upon conviction (see Becker, 1968).

[13]   Recall that we are trying to understand why there is a separate class of wrongs called crimes—why, that is, mere civil liability may be inadequate at achieving an optimal amount of some bad thing.

[14]   There may be a connection between those behaviors and the *other* reasons for imposing criminal liability, such as intending to do harm.

[15]   For example, suppose that the award of punitive damages becomes a routine method of dealing with the under-apprehension and failure-to-sue problems. There may be some potential wrongdoers who become so fearful of being held liable for punitive damages that they may take *too much* precaution. Note that this objection applies equally to *any* policy that leads to the expected cost of crime's being too high.

[16]   This is not to mention the troubling issue of the optimal amount of crime to deter. If we decide to raise the expected cost of crime by expending real resources on criminal justice system variables, then we should have in mind just how much crime we seek to deter. In economic jargon, we need to know the "optimal amount of crime." One of the reasons for being skeptical about getting the expenditure of crime-deterring resources right is that there is a strong tendency to want to eradicate *all* crime—that is, to assume that the optimal amount of crime is zero or that the optimal amount of deterrence is 100 percent. But economics can show the error of this way of thinking. The marginal cost of catching an increasing percentage of wrongdoers rises. It is not that expensive to apprehend the first 10 percent of all wrongdoers, but it is extremely expensive to apprehend the last 10 percent. Moreover, the marginal benefit to society of apprehending an increasing percentage of wrongdoers is likely to decline. Thus, the benefit of getting rid of the first 10 percent of wrongdoers is likely to be greater than the benefit of getting rid of the last 10 percent. If we combine these two points, we conclude that the net benefit (marginal benefit minus marginal cost) of apprehending increasing percentages of wrongdoers eventually falls below zero. Thus, the socially optimal percentage of wrongdoers to apprehend is less than 100 percent. (On a similar troubling tendency of public decisionmakers to try to eradicate *all* risk, see Breyer, 1993).

[17]   There is an old legal adage that captures this: "Even a dog recognizes the difference between being stumbled over and kicked."

[18]   There has always been a debate, since Professor Becker's seminal article (Becker, 1968), as to whether the criminal's pleasure or benefit from committing the criminal wrong should be counted in the calculation of the net social benefit of the crime. Most commentators believe, as do I, that the criminal's pleasure or benefit from doing wrong should *not* count.

[19]   For an economic investigation of *mens rea*, see Parker (1993).

[20] Note that this reason for criminal liability calls for sanctions to be even larger than the *supra*-compensatory amounts called for by the under-apprehension and failure-to-sue justifications.

[21] The importance of the distinction is the focus of Coffee (1991). (The article is part of an important symposium, "Sentencing of the Corporation.") Professor Coffee argues that American law has increasingly blurred the distinction between tort law and criminal law and that this may be a bad thing. He notes that the purpose of tort law is to "price" behavior (i.e., to get otherwise valuable activity to take into account its external costs) but that the purpose of criminal law is to prohibit behavior. While this might be taken to imply that criminal sanctions in the form of monetary fines are inappropriate, that is not necessarily Coffee's point. I have already pointed out the economic pitfalls of failing to distinguish between intentional and unintentional wrongs, but that discussion said nothing about the form of the sanction that ought to be imposed. I shall turn to that topic in the next section.

[22] I am focusing on the expected cost of crime as the method of deterrence. In a more complete analysis, I would also deal with the possibility of reducing the incentive to commit crime by raising the opportunity cost of crime—i.e., by raising the returns from legitimate endeavors.

[23] Recall that law and economics distinguishes between positive (descriptive) analysis and normative (prescriptive) analysis. The question I am going to avoid in this section is a *normative* matter—"What is the optimal amount of crime?" This section will look at the sanctions issue from a positive point of view.

[24] By "uncertain marginal results" I mean that the benefit, in terms of increases in the probabilities of detection, arrest, and conviction, of spending on, say, more police and prosecutors are not know with certainty. It makes intuitive sense that, if there are more police, then the probabilities of detection and arrest will be greater. But it is not at all clear by how much. As a result, the increase in the expected cost of crime may or may not be worth the resources expended. We usually do not know.

[25] I do not want to push this argument too far. Clearly, recent history in the United States suggests that stiffening criminal sanctions has had a profound effect on the real resources of the criminal justice system and, possibly, on its efficiency. I am referring to the fact that the prison population of the U.S. has tripled in the last 15 years, largely because of the more swift and certain sanctions imposed for drug offenses. This increase has caused a boom in prison-building and, perhaps, a deterioration in police and prosecutorial services devoted to non-drug offenses. Why this increase in the level of criminal sanctions should have had a *real* effect (i.e., in creating a demand for more prisons) rather than, as the text suggests, merely causing a reduction in the amount of crime, is a subject to which I shall turn in the next section when I compare the economics of individual and corporate crime.

[26] For a fuller discussion of these general points, see Cooter and Ulen (1996:535-559), Block and Lind (1975), and Shavell (1987).

[27] The discussion thus far has been entirely theoretical, and the reader may wonder if there is any empirical support for the economic theory of crime. Indeed, there is.

Those who would like a summary of that literature might see Cooter and Ulen (1996), Chapter 12. I shall discuss some of that empirical literature in the next section of this chapter.

[28] The material in this section is based on Cooter and Ulen (1996).

[29] Those who suffer from temporal inconsistency frequently act in ways that are contrary to their true long-term interests. An example is to be found in the behavior of someone who values the immediate pleasure of a cigarette and ignores the adverse long-term consequences.

[30] Two-thirds of the prisoners had reasonably stable jobs when they were not in prison. On average, the prisoners believed that they made $5.78 per hour at those legitimate jobs.

[31] For a study of the discount rates of criminals, see M.K. Block and V.E. Gerety (1995).

[32] I summarize some of the literature on the imperfections in corporate decision-making in Ulen (1994).

[33] Nor do courts do a particularly good job of discounting to present value. For an example of the difficulties that inflation presented to courts and the odd solutions some of them chose, see *Beaulieu v. Elliott*, 434 P.2d 665 (1967).

[34] The suggestion is that, left to their own devices, employers and employees might voluntarily agree to the employer's vicarious liability for his employees' wrongs. That is, vicarious liability could be mutually beneficial.

[35] I have observed anecdotal evidence of these reactions. University administrators are sometimes unsure about whether they are personally liable or have an absolutely immunity from liability for actions taken in the course of their jobs. That uncertainty has made some administrators squeamish about making potentially injurious decisions. Surely, there is far more systematic evidence than this, but if so, I am unaware of it.

[36] For a full discussion of the economics of this issue, see Sykes (1984).

[37] See Cohen (1991:258). As we have already seen, the average corporate fine greatly increased after the imposition of the federal corporate sentencing guidelines.

[38] The notion of *over*-deterrence is transparent to economists but not necessarily to others. What it means is that firms become so fearful of the losses from being accused and convicted of a crime that they take too much precaution against being found guilty. For example, they may take resources away from otherwise productive uses to monitor their employees' behavior.

[39] Professor Arlen (1994) goes on to explore three alternative legal rules (negligence liability, mitigation provisions, and corporate criminal immunity for criminal information developed through internal audits) that might induce efficient enforcement against corporate criminal actions. The relative efficiency of these alternatives—and of vicarious criminal liability—depends on several factors, among which is the possibility of corporate insolvency.

7

Structural Sanctions:
Corporate Sentences Beyond Fines

Richard S. Gruner[1]
University of Southern Calfornia Law School and *Whittier Law School*

INTRODUCTION: DIFFERENCES BETWEEN
STRUCTURAL AND ECONOMIC SANCTIONS
FOR CORPORATE OFFENSES

Compelled changes to corporate practices and organizational structures (hereinafter referred to as structural sanctions) provide a non-market alternative to fines in the control of corporate crime (Braithwaite & Geis, 1982; Coffee, 1977; Coffee, 1981; Fisse, 1973; Fisse, 1978; Fisse, 1983; Gruner, 1988; Gruner, 1993). The primary focus of corporate fines is on pricing criminal activity at a level that will either (1) deter corporate managers and employees from such activity, or (2) significantly disadvantage firms whose agents commit offenses relative to competing concerns that operate lawfully (Gruner, 1992; Gruner, 1994a; Gruner, 1994b). Higher prices for illegal conduct are expected to cause corporate managers and employees to choose lawful conduct (and practices promoting that conduct) when considering alternative business practices, investors to choose law abiding firms in marketplaces for investments, and consumers to choose suppliers that do not pass on offense costs in marketplaces for products. By contrast, internal reforms imposed through mechanisms like corporate probation sentences represent a measure of focused government control over narrow aspects of corporate conduct in circumstances where a conviction reveals a major deficiency in voluntary corporate law practices (Coffee, 1977; Coffee, 1981).

143

Even if one assumes a preference for pricing mechanisms over government controls where these both are effective, there are a variety of reasons why deterrent fines and pricing mechanisms may be insufficient to prevent many corporate crimes. First, detection rates for many types of offenses committed by corporate employees may be small, making expected costs of criminal activity too low to trigger offense pricing impacts either inside or outside of firms.[2] Second, even if an average firm might be deterred by the threat of market discipline associated with a given level of fines, the managers of a particular firm may be risk-preferring, meaning that market pressures will not have their desired crime prevention effect with respect to that firm. In such a firm, direct restraints on illegal practices may be needed as a substitute for fines. Third, the source of some corporate crimes are low-level employees whose conduct may not be directly affected by market pressures imposed on their firms and who will need direct compulsion and monitoring to change their behavior and prevent future crimes. Fourth, fines and market forces alone may be insufficient to deter corporate crimes because of corporate practices isolating internal corporate practices from outside scrutiny. In such cases, monitoring and disclosure requirements imposed through probation terms may enhance market mechanisms. Monitoring and disclosure requirements can further these ends by ensuring that fines are more accurately focused to reach a higher percentage of all organizational offenders and by raising the apparent price of each offense through elevated detection rates and expected fines.

This chapter examines the availability and desirability of structural sanctions as sentencing alternatives to corporate fines. It describes the policies supporting structural sanctions for corporations, provisions of federal statutes and sentencing guidelines authorizing such sanctions, and specific types of structural sanctions that can ensure proper corporate reactions to past offenses and reduce the likelihood of future misconduct in corporate environments. Overall, this chapter explains why structural sanctions are sometimes superior alternatives to corporate fines. The chapter uses the particular organizational sentencing practices now authorized under federal sentencing guidelines to illustrate how a sentencing system can implement structural sanctions.

A POLICY ANALYSIS OF STRUCTURAL SANCTIONS

Corporate law compliance is necessarily an agency process. Corporate compliance with applicable laws—like other aspects of corporate performance—must be carried out by employees and managers acting as agents for their corporate principals. The conduct of these individual corporate agents is shaped by organizational structures and practices that define agency relationships between the individuals and their firms. These structures and practices ensure that the relationships are productive by directing corporate agents toward actions that will further corporate interests, monitoring whether those actions are undertaken, and rewarding desirable actions by agents to create incentives for further such actions (Arrow, 1985).

Agency processes to further corporate law compliance should follow a similar pattern. Company managers with control over operating structures and practices should shape these corporate features to ensure law compliance by corporate employees and other agents. In particular, operating structures and practices should inform employees about applicable legal requirements, monitor their adherence to those requirements, and reward lawful conduct (or create similar incentives by punishing unlawful conduct) (Gruner, 1994a; Roberts, 1991; Sigler & Murphy, 1988).

Where these types of organizational structures and practices are lacking, the risk of unchecked, self-interested misconduct by individual corporate agents may be high. This is particularly true where other corporate management practices—such as promised bonuses for high sales volumes or effective cost containment—provide individuals with personal reasons to increase corporate profits illegally. Given the importance of corporate operating structures and practices that promote law compliance by corporate agents, a primary goal of corporate legal standards should be to ensure that firms adopt these structures and practices. Both corporate fines and structural sanctions are aimed at furthering this goal, but through substantially different mechanisms.

Structural sanctions for organizational crime ensure that, with respect to law compliance, organizational form follows function (Chandler, 1962). That is, given law compliance as a necessary corporate goal,[3] firms need to adopt corresponding management structures and practices if they are to effectively pursue that goal. Ideally, these steps should be voluntarily undertaken, either out of a sense of moral obligation or in response to economic pressures of potential liability and lost reputation. However, in situations where these pressures are not adequate to produce organizational structures that promote law compliance and public protection, structural sanctions following corporate criminal liability offer means to force recalcitrant firms to adopt the operating structures and methods that are needed for law compliance.

Structural sanctions are but one of many legal devices aimed at ensuring that corporations and other organizations adopt structures and practices aimed at ensuring law compliance. For example, standards for contract formation and enforcement give many parties affected by corporate activities means to negotiate and enforce contract terms that obligate corporations to comply with laws that protect their contracting partners. Obviously, these protections are limited to parties who have sufficient economic clout to insist that corporations undertake protective steps, sufficient information to know what steps to specify, and sufficient monitoring opportunities to detect when protective obligations are not being met.

Tort laws provide additional incentives for corporations to adopt protective structures and methods. Negligence standards impose liability for failures to exercise due care in corporate activities. Typically, due care entails expenditures of resources to prevent harms where such expenditures are less costly than the losses the expenditures will prevent (Posner, 1992). Where particular corporate operating structures promote law compliance and injury minimization better than other available structures involving comparable operating costs, due care will include the adoption of the improved structures. Hence, the threat of negligence liability for breaches of due care tends to encourage firms to adopt efficient injury prevention practices. Similarly, strict liability places the costs of all losses from certain harmful conduct on corporate actors, giving them direct economic incentives to adopt efficient structures for preventing those losses.

The threat of these tort remedies imposes powerful pressures for injury prevention and compliance with related laws. However, these pressures are only as strong as the levels of tort claim enforcement which create the pressures. There are certain circumstances in which tort claims are unlikely to be brought and where tort laws will be ineffective in promoting injury prevention and law compliance. One such setting involves corporate activities with widespread damage comprised of small injuries to numerous parties. Environmental pollution often fits these criteria. In such circumstances, no one person or group may have sufficient injuries to justify a tort action seeking relief. The overall problem is severe, yet undeterred by the threat of tort liability.

A similar result may occur where a few victims have large, quantifiable injuries, but the causal mechanism that produced those injuries is obscure, meaning that the party which is the source of a particular injury can not be identified. This type of problem will also frustrate tort actions, leaving harmful conduct undeterred. Criminal prosecutions aimed at conduct threatening these types of injuries may create greater deterrents and reduce related injuries.

A further type of problem relates to the nature of injuries from some types of organizational conduct. Some injuries are non-quantifiable as with injuries to wildlife and landscape esthetics stemming from some environmental crimes. In other instances, injuries may ultimately be measurable in economic terms, but not be presently quantifiable because the full scope of the injuries depends on future contingencies. Injuries from fraud by stock market professionals often fits this model since the full scope of the injuries that result from such fraud often depends on the reductions in investor confidence that follow and the resulting drop in beneficial stock transactions.

In these types of cases, the lack of economic incentives for victims to bring tort actions (and the corresponding lack of incentives for potential victims to engage in monitoring to detect injurious corporate behavior) make tort claims inadequate means to prevent public harm. Where such mechanisms fail, criminal prosecutions of corporations and individual offenders within firms can fill the deterrence gap. When directed towards corporations, such prosecutions are aimed at crime prevention in two senses. First, the threat of these prosecutions will cause corporate managers to select business practices that are not illegal of themselves and that do not inadvertently promote or tolerate illegal activities in the course of company business. Second, these prosecutions will encourage firms to actively seek out illegal conduct and practices that conceal such conduct. Once detected, firms will have strong motivations to stop illegal activities and thereby cut off potential corporate liability. Hence, in this last respect, corporate criminal prosecutions can have an important role in promoting crime prevention structures and practices within corporate organizations.

In many settings, corporate prosecutions will promote these ends through the threat of corporate fines. In theory, a threatened fine that is greater than the cost of offense prevention structures and practices should be sufficient to encourage a corporation to implement those structures and practices. However, a number of features of the economics of this area make it difficult to specify the level of corporate fines that will have this effect (Coffee, 1981; Comment, 1979; Fisse, 1973; Fisse, 1983; Gruner, 1992; Nader, Green & Seligman, 1976; Stone, 1975; Stone, 1980).

Fine levels that are sufficient to promote effective crime prevention structures and practices in corporate operations must exceed the costs of those structures and practices. Since the details of these structures and practices are often difficult to assess from outside corporate environments, the costs involved in adopting these methods are also difficult to estimate. Hence, the proper corporate costs to consider in setting fines are often difficult to establish.

Furthermore, corporate fines must be not just greater than operating costs of crime prevention structures and practices, the perceived level of threatened fines must exceed those operating costs. The difference here is that the threat posed by threatened corporate fines in the eyes of particular corporate managers or employees will be discounted by the possibility that no fine will be imposed for a given instance of misconduct.

For example, if a $1 million fine is likely for a given type of offense, but that fine is only imposed (on average) in one of every 10 instances the crime is committed, then the expected value or threat of the fine in connection with each offense is only $100,000. Put in preventive terms, if a firm is conducting activities in which this type of offense may be reoccurring, it would not appear beneficial for the firm to adopt preventive practices that cost more than $100,000 per offense prevented. If a corporation did adopt practices that were more expensive than this, it would spend more than $1 million to prevent 10 offenses. Yet it would have suffered a fine of only that amount had it done nothing, let the 10 offenses occur, and paid the fine on the one in 10 (on average) that was detected and punished.

What this example illustrates is that increasing corporate fines to reflect partial detection and punishment rates is critical if sentencing courts are to impose fines that are large enough to promote crime prevention. Yet these detection rates are particularly difficult to assess with any degree of precision. Detection rates certainly vary from crime to crime. Environmental reporting violations are undoubtedly detected less frequently than manslaughter offenses involving unsafe workplaces. These detection rates also vary from firm to firm and region to region based on differences in corporate information disclosure policies, recordkeeping practices, investigative procedures, and prosecutorial priorities. Detection rates may even vary for a given type of crime based on the scale of the activity. An illegal oil spill involving a single barrel of oil may easily go undetected, while an offense involving a major spill on the order of the Exxon Valdez disaster is unlikely to be overlooked.

Given the complexity of determining these critical detection rates, it is hardly surprising that there remains great controversy over the proper levels of corporate fines. The fines necessary to gain the attention of corporate managers are undoubtedly large, however. Indeed, fines large enough to be deterrents in future cases may be so large that the particular corporate defendants who are subject to the fines will not survive as business entities.

Structural sanctions are means to overcome these deficiencies of corporate fines and to ensure that corporations adopt crime prevention structures and practices that are appropriate for the scope and nature of those concerns' business activities (Fisse, 1983). Beyond just ensuring that specific and effective corporate reforms are implemented following an offense,[4] structural sanctions have several other advantages in preventing corporate crimes. These sanctions offer sentencing courts a variety of sentencing options that will avoid the crippling effects of large corporate fines, while still promoting the prevention of subsequent corporate offenses. The law compliance mechanisms that are imposed through structural sanctions will tend to reveal a greater percentage of offenses by corporate employees than would otherwise have come to light, thereby facilitating greater law enforcement efforts and deterrence concerning individual employees.

In addition, structural sanctions force corporations to operate law compliance systems in conjunction with their other business activities, thereby ensuring that these firms (rather than taxpayers generally) bear the sometimes unusually high law enforcement costs associated with operations conducted in an organizational form. These unusual expenses stem from a variety of sources, including the ability of corporations to undertake activities on a scale beyond that of other actors, the tendency of corporations to act through secretive, impenetrable bureaucracies, and the commonplace use in corporate operations of agency processes (such as delegating work through sales quotas tied to performance bonuses) that can promote offenses. Absent internal law compliance efforts, exceptional law enforcement costs related to these corporate features would be born by the government, potentially frustrating effective law enforcement. Under a court-compelled law enforcement program, these costs are imposed on firms on an ongoing basis, effectively tying a law enforcement "tax" to the scope of corporate operations and giving firms a clear economic incentive to develop law compliance methods that are both efficient and effective.

The costs of conducting equivalent law enforcement activities from outside large firms typically would be far greater. Corporate managers operating internal law enforcement programs have more extensive abilities to coordinate essential fact-finding and reporting practices with other corporate activities than would outside investigators or regulators. Outside investigators, by contrast, would often waste considerable sums on mistargeted investigations. Corporate insiders monitoring law compliance results will be much more effective and efficient fact-finders than outsiders since corporate personnel can interpret the findings of an investigation in terms of accumulated knowledge and expertise about corporate activities. Corporate insiders may also have greater access to information within corporate bureaucracies that bears on the detection of law compliance problems. Outside investigators' access to the same information will be limited in most cases by the need to have sufficient advance information about an offense to support a finding of probable cause and a corresponding search warrant. Private fact-finders can also gain greater information by imposing private sanctions (such as salary cuts, demotions, or dismissals) on persons who do not fully cooperate with internal investigations of corporate law compliance.

To summarize, given the administrative costs associated with externally-imposed structural sanctions and our general hesitancy to undertake direct judicial intervention in corporate affairs where less intrusive governmental sanctions will suffice, structural sanctions may be less desirable corporate sentences than fines where the latter will serve deterrence and crime prevention goals. However, there are reasons to believe that fines which are adequate to serve these goals cannot be specified in many cases, either because relevant considerations such as offense detection rates cannot be ascertained or because the necessary fines are so large that to impose them would be disastrous for the corporations involved and others who depend on them. Given the failure of fines in these cases, structural sanctions may be the most desirable sentence candidates.

The merit of a structural sanction in a given case will turn on other factors. One is the ability of the court to fashion a policable probation order or other vehicle for imposing the structural sanction. This means that the court must have viable structural sanction alternatives presented to it and be able to evaluate the merit of those proposals in preventing subsequent corporate crimes. Often, these presentations and evaluations will be made by defendant organizations and court-appointed experts for use by the court in fashioning its order. Ultimately, the court's order will need to identify specific changes in corporate reporting, monitoring, or operating practices that will reduce the risk of future misconduct. These changes will need to be described sufficiently, particularity to provide guidance to the corporate probationer as to what is required and to establish a clear compliance standard for use by persons such as probation officers and experts serving as outside monitors who must determine if the firm is complying with its probation terms.

Beyond the form of the order, a sentencing court will need to be concerning about the reasonableness of structural sanctions in light of both the benefits they will entail and the burdens they will impose. In general, the sanctions should specify the least expensive means to achieve a given level or likelihood of law compliance. Expensive procedures should not be imposed if they will only be likely to achieve a speculative or socially insignificant gain in law compliance. Burdens imposed under probation terms should be evaluated in terms of (1) the public risks that will be reduced through compliance with the terms, (2) the likelihood of further offenses by the defendant firm taking into account both the firm's past record and post-offense reforms, and (3) the probability that further offenses will be deterred and remedied through other private processes such as contractual enforcement or tort actions. Where, on balance, these factors suggest that the burdens of required activities under probation terms are justified by the probable crime prevention gains that will follow from those activities, the terms should be imposed. Once imposed, these probation terms will establish a law compliance framework within which the probationer must operate. The probationer will still have the ability to adjust law compliance methods within this framework to make its law compliance program more effective and efficient. The probationer will also have the opportunity to reassess the profitability and importance of corporate activities that obligate it to undertake corresponding law compliance efforts. This last reassessment may cause firms to realign the mix of various corporate activities in accordance with their law compliance costs.

SUPPORT FOR STRUCTURAL SANCTIONS IN FEDERAL STATUTES AND SENTENCING GUIDELINES

The Sentencing Reform Act of 1984[5] strongly supports offender reform as a central goal of federal sentencing. The Act identifies the specific deterrence and reform of offenders as primary sentencing objectives (Sentencing Reform Act, 1985; Senate Report No. 225, 1994). The drafters of the Act recognized that these goals should be served in corporate as well as individual sentencing. For example, they anticipated that probation restrictions on organizational operations would be used to prevent repeat offenses.[6]

In its corporate sentencing guidelines, the United States Sentencing Commission built on this statutory base by recommending that sentencing courts impose a number of structural sanctions aimed at corporate reform and specific deterrence. These include (1) mandatory publicity by a corporate offender about its offense to encourage heightened monitoring of offender behavior in private relationships, (2) court ordered law compliance programs for firms having 50 or more employees that have not adopted such programs before sentencing, and (3) additional law compliance measures where the nature of a firm's offense, as measured from a pattern of similar offenses, the involvement of high-level officials, or other factors, indicates that changes are needed to reduce the likelihood of future criminal conduct (Sentencing Guidelines, 1994:§§8D1.1(a), 8D1.4(c)).

Given their elaborate nature in comparison with a simple order to pay a fine, innovative corporate sentences may involve unusual judicial administration costs. However, these appear to be costs which Congress intended sentencing courts and convicted firms to bear in the interest of reducing corporate crimes and preventing repeat offenses. Furthermore, since corporate probationers can be required to undertake or pay for many of the most expensive steps in developing and administering probation sanctions, most if not all the exceptional costs of innovative sanctions can be placed on corporate offenders, rather than on sentencing courts or government agencies.[7]

Even if some costs of changed offender behavior (for example, the business impact of probation terms precluding certain sales tactics) are significant, the notion of imposing exceptional burdens and costs on convicted parties to ensure that they avoid future crimes is not peculiar to corporate defendants. Sentencing courts impose many costly probation restrictions on individuals to prevent further offenses and encourage offender rehabilitation.[8] Where they are directly related to the specific deterrence and rehabilitative goals of federal sentencing, these added burdens on individual or corporate probationers are both fair consequences of the criminal behavior leading to sentencing and necessary expenses to implement federal sentencing statutes.

The United States Sentencing Commission's sentencing guidelines for organizational offenders also authorize a number of corporate sanctions aimed at preventing future corporate offenses. These sanctions are recommended for firms with offense histories or other organizational features suggesting that the companies are unusually offense-prone.[9] Even though a single corporate offense does not conclusively indicate a likelihood of further corporate crimes, the guidelines adopt the view that an offense indicates the need for a detailed examination of the corporate offender's internal law compliance standards and procedures, coupled with compelled improvements in those standards and procedures where improvements are necessary to avoid further misconduct. As a corollary, the guidelines support the notion that managers of corporate defendants should have the first opportunity to evaluate their own law compliance programs and make corrective adjustments following an offense. Sentencing courts are instructed to determine the sufficiency of corporate responses and to step in to compel changes only when firm managers do not adopt needed reforms voluntarily.

Restrictive probation sentences constraining corporate conduct during a period of court supervision can further several types of offender reforms. Probation terms can directly constrain post-offense conduct by corporate personnel in ways that make further offenses less likely. Probation sentences can also ensure that sources of corporate misconduct are identified and revealed to shareholders, employees, and other interested parties, thereby permitting this information to be taken into account in corporate governance and accountability processes. The aim of such disclosures is to assist private processes that tend to constrain corporate conduct within legal bounds. An additional type of preventive sentence that is authorized under the guidelines involves adverse publicity aimed at transmitting information about a firm's offense to a broad range of parties such as potential consumers of a firm's products or services. With greater information about an offense, these parties can adjust their subsequent dealings with a convicted firm to better detect and prevent corporate crimes. Furthermore, the threat of adverse public reactions due to offense publicity creates substantial crime deterrents for corporate managers.

STRUCTURAL SANCTIONS ENHANCING OFFENSE DISCLOSURES

Corporate probation terms can indirectly further post-offense reforms in convicted firms by aiding corporate governance and other private monitoring and discipline processes. If the circumstances surrounding an offense, including the possible involvement of senior officials, have not been adequately clarified, probation terms can require critical evaluations of the offense and disclosures of the results (Coffee, Gruner & Stone, 1988). Sentencing courts can direct an agent of the corporation or an outside expert such as special counsel to undertake an offense study for this purpose. Such a study should produce a report that sets forth a factual account of the criminal behavior underlying a corporate offense, the involvement of corporate personnel in the offense, and an evaluation of existing and potential control systems to prevent similar offenses in the future. When completed, such a report should be filed with the sentencing court for use by shareholders in holding corporate officials accountable for their actions and by employees, customers, suppliers, or others wishing to redefine their dealings with the firm in light of its illegal conduct.

The goal of this form of probation sentencing is to implement in a sentencing context a parallel to the Securities and Exchange Commission's practice of requiring an internal investigation and report on securities law violations as part of case settlements under consent decrees (Coffee, 1977). The objective of both the SEC's practices and similar studies under probation terms is to enhance corporate governance and accountability processes to the benefit of both shareholders and the public. Internal accountability within a convicted firm generally cannot be restored unless the corporate offender's board of directors and its shareholders have an adequate understanding of the corporate conduct leading to the conviction. Probation terms of the sort described here will help ensure that shareholders and directors have an independent source of information not limited by corporate managers' neglect or active suppression of offense studies and revelations.

Mandated offense studies and disclosures are particularly important to counteract "an unfortunate plea bargaining dynamic" that tends to conceal the substance of corporate offenses (Coffee, Gruner & Stone, 1988). Often, when a firm and its top corporate officials are both prosecuted, the firm will agree to plead guilty in exchange for an agreement by prosecutors to drop charges against the individual officers. The corporation's plea may reveal little about the circumstances of its offense or about the identity of those within the corporate organization who were primarily responsible. To the extent that one important goal of federal sentencing is "to promote respect for the law" (Sentencing Reform Act, 1985:§3553(a)(2)(A)), sentencing courts should not permit the plea bargaining process to become a barrier to public understanding of the culpability of individuals responsible for corporate crimes. Sentencing courts can avoid this result by accepting corporate plea bargains, but ensuring through probation sentences that the circumstances of an offense are thoroughly investigated and revealed.[10]

STRUCTURAL SANCTIONS MANDATING OFFENDER REFORMS

Probation sentences requiring specific reforms by corporate offenders serve several sentencing goals that are poorly addressed by other sanctions. One important function of such probation sentences is to ensure changes in conduct at a corporate rather than an individual level when the nature of an offense suggests that more than one individual was responsible. Systemic reforms of corporate practices are particularly appropriate if individual responsibility for an offense is difficult or impossible to assign. Compelled improvements in management practices may also be needed if corporate managers bear some responsibility for an offense. For example, mandatory reforms may be needed where managers adopted a policy or practice that promoted an offense, failed to detect and prevent an offense through reasonably available means, or did not respond to prior offenses by investigating those offenses and developing new corporate practices to avoid repetitions.

Compelled reforms of corporate operating practices may be the only effective means to serve the preventive goals of federal sentencing in some cases. Even if threatened corporate fines create sufficient incentives to deter corporate managers from encouraging or tolerating corporate offenses, individuals within a corporate organization may still believe that illegal conduct is personally advantageous. Individual employees may view discipline by corporate managers or personal criminal liability as distant and contingent threats that do not outweigh immediate corporate rewards for performance achieved through illegal conduct. Compelled reforms to heighten monitoring and deterrence of illegal conduct at operating levels may be needed to overcome these limitations of corporate fines.

In addition to ensuring conduct reforms that corporate fines may be insufficient to achieve, mandated reforms sometimes involve other advantages. Reforms increasing outside monitoring of employee behaviors related to corporate law compliance may be necessary to balance management-created internal pressures to attain profit-oriented performance, particularly in times of corporate financial distress. Continuous monitoring can also help ensure that reforms adopted after an offense are maintained throughout a term of probation, rather than being ignored once the heightened attention associated with a criminal prosecution is no longer focused on a firm. Probation arrangements involving monitoring of corporate conduct may raise the perceived likelihood of crime detection in the minds of corporate employees. This will heighten expected fines and deterrents considered by individuals contemplating subsequent offenses. Finally, probation restraints may be an efficient means to allocate limited government law enforcement resources since they focus law enforcement expenditures on a few firms self-identified through their offenses as either risk-preferring or lacking adequate law compliance controls.

Mandated probation reforms raise certain risks. Even with the aid of outside experts, sentencing courts may fail to require corporate behaviors likely to promote law compliance. Probation-imposed monitoring may be insufficient to detect deviations from required conduct. While reforms mandated under probation terms may achieve some improvement in corporate law compliance, the judicial and law enforcement resources expended to achieve this result might be better utilized elsewhere. Corporate probation conditions may restrict both legitimate and illegitimate business activities, producing spillover damage in weakened corporate competitiveness, business failures, and associated disruption to shareholders, employees, customers, suppliers, and surrounding communities.

While these risks are real, they should be taken as dangers to avoid in formulating and administering corporate probation terms rather than as reasons to forego corporate probation altogether. Given its many potential advantages as discussed above, corporate probation is too valuable to be ignored as a sentencing alternative. To reduce risks of harmful constraints on legitimate corporate activities, sentencing courts need to impose corporate probation terms in ways that maximize opportunities for corporate personnel to participate in shaping and enforcing mandated reforms. In addition, sentencing courts need to minimize the impact of their own limited managerial expertise by relying on appointed experts, compensated by the probationer, to evaluate probation restrictions and monitor probation compliance.

CIRCUMSTANCES WARRANTING COMPELLED REFORMS

Federal sentencing guidelines for organizational offenders provide a concrete illustration of how circumstances warranting compelled reforms can be identified. A corporate probation sentence is required under the guidelines in several circumstances where the nature of an offense or the history of the offender indicates an unusual likelihood of further offenses. Circumstances triggering mandatory probation include (Sentencing Guidelines, 1994:§8D1.1(a)):

1. The failure of an organization having 50 or more employees to adopt an effective program to prevent and detect violations of law;[11]

2. Similar misconduct by corporate employees or agents within the five years prior to sentencing that resulted in an adjudication of corporate criminal liability;

3. Similar misconduct by high-level personnel in the organization, or the unit of the organization within which the instant offense was committed, during the five years prior to sentencing that resulted in an adjudication of individual criminal liability; and

4. Any circumstances indicating that probation requirements are necessary to ensure changes within the organization that will reduce the likelihood of future criminal conduct.[12]

Types of Required Reforms

Federal sentencing guidelines also describe several desirable corporate reforms that can be imposed through structural sanctions. The guidelines provide for two types of corporate probation terms aimed at preventing future criminal conduct. The first involves terms requiring an offender to adopt a general law compliance program if one is absent at the time of sentencing. The second involves the requirement or prohibition of specific business activities or reporting practices that will help prevent further offenses like that under sentencing.

Mandated Compliance Programs

If a sentencing court finds one or more of the above circumstances to be present, the guidelines recommend that the court require an organizational offender to adopt and maintain a program to detect and prevent future violations of law (Sentencing Guidelines, 1994:§8D1.4(c)). An acceptable program should be reasonably calculated to prevent criminal conduct in the organization. The guidelines do not require a convicted firm to adopt any particular type of compliance program. It seems clear, however, that the Commission felt an offender should adopt an effective compliance program following an offense, and anticipated that sentencing courts would compel this result under probation terms if an offender does not pursue it voluntarily.

A new compliance program, whether voluntarily adopted or court imposed, should meet the standards for an effective compliance program articulated in the Commission's corporate sentencing guidelines (Sentencing Guidelines, 1994:§8A1.2).[13] To be deemed effective under those standards, a corporate law compliance program must include reasonably designed, implemented, and enforced law compliance efforts that are generally effective in preventing and detecting criminal conduct. This is the equivalent of saying that an effective law compliance program must reflect due diligence on the part of corporate managers to prevent offenses by corporate employees and agents in the course of their business activities. In addition to these general features, a law compliance program must incorporate seven key components to be deemed effective under the guidelines. These required features include: (1) compliance standards and procedures defined in conduct codes and other corporate policy statements, (2) high-level managerial responsibility for compliance with such standards and procedures, (3) due care by managers to prevent delegation of substantial discretionary authority to individuals who have a propensity to engage in illegal activities, (4) steps to communicate law compliance standards and procedures to all employees and other agents, (5) monitoring and auditing systems reasonably designed to detect criminal conduct by corporate employees and agents, (6) consistent enforcement of compliance standards through disciplinary mechanisms, and (7) active organizational responses to misconduct to prevent further offenses.

The guidelines recommend several steps that sentencing courts should use in implementing and policing probation terms requiring the operation of a compliance program. An organization should be given an opportunity to develop a proposed compliance program, including a schedule for implementation that will, if approved by the sentencing court, form the basis for the convicted organization's probation terms (Sentencing Guidelines, 1994:§8D1.4(c)(1)). A sentencing court is authorized to engage experts to aid the court in reviewing the efficacy of a compliance program submitted by a convicted concern. Such experts must be afforded access to all material possessed by the organization that is necessary for a comprehensive assessment of the proposed program.

The guidelines also recommend that sentencing courts require certain actions by offenders to ensure the proper implementation and maintenance of an approved compliance program. Upon approval of its compliance program by a sentencing court, an organization should be required to notify its employees and shareholders of its criminal conduct and its program to prevent and detect further violations (Sentencing Guidelines, 1994:§8D1.4). This notice should be in a form prescribed by the court. The organization should also be required to make periodic reports to the court or the offender's probation officer, at intervals and in a form specified by the court, regarding the organization's progress in implementing its compliance program. Finally, to monitor its adherence to its compliance program, the firm should be obligated to submit to a reasonable number of regular or unannounced examinations of its books and records by a probation officer or experts engaged by the court and to allow the interrogation of knowledgeable individuals within the organization. The costs of any experts engaged by the court for purposes of these examinations or interviews will be born by the corporate probationer.

Business Practice Reforms

In addition to requiring a corporate offender to operate an effective law compliance program, a sentencing court can restrict specific business practices of the offender to help ensure that repeat offenses do not occur. Although a sentencing court cannot completely exclude a convicted firm from a line of business,[14] it can require a corporate offender to conduct specific business activities in a restricted fashion. A corporate probationer can be required to engage in particular business activities only to a stated degree or under specified circumstances (Sentencing Reform Act, 1985:§3563(b)(6)). Business practice restrictions should be aimed at compelling changes that will prevent the continuation or repetition of particular abusive practices. For example, "an organization convicted of executing a fraudulent scheme might be directed to operate that part of the business in a manner that was not fraudulent" (Senate Report No. 225, 1984:96). The types of probation restraints that are appropriate in a given case obviously will depend on the nature of the offense under sentencing and the circumstances that prompted it. However, conduct restraints drawn from three sources will provide convicted corporations, court-appointed experts, and sentencing courts with valuable suggestions regarding potential probation terms.

The first and most useful source of examples will be the practices that similar firms use to ensure law compliance. Business practices already used by other firms to combat the type of illegal conduct observed in a convicted firm ought to be considered as candidates for probation requirements. Of course, the similarity of the settings in which these practices are used to the offender's circumstances, along with the degree of success they have achieved in assuring law compliance, ought to be considered by a sentencing court before imposing other firms' practices as probation requirements. Because they reflect the inventiveness and business experience of others (as well as, perhaps, a greater willingness to try law compliance measures than is present in the defendant organization), law compliance techniques of other firms are valuable candidates for probation requirements.

A second source of possible probation restrictions lies in the experience of the convicted firm itself. The offense under sentencing is one instructive bit of corporate experience, since it may reveal defects in corporate policies or practices that need repair to help avoid repeat offenses or to make later offenses more easily detected. Therefore, a full understanding of the offense under sentencing, its sources, the internal procedures that might have prevented it, and the detection methods that might have revealed it earlier should be considered by a sentencing court in identifying desirable probation constraints. However, studies leading to probation terms need not be limited to the offense under sentencing. Rather, corporate managers or outside experts should be required to assess whether other corporate indicators like civil claims, complaints, or aborted transactions suggest patterns of behavior like that reflected in the firm's offense. These claims, complaints, and transactions can be further indicators of law compliance disfunction, suggesting the need for alternative practices to prevent the repetition of similar conduct. If firm managers have not responded to these indicators of potential illegal conduct, courts should compel them to do so by appointing outside experts to propose appropriate new constraints and by requiring compliance with those constraints as corporate probation conditions.

General corporate management principles are a third source of information on desirable corporate probation constraints (Gruner, 1988). By treating the illegal behavior present in a firm's offense as a type of corporate activity that should be discouraged or prevented by management processes, established management principles can identify corporate probation terms that will help prevent further instances of such behavior.[15] In general, business management principles suggest means to increase the likelihood that individual corporate employees will undertake activities promoting corporate interests. Focusing on the particular corporate interest of law compliance, management principles can identify practices that reduce illegal conduct by restricting the discretion of individual employees to select illegal conduct or by shaping their situational incentives to discourage such choices (Williamson, 1970). Changes to further these ends can be made in organizational, motivational, informational, personnel selection, performance monitoring, and control features of corporate practices (Gruner, 1988). If court-appointed experts, managers of the corporate probationer, or government attorneys can articulate why, in terms of established management principles, specific corporate changes are reasonably calculated to prevent and detect further offenses, sentencing courts should rely on those principles and impose the indicated reforms.

CONCLUSION: A COLLABORATIVE APPROACH TO THE DEVELOPMENT, IMPLEMENTATION, AND ENFORCEMENT OF STRUCTURAL SANCTIONS

Corporate probation and other sanctions authorized under federal sentencing guidelines can create a range of incentives encouraging managers to respond to corporate crimes. To maximize the beneficial effect of probation sentences, sentencing courts need to match the form of probation sentences to the degree of cooperation by managers of convicted firms in voluntarily undertaking post-offense reforms.

The overall probation sentencing strategy that will best further this goal is a "tit-for-tat" enforcement pattern (Ayres & Braithwaite, 1992; Braithwaite, 1985). Under this strategy, the extent and detail of court control over a corporate probationer should vary in an inverse relationship to the extent of voluntary efforts by corporate managers to formulate and institute post-offense reforms. That is, a sentencing court should defer to firm managers to the extent that managers voluntarily pursue substantial internal reforms following an offense. However, if managers resist reform efforts, sentencing courts should impose detailed, demanding, and heavily monitored probation terms. By shifting enforcement strategies in parallel with corporate cooperativeness, a sentencing court can ensure that firm managers with varying attitudes about the desirability of voluntary corporate changes have meaningful incentives to pursue and maintain post-offense reforms.

A range of specific probation enforcement strategies can be pursued within this "tit-for-tat" framework. At one extreme lies voluntary adoption of compliance plans and other reform measures by a corporate offender prior to sentencing. Federal sentencing guidelines encourage this process strongly, if indirectly. The guidelines make the threat of court-ordered probation and reforms clear to corporate managers once a corporate conviction is likely. However, the guidelines give corporate managers an opportunity to act to improve their firm's position at sentencing by providing that post-offense responses should be considered in setting fines and probation terms. If managers adopt substantial compliance programs voluntarily following an offense, their efforts can avoid corporate probation entirely.

Voluntary Compliance

A voluntary compliance approach to meeting federal sentencing goals involves cooperative efforts by both sentencing courts and corporate executives. In probation sentencing, a court can cooperate with corporate managers by granting relatively unrestrictive probation terms. For their part, managers of a corporate offender can cooperate in achieving federal sentencing goals by formulating and implementing substantial corporate reforms prior to sentencing. This will require substantial corporate self-studies to identify sources of corporate offenses, further analyses of reform alternatives and their probable effectiveness, and the implementation of the reforms identified as probably the most effective. If managers respond to a corporate crime this way prior to sentencing, their firm deserves light probation restrictions or no probation sentence at all.[16]

Even if their organizations have voluntarily adopted substantial law compliance reforms, corporate offenses will be minimized only if firm managers still feel that they have something to lose from poor law compliance.[17] One way to enhance this motivation is for sentencing courts to require convicted firms to avoid and report any subsequent criminal offense during their probation periods. Any pattern of similar offenses reported by a corporate probationer should trigger a thorough judicial review of the adequacy of the firm's ongoing compliance efforts and resentencing to more demanding probation terms if the firm's efforts are inadequate.

Enforced Self-Regulation

If firm managers hesitate to respond to a corporate offense with voluntary studies and reforms, some suspicion about the depth of management's commitment to law compliance is justified. In these circumstances, a sentencing court should adopt a less cooperative probation approach. If managers of a corporate offender have not voluntarily examined the need for post-offense reforms as of sentencing, a sentencing court should consider a probation strategy involving enforced self-regulation of law compliance standards.[18] Under this arrangement, managers of a corporate offender would be compelled to develop and adopt law compliance standards and procedures which, upon review by prosecutors, court-appointed experts and the sentencing court, appear sufficient to ensure a reasonable probability of subsequent law compliance. Compliance with the resulting standards would be made a condition of the corporation's probation. Further probation terms would require the probationer to adopt internal corporate mechanisms for enforcing compliance with the new standards and procedures. These enforcement arrangements might include the creation of a probation compliance staff within the corporate offender, the specification of the duties of this compliance staff and arrangements to isolate the staff from line-management control, and the requirement of external reporting on compliance monitoring activities undertaken by the internal staff and the results of those activities.

Such internal enforcement efforts could be coupled with probation terms providing for external probation monitoring by probation officers or regulatory officials (Braithwaite, 1985). External monitoring would be aimed at detecting gross abuses of the probationer's internal compliance systems. Appropriate external monitoring activities would include: (1) assessments of whether company law compliance standards and procedures continue to be sufficient to ensure compliance with applicable laws, (2) analyses to determine if company compliance officials are free to identify compliance problems without pressure from corporate superiors to downplay those problems, (3) analyses of types of monitoring undertaken by internal compliance monitors, (4) spot inspections to check that compliance personnel are detecting and remedying most or all violations of probation terms and other legal requirements, and (5) investigations and reports to the sentencing court if a firm fails to comply with its probation terms.

By adopting these types of probation terms, sentencing courts will establish systems of privately developed and publicly ratified standards for ensuring compliance with the criminal laws addressed. Probation conditions developed in this manner will restate criminal law demands in terms particularized and strengthened for convicted firms. These probation standards will serve as both targets for corporate action and measures of corporate law compliance success. Particularized probation terms will make later assessments of many probation violations simpler than related analyses of criminal violations.

Under a system of "tit-for-tat" enforcement, corporate probation sanctions should be tailored to rely on reform efforts by corporate managers to the extent that cooperation is shown in return. Giving corporate managers the opportunity to shape compliance standards to minimize disruption of legitimate business activities will motivate them to actively participate in constructing probation terms and enforcing those terms as internal corporate standards. Of course, if internal enforcement efforts falter during a term of probation, a sentencing court can again adopt a "tit-for-tat" enforcement philosophy and either impose more demanding probation terms or resentence the firm involved to a harsher fine.

Reliance on enforced self-regulation as a probation strategy has many advantages over a system relying exclusively on external formulation and enforcement of probation restrictions. It allows probation constraints to be carefully matched to a particular firm's operations and law compliance problems. At the same time, it should help to minimize the administrative burdens of compliance measures by allowing firm managers to coordinate these measures with other corporate activities. Because company personnel will undertake most compliance enforcement and monitoring activities, this approach will cause corporate probationers to bear most probation enforcement costs. Furthermore, corporate managers will have a stake in making a self-enforcement system work effectively because the failure of this process will place their firm at risk of resentencing and the imposition of more restrictive probation terms or harsher fines. With this motivation, corporate managers should be willing to apply internal sanctions and investigative capabilities to ensure compliance with probation terms.

Mandated Restrictions with Enforcement Discretion

As a more onerous form of corporate probation, sentencing courts can mandate probation restrictions developed for resistant firms by outside experts. If a corporate probationer violates externally developed probation standards, a sentencing court will have the discretion to specify a wide range of sanctions. The threat that a court may impose severe sanctions on a firm that undertakes few efforts to comply with probation terms should encourage firm managers to seek methods to comply with those terms. Hence, even in the absence of initial cooperation by firm managers, mandated probation restrictions coupled with discretionary choices about sanctions for violations constitute another valuable "tit-for-tat" variant of corporate probation sentencing.

Because externally imposed probation terms may not be supported by internal enforcement mechanisms, extensive external disclosures and studies will be typically needed to monitor compliance with such probation terms. However, to the extent that external compliance monitors have substantial discretion regarding compliance findings, they may be targets of co-option by the corporations they scrutinize. Mechanisms like peer reviews of efforts by external monitors or rotations of monitoring assignments may be necessary to ensure accurate probation monitoring. While enforcement processes located outside corporate probationers' organizations will typically be more expensive to maintain than internal enforcement arrangements, probationers can be forced to pay the costs of experts appointed to serve as external probation monitors. Even if the government bears some incremental costs from imposing externally monitored corporate probation arrangements, a viable threat of externally developed and enforced probation schemes should be maintained to encourage firm managers to make good faith proposals of probation terms when they have the opportunity to do so and thereby avoid externally imposed probation arrangements.

Mandated Restrictions with Defined or Presumed Sanctions

At an even higher level of compulsion, particularly recalcitrant firms can be subjected to externally developed probation terms coupled with pre-selected sanctions for failures to comply with particular probation conditions. Alternatively, probation terms might be tied to presumed sanctions that will be imposed following a probation violation unless the probationer presents convincing reasons why those penalties are inappropriate.

The advantage of these arrangements lies in guaranteeing harsh sanctions for particularly serious probation violations. Serious probation violations include violations that are part of patterns of offenses that reflect weak law compliance monitoring or enforcement efforts by corporate managers or violations involving a flagrant disregard of probation restrictions related to significant public risks. By promising harsh sanctions for probation violations like these, sentencing courts can define the serious consequences of such misconduct and create corresponding deterrents. Even managers who are otherwise resistant or oblivious to probation requirements may respond to clear statements of draconian consequences for specific probation misconduct.

Threatened sanctions will often need to involve very serious consequences to have this effect. Federal sentencing guidelines include a good example of the type of strong sanction that sentencing courts can specify as a consequence of serious probation violations.[19] The guidelines provide that "[i]n the event of repeated, serious violations of conditions of probation, the appointment of a master or trustee may be appropriate to ensure compliance with court orders" (Sentencing Guidelines, 1994:§8D1.5). Because the appointment of a master or a trustee would directly displace the powers of corporate managers,[20] the possibility of such an appointment will be a powerful and meaningful threat to corporate leaders and encourage them to take substantial efforts to avoid its realization (Galbraith, 1971).

Toward a General Law Compliance Methodology: Law Compliance as Good Management

Regardless of the sentencing strategy used, the ultimate objective of most probation sentencing is to ensure that a corporate offender adopts and maintains effective law compliance practices. In evaluating and monitoring law compliance programs, corporate officials and courts alike should be guided by the fundamental principle that law compliance is an aspect of high quality corporate performance and that the degree of law compliance achieved by a firm is, in essence, a specialized quality control issue. Corporate law compliance programs are a variety of quality control programs with a particular emphasis on ensuring high quality law compliance in corporate operations. By viewing corporate law compliance programs in this way, managers and courts can use quality control principles developed in other corporate settings to construct and evaluate law compliance systems. Indeed, existing government standards (Comptroller General, 1994; U.S. Department of Defense, 1960; U.S. Department of Defense, 1963) and industry guidelines (ANSI & ASQC, 1987; U.S. Department of Commerce, 1994) for evaluating quality control systems can supplement legal standards for law compliance programs and produce useful tests for due diligence in corporate law compliance efforts.

At the heart of every law compliance program is the recognition that law compliance, like other aspects of corporate performance, is ultimately a responsibility of corporate line managers who control day-to-day business operations. The essential objectives of a law compliance program are to ensure that line managers give attention to law compliance matters in their oversight of corporate operations[21] and that law compliance efforts are integrated with other day-to-day management practices and procedures.[22]

This definition of law compliance due diligence suggests a number of the features that an effective law compliance program should have.[23] In general, an adequate law compliance program that supports confidence about corporate law compliance will have the following characteristics (ANSI & ASQC, 1987):

1. Performance demands imposed by the system are well-understood and generally met by corporate employees;

2. The performance required by the system is effective in satisfying legal requirements; and

3. The system fosters an operational emphasis on preventing legal offenses rather than on detecting offenses after the fact.

The scope of performance controls and monitoring that are necessary to make a law compliance program effective will depend on the extent of corporate activities within a firm, the diversity of those activities, and the nature of the legal risks raised by those activities. The more likely legal violations are in terms of these factors, the more extensive a firm's law compliance practices should be in order for top managers and directors to be reasonably assured that law compliance is being maintained. Likewise, the more extensive the history of offenses is in a particular firm or industry, the more extensive law compliance practices should be to maintain a reasonable certainty that additional offenses of a similar sort are being prevented. Finally, when a firm's activities threaten illegal conduct with particularly harmful consequences (such as, for example, illegal waste discharges by a chemical manufacturing firm that would threaten a nearby town), the public dangers involved will require expanded law compliance efforts to achieve a reasonable certainty of law compliance. In such settings, the extreme public risks associated with firm activities will raise the level of compliance efforts necessary to achieve a reasonable certainty of law compliance.

Corporate law compliance programs reflect systematic efforts to confront these issues and to ensure that corporate business practices are matched with law compliance safeguards. Structured sanctions are means to compel reticent corporate managers to adopt new compliance measures for corporate activities entailing significant risks of unlawful conduct. Given the often weak threat of corporate fines as incentives for further action, structural sanctions such as probation sentences frequently offer sensible and effective means to ensure improved law compliance in the operations of convicted concerns.

NOTES

[1]   Professor of Law, Whittier Law School. Professor Gruner is the author of the treatise "Corporate Crime and Sentencing" published by The Michie Company. He is a former inside counsel to the IBM Corporation and consultant to the U.S. Sentencing Commission concerning corporate sentencing standards.

[2]   The perceived economic threat of a fine will typically be discounted or lowered to reflect the likelihood that the fine will not be imposed (Parker, 1989). This will reduce the deterrent impact of threatened fines, which will in turn limit the impact of potential fines on internal corporate decisions about what activities to pursue and external decisions by investors about what stocks to buy.

[3]   By viewing corporate law compliance as a business goal, it is possible to analyze corporate offenses as defects in corporate performance that often stem from the same types of sources as other types of corporate performance defects (Gruner, 1994a).

[4]   Structural sanctions in the form of corporate probation conditions can ensure that operating reforms are adopted and continued by imposing substantial law compliance monitoring and reporting requirements on corporate probationers (Gruner, 1988).

[5]   The Sentencing Reform Act of 1984 was enacted as part of the Comprehensive Crime Control Act of 1984 (Public Law 98-473, 1984).

6   The legislative history of the Sentencing Reform Act notes that "an organization convicted of executing a fraudulent scheme might be directed to operate that part of the business in a manner that was not fraudulent" (Senate Report No. 225, 1984:96).

7   If the development or enforcement of innovative sanctions requires special expertise or monitoring of offender conduct, sentencing courts can often shift associated burdens to offenders under probation terms providing for the appointment of experts to aid the court and requiring offenders to pay associated costs.

8   Many of the probation conditions authorized for individual defendants under federal law involve limitations on individual conduct that entail losses of income or costly conduct by probationers. These include restrictions on work activities, required support payments to family members, and mandated community service (Sentencing Reform Act, 1985:§3563(b)(1), (5), (6), (13)).

9   Although rehabilitation of individual offenders within the federal penal system is viewed by many as a failed approach to street crime, rehabilitation of corporate offenders through probation sentences compelling improvements in offender practices is more likely to succeed. Although it may be difficult to reorient or rehabilitate a human psyche, "it is much easier to rearrange a corporation's standard operating procedures, defective control systems, inadequate communication mechanisms, and in general its internal structure" (Mokhiber, 1988:33).

10   Of course, to the extent that corporate officers are concerned about additional reputational harm or civil liability that may follow these investigations and disclosures, the officials may be somewhat more hesitant to enter into related plea agreements.

11   A firm may avoid probation on this ground by adopting a law compliance program at any time prior to sentencing, meaning that managers have strong incentives to make voluntary post-offense improvements in compliance systems. Federal sentencing guidelines specify the basic features that should be included in an effective law compliance program (Sentencing Guidelines, 1994:§8A1.2 (Application Note 3(k))).

12   While the guidelines do not indicate the types of circumstances covered by this provision, the absence of corporate self-studies concerning the causes of a corporate offense or a lack of follow-through on the results of such studies would be logical grounds for determining that changes will not occur absent court compulsion.

13   These standards are utilized elsewhere in the guidelines for determining whether a firm warrants a fine reduction due to its operation of a generally effective law compliance program at the time of an offense (Sentencing Guidelines, 1994:§8C2.5(f)).

14   Congress rejected the proposed language in the Sentencing Reform Act of 1984 that would have authorized sentencing courts to bar a convicted organization from engaging in a particular occupation, business, or profession. It removed this provision from the final bill, in part because of complaints by business leaders that sen-

tencing courts might use this authority to put legitimate enterprises out of business following a regulatory offense (Senate Report No. 225, 1984:69, 96-97).

> Even though they cannot be excluded from a particular line of business under probation terms, organizations operated primarily for illegal purposes or primarily by criminal means can be precluded from all further business operations. Such organizations—dubbed "criminal purpose organizations" in the Sentencing Guidelines—are subjected to draconian penalties aimed at putting the organizations out of business (U.S. Sentencing Commission, 1991b). The fines for these organizations are set at amounts sufficient to divest them of all their net assets (Sentencing Guidelines, 1994:§8C1.1).

[15] Management actions that further a particular corporate goal like law compliance can only be specified in terms of relative merit. No single, best selection exists, but techniques that tend to promote a desired end better than others can be identified (Galbraith, 1977; Lorsch & Lawrence, 1970).

[16] If such reform efforts are underway, but uncompleted at sentencing, a sentencing court can impose demanding probation terms while indicating to the managers of the sentenced corporation that they should continue to develop their own probation proposals for submission to the court in a motion seeking altered probation terms or a dismissal of probation terms altogether in light of the organization's reforms.

[17] The likelihood that illegal conduct will be detected by public authorities will significantly affect managers' assessments of crime risks. In some settings, such as small firms with frequent public contracts or firms in heavily regulated and inspected industries, illegal conduct may be likely to be detected and deterred accordingly. More substantial detection problems are likely to arise in large corporate organizations operating in unregulated fields and in substantial isolation from public scrutiny.

[18] The notion of enforced self-regulation was first proposed as a strategy for regulatory reform (Ayres & Braithwaite, 1992; Braithwaite, 1985).

[19] A sentencing court might wish to frame a designated sanction in presumptive rather than guaranteed terms to signal corporate managers that it is willing to adopt a lesser sanction for good cause, thereby giving probationers an incentive to make improvements following a probation violation.

[20] While it was "not the intent of the Committee [reporting the Sentencing Reform Act of, 1984] that the courts manage organizations as a part of probation supervision" (Senate Report No. 225, 1984:99), the legislative history of the Act indicates that Congress envisioned probation arrangements entailing "effective supervision of a convicted . . . union, . . . or brokerage house," which could be undertaken by probation officers "from the requisite profession" (Senate Report No. 225, 1984:131). Thus, auditors, accountants, lawyers, engineers, or experienced executives in the field of a convicted firm could serve as probation officers.

21   For example, an effective environmental law compliance program should reflect the following sorts of line management attention to law compliance (Advisory Group, 1993):

> *Line Management Attention to Compliance.* In the day-to-day operation of the organization, line managers, including the executive and operating officers at all levels, direct their attention, through the management mechanisms utilized throughout the organization (e.g., objective setting, progress reports, operating performance reviews, departmental meetings), to measuring, maintaining and improving the organization's compliance with environmental laws and regulations. Line managers routinely review environmental monitoring and auditing reports, direct the resolution of identified compliance issues, and ensure application of the resources and mechanisms necessary to carry out a substantial commitment [to law compliance].

22   Thus, an environmental law compliance program should include the following features (Advisory Group, 1993):

> *Integration of Environmental Policies, Standards and Procedures.* The organization has adopted, and communicated to its employees and agents, policies, standards and procedures necessary to achieve environmental compliance, including a requirement that employees report any suspected violation to appropriate officials within the organization, and that a record will be kept by the organization of any such reports. To the maximum extent possible given the nature of its business, the organization has analyzed and designed the work functions (e.g., through standard operating procedures) assigned to its employees and agents so that compliance will be achieved, verified and documented in the course of performing the routine work of the organization.

23   Legal standards presently describe the minimum features of effective law compliance programs for consideration in corporate regulation (U.S. Environmental Protection Agency, 1986; U.S. Environmental Protection Agency, 1991), prosecution (U.S. Department of Justice, 1991), and sentencing analyses (Sentencing Guidelines, 1994:§8A1.2 (Application Note 3(k))).

Section IV

REGULATORY RELATIONS

Until recently, scholarly attention to regulatory relations was limited. The possibility that the posture of the state toward business could effect corporate behavior was largely overlooked in favor of attention to the capacity of the state vis-à-vis business. Effective control of corporations was, and still is in many cases, theorized as a product of the extent of the threat presented to business by the state. In large part due to the growing influence of European and Australian scholars in the study of corporate crime, the possibility of alternative regulatory postures and the role of these postures in corporate crime control has begun to receive widespread attention. At the center of this debate is whether a negotiative regulatory posture designed around a structural understanding of corporations could reduce corporate crime.

The next two chapters of this book address the issue of regulatory relations by providing contrasting approaches to this debate. Heretofore, the agency model has been presented exclusively from the perspective of law and economics, clearly the dominant modes of expression of this model. As criminologist Leo Barrile makes clear in this section, however, an alternative, leftist agency model also exists. In fact, Barrile develops a useful typology of agency and structure theories, which clearly distinguishes his version of agency theory from classical economic versions of this theory. Barrile's application of agency theory shares with law and economics a belief in the fundamental rationality of individual and organizational actors. However, by questioning the legitimacy of the economic institutions in which these actors are located, their rational actions are viewed as socially harmful. In direct contrast to Parker, for example, Barrile views corporate crime as a widespread and serious problem. As a result, the state must act aggressively to limit these harms. The market, which is the location of regulation for law and economists, is inadequate because the market mechanism is so centrally implicated in the generation of social harms. It is the state, through aggressive, adversarial action, which must seek to limit corporate wrongdoing.

British socio-legal scholar Bridget Hutter introduces an additional level of complexity to this debate by considering the role of state posture, not just state capacity, in corporate crime control. Arguing from a structure perspective, Hutter asserts that the state must structure its relationship toward business in a manner that recognizes the strength of business in lawmaking and in resisting regulation, the superior knowledge of managers of the operations of their corporation, and the interest of business persons in abiding by the law. Given these considerations, the state is best off working in a negotiative manner with business in crafting and enforcing regulations, providing business a central role in enacting compliance plans consistent with their corporate structure, while the state approves and provides secondary enforcement of such plans. Whether one shares Hutter's pluralist view of the state, in which business functions as a non-privileged interest group, or an elite theory more consistent with Braithwaite's contributions to the regulatory relations debate, the central point remains the same—the state should approach business in a manner designed to maximize the likelihood of law compliance by minimizing the likelihood of resistance. This cooperative approach to regulation is in direct contrast to the largely adversarial role of government that Barrile advocates.

8

Agency Model: Improving Prevention[1]

Leo G. Barrile
Bloomsburg University

Over the past three decades, the regulatory apparatus in the United States and other industrialized countries has attempted to reduce the injurious and lethal consequences of business decisionmaking, the "negative externalities" of business, by establishing national safety standards for the workplace, the environment, and consumer products and by backing those standards with abatement orders, consent decrees, fines and ultimately the referral of individuals and companies to district attorneys for civil action or criminal prosecution (Smith, 1976, 1979; Reiner & Chatten-Brown, 1989; Jones, 1990/91; DiMento, 1993). States such as California, New Jersey, New York, and Michigan have been forerunners in government intervention of business crime, using administrative, civil, or criminal courts more extensively than other states and the federal government (Curington, 1988; Benson, Cullen & Maakestad, 1992).

It is the contention of this chapter that regulatory diligence is directly related to health and safety, that is, when there is greater adherence to regulatory law and other statutes through aggressive investigation, enforcement, and criminal prosecution, better health and safety conditions prevail. By contrast, when enforcement is relaxed as during periods of government underfunding and deregulation, there is either a hiatus or a decline in the health and safety of the public.

Still, some insist that nonadversarial tactics such as "flexible" interpretations of regulations, voluntary compliance, collaborative arrangements, and encouraged self-policing are more efficacious at altering the decisionmaking of business agents than punitive measures which, they say, are often unreasonable and likely to produce defensiveness and litigious resistance (Kagan & Scholz, 1982; Bardach & Kagan, 1982; Hawkins, 1984). Others, however, are skeptical of the use of informal pressures and coaxed compliance, of the assumption that most businesses and their agents are "good apples" willing to self-police, to alter the fundamental rationality of their decisionmaking, namely, capital accumulation (Pearce & Tombs, 1990, 1992). Rather, they favor deeper state interventionism, retributive, or deterrent strategies such as punitive fines and even imprisonment, because, on the one hand, these punishments are equitable and deserved (Schlegel, 1990), and, on the other hand, as more radical thinkers contend, they are a first step toward altering the criminogenic nature of economic institutions (Pearce, 1993; Tombs, 1992; Barrile, 1993, 1995).

Indeed, the most invasive intervention, the criminal accountability and punishment of corporate agents, has much to recommend it. The truly victimizing nature of corporate violence would be publicly acknowledged as more than a technical violation, and those who suffer would not be invisible "victims without crime" (Reasons, Ross & Patterson, 1981; Bros, 1989; Frank, 1993; Bixby, 1990; Maakestad, 1990; Tombs, 1992). Criminal punishment would satisfy the demand for retribution—condemning wrongdoing, affirming morality, and avenging victims (Miester, 1980; Koprowicz, 1986; Edelman, 1987; Reilly, 1987; McDonnell, 1989; Humphreys, 1990; Schlegel, 1990). It might better deter companies and business agents (Dutzman, 1990; Boston College Law School, 1988) who are more affected by the stigma and humiliation of adjudication than are lower class defendants (Benson, 1990). It might better dovetail with rehabilitation and individual reform programs because corporate criminals typically possess far more personal capital, such as education, training, and occupational opportunities, than do lower class convicts (Braithwaite & Geis, 1982; Paternoster & Simpson, 1993). It would pierce the veil of invulnerability from enforcement and prosecution that normally insulates corporate crime (Pearce, 1993). It would avert the collateral consequences of punitive civil suits, and large criminal fines, the effects of which can be "passed through" to stockholders, workers, and the general public (Coffee, 1992; Barnett, 1993). It would prevent the corporation from "getting off the hook" by paying a nominal regulatory fine. And it would preclude "agency capture" and "clientism" (Passas & Nelken, 1993) which occur when regulators rely on voluntary compliance and the corporation's perspective, in some cases to such an extent that their agencies become increasingly isomorphic with the corporation, losing sight of their primary goals (DiMaggio & Powell, 1983).

In this chapter, the case will be made for a greater use of criminal punishment of corporate agents and corporations by a better armed regulatory apparatus, one to which criminal sanctions are more readily available, one which supplements and is supplemented by the criminal justice system, and one which is supported by an involved and progressive state and an activist community. I will discuss various strategies and why increased criminalization might be the most eliciting of long-term prevention. I will address the social and practical obstacles in the path of criminalization. And I will consider the social reality of corporate crime, specifically, that since corporate crime is largely a consequence of modern capitalism, criminal punishment (and any other proposed interventions and solutions) must include a democratization of the economy and company decisionmaking to have a long-term preventive effect. Using a left realist perspective, the criminal punishment of corporate agents is seen as a first step in the transformation of the relations among the state, the corporate class and civil society. Without changes in the political economy, all social control strategies from agent imprisonment to organizational restructuring will take a short-armed swipe at prevention.

MODELS FOR CONTROLLING CORPORATE CRIMINALITY

As with all other crimes and social problems there is a great deal of debate among social scientists and legal scholars about how to prevent corporate crime. The strategies range across political and theoretical perspectives from classical utilitarianism to revolutionary Marxism. We can typologize the major arguments about corporate crime using three main political perspectives, conservative, liberal, and radical; and the degree of state interventionism that each advocates. Using these variables, I have constructed a two by three table consisting of six "ideal types" of policy positions on corporate crime: laissez-faire; desert/deterrence; voluntary compliance; social reform; class conflict; and left realism (see Table 8.1). While typologies run the risk of oversimplifying the complexity of researchers' intellectual positions, I believe that this ideal typology renders a clear view of how the major analytical approaches and socio-political perspectives intersect in the study of and policy recommendations for preventing corporate wrongdoing.

Table 8.1
Criminological Strategies for Combatting Corporate Crime

PERSPECTIVES	STATE INTERVENTIONISM	
	LOW	HIGH
Conservative	Laissez-Faire Market Self-Control	Retribution Deterrence
Liberal	Voluntary Compliance Encouraged Self-Regulation	Organizational Reform Individual and Corporate Responsibility
Radical	Class Conflict Group and Community Activism	Democratization of the Corporation and Socialization of the Economy

Noninterventionistic Conservatism: Market Based, Laissez-Faire

Using a classic laissez-faire capitalist perspective, these conservatives contend that the market acts homeostatically. It corrects itself. It weeds out nefarious players. For those who are wronged, for those incidents in which consensual exchanges have been violated, there are avenues open to those in the existing civil laws. Businesses can be sued for injuries, environmental destruction, breaches of contract and other ill-conceived decisions of its agents by individual customers, communities, or other companies (Coase, 1960; Cooter & Ulen, 1988). Most of the external consequences of companies are thought to be remediated by tort action or by other social pressure from participants in the market, such as boycotts or negative publicity from consumer groups or other companies. The existing regulatory laws are described as overly intrusive and often dysfunctional for business and the society (Howard, 1994), and the criminal law is described as particularly inappropriate because: first, the corporation cannot generate criminal intent and thus its actions are not specifically criminal (Mueller, 1957); second, the vast majority of this behavior is not criminally intended but rather a technical violation of law (Coffee, 1981, 1992); third, what some call violations are really "acceptable risks" of doing business from which the benefits are a healthy economy—economic production and resource dependency outweigh other issues (cf. Liska, Chamelin & Reed, 1985).

This position is panderingly pro-business, anti-regulatory, and dismissive of the harm that is caused by businesses and their officials. It ignores the historical record in which business has consistently trivialized the risks to the public and has relented in dangerous practices only when forced to by law. Individual suits and community action are simply not enough to counteract the power and continuing victimization by companies (Epstein, Brown & Pope, 1982; Brown, 1981).

Interventionistic Conservatism: Desert and Deterrence

While the desert and deterrence approaches have different assumptions and goals, they are both agency model, punishment-based perspectives and advocate the use of state imposed sanctions such as imprisonment and fines for corporate agents and corporations themselves. Desert theorists maintain that punishment ought to be proportional to the harm caused by an individual, ought to morally censure the individual, and ought to be sufficiently painful or depriving as to have a dissuasive function (von Hirsch, 1976, 1985, 1993; Newman, 1983). When the state retributively punishes crime, it affirms the collective morality and norms, vindicates the victim, and demonstrates fairness and justice.

Using the desert model, one would advocate criminal punishments, from punitive fines to imprisonment, for corporate agents that would be geared to their level of blameworthiness and the amount of harm caused by their decisions (Miester, 1980; Koprowicz, 1986; Edelman, 1987; Reilly, 1987; McDonnell, 1989; Maakestad, 1990; Humphreys, 1990; Schlegel, 1990). So, for instance, criminal prosecutions are particularly appropriate when company officials demonstrate a disregard for health and safety exposing workers, consumers, and the general public to known hazards, causing injury, disease, or death.

While deterrence theorists also advocate the use of criminal punishments, the ultimate goal is prevention of crime in the specific individual and in the general population. Deterrence theory is based upon the assumptions first proposed in classical criminology by Beccaria (1986) and Bentham (1970), that if punishment were rational, certain, swift, of appropriate duration, and humanely executed, an individual would be more likely to desist committing crime because the disadvantages of the punishment would outweigh the benefits of the crime. Most deterrence researchers and theorists today admit to the difficulty in attaining celerity and certainty in punishments (Wilson & Herrnstein, 1986). Furthermore, the evidence on the deterrent effects of imprisonment and other criminal sanctions is inconclusive, particularly when confounded by other variables such as perceived risk, informal social control, internal social control, and personal capital differences (Paternoster, 1987; Paternoster, Saltzman, Waldo & Chiricos, 1983; Paternoster & Simpson, 1993; Nagin & Paternoster, 1994).

However, for some desert and deterrence advocates, the greater societal purposes served by severe sanctions of corporate crime outweigh their cost, time consumption, and infrequency. They see the admonishments of business that harsh sanctions will irreparably disrupt the economy as hollow and as unnecessarily immobilizing the state from punishing truly unethical and criminal behavior, and as contributing to the agents' insouciant disregard for regulations, standards, and the law. Barnett contends that both desert and deterrence can be accomplished by a strict enforcement and sanctioning strategy, which, while not as efficient as less punitive or less retributive measures such as negotiation and voluntary compliance, squarely stigmatize those who are blameworthy for harmful actions, thereby increasing the perceived costs of potential violations and averting the "socialized costs" of cleanup to the public. Barnett (1993:133) concludes that:

> If industry's equity or equity efficiency trade-off arguments
> prevail, those responsible for environmental damage will
> avoid both stigma and substantial liability for past actions
> and may feel free to pursue environmentally unsound prac-
> tices in the future. Organized public resentment will have
> promoted cleanup but will not have toppled barriers to
> sanctioning the powerful. . . . Congress is faced with a
> decision either to accept the high social cost of imposing
> sanctions on polluting corporations or to simply pay for
> cleanup and hope that history will not repeat itself.

The strength of the desert and deterrence models is that they attempt to attain fairness in social control by proposing the criminalization and punishment of organizational victimizers in the same way as traditional victimizers, and to the veil normally covering corporate crime. On the other hand, in focusing on individual human or organizational violators, the position does not address the issue of social change, that is the types of structures we might create to reduce the causes of corporate crime.

Noninterventionistic Liberalism: Voluntary Compliance

Voluntary compliance advocates maintain that most corporate agents and companies are not amoral calculators but rather good citizens, a few of whom occasionally engage in "deviant" violations of regulatory laws, and in rare cases who act criminally (Kagan & Scholz, 1984; Ermann & Lundman, 1982). It also assumes that most business officers are more likely to cooperate with regulatory agencies when they are encouraged to voluntarily comply with laws and when they are educated or counseled rather than being punished (Hawkins, 1984; Scholz, 1984; Gattozzi, 1986/87; Sigler & Murphy, 1988; Porter, 1990; Rakoff, Blumkin & Sauber, 1993). The assumption is that "real" criminal activity (*mens rea* crime) is far less common than incompetence, inattention, and ignorance from the organizational decentralization of managers (Stone, 1975, 1980) and that if companies and agents are all treated adversarially with the suspicion and distrust of a criminal suspect, then they will become defensive, litigious, and concealing (Kagan & Scholz, 1984; Reiss, 1984).

Compliance strategists believe that the role of the regulator should be non-adversarial, as an "educator," "politician," and "counselor," rather than as an enforcer because these resonate with the business agent's self concept as a rational, moral, and socially integrated individual, and with their company image which they wish to protect from scandals or negative publicity (Hawkins, 1984; Kagan & Scholz, 1984). Instead of intensive interventionism, compliance strategists recommend that regulators engage in "discriminating rule enforcement," that they be flexible in their requests for compliance, and even that they consider waivers and exceptions to full standards if some seem overly burdensome or costly to a company without producing much payoff in safety (Kagan & Scholz, 1984), thus manipulating rewards to elicit corrective actions rather than punishments to settle individual harms (Reiss, 1984). If "regulatory unreasonableness" prevails rather than encouragement and criminal intervention is rare then, violations are likely to be more frequent.

I believe that the notion of regulatory unreasonableness is itself an unreasonable notion. It grossly understates the devastating and violent victimization generated by businesses; it egregiously overestimates the trustworthiness of business officials by underestimating the hold that profits have over their decisionmaking; it sidesteps the issue of fairness in not punishing corporate crime like street crime. Moreover it blinds itself to "agency capture" and "clientism" which are likely to occur when regulatory inspectors are so accommodating to company agents that they accept as fact the corporation's definition of "reasonableness" in regulation, in harm, in risks, in costs, and in benefits, regardless of the real social costs, risks, and harm.[2]

Interventionistic Liberalism: Social Reform of the Company and its Agents

This more structural position is based on the assumption that individuals and organizations are reformable and that individuals and corporations can be made accountable for their actions. Criminal punishment is necessary only on the presumably rare occasions when a heinous crime has been committed or as the ultimate threat. Internal self-policing is more effective and practical than criminal sanctions for preventing corporate crime (Fisse & Braithwaite, 1993; Kynes & Markman, 1989; Geraghty, 1979; Rush, 1986). The most cited proponents of this approach, Fisse and Braithwaite (1993), propose an "accountability model" which holds agents and corporations responsible for crime, but which allows companies the chance to pursue individual and collective reform first, cost effectively without undue burden on the company and individuals. Rather than abandoning individual responsibility for corporate punishment or reform, Fisse and Braithwaite recommend that businesses, by arrangement with regulators or prosecutors, establish an internal, private policing, and justice system that would identify and hold officials culpable for their actions and require specific changes in behavior and structure to accommodate regulators' and prosecutors' complaints. If all else fails then more serious punishments ought to be considered. They assume that most of the cases can be handled by an agreement between the company and public enforcers rather than an adversarial attack on the company and its agents. The conclusion drawn from research on Australian nursing home directors is that a business agent's guilt has a greater deterrent effect than formal punishments or informal social controls (Makkai & Braithwaite, 1994).

Would enforced self regulation work, particularly in a global economy? The scant evidence is mixed. Braithwaite (1993) claims that international business and professional groups, the United Nations and the World Health Organization (WHO), and regionalized influence from countries affect the decisionmaking of pharmaceutical companies. Gerber's (1990) findings about enforced self regulation are more sobering. He found that the strategies by activist groups and WHO to use boycotts, negative publicity, and pressure to make Nestle Corporation more responsible in the marketing and sale of infant formula in Third World countries was in the long run unsuccessful. The company responded with "counter publicity," establishing an impotently tokenistic self-regulating committee. "Without a multinational government agency capable of functioning in a supervisory role," (Gerber, 1990:107) there is no enforcement of the self regulation, and a sense of professional ethics or guilt is either inadequate or nonexistent.

While this model proposes to reduce the harm created by corporate crime by reforming the organizational structure and its agents to make them more accountable for their actions, it largely ignores the role of the capitalist economy in seeding corporate crime. Liberal reformers have not adequately addressed the inherent value contradiction between, on the one hand, the quest for capital accumulation and stabilization of the market, and, on the other hand, the ethical concerns for the well-being of others.

Noninterventionistic Radicalism: Class Conflict Model

Radical models, despite varied explanations and strategies, contend that corporate crime is endemic to capitalism itself, not to individual deviance, deficient organizations, nor to a lack of pressure from or involvement in moral communities. Indeed corporate crime is seen as: a symptom of the political economy; a crime of domination over labor and the public; a mechanism to rationalize capital accumulation by, for instance, creating stable organizational fields that rein in prices and wages and attempt to diminish the effects of boom and bust market cycles; and as a way to pressure the state to protect the interests of the most concentrated and corporate fraction of the dominant class (Quinney, 1974, 1980; Fligstein, 1990; Kolko, 1963; Domhoff, 1986; McCormick, 1979). Thus, corporate crime can be reduced or eliminated only when the inordinate power of the dominant corporate class is substantially siphoned off and the economy is democratized (Kramer, 1989).

Radical models differ in their theoretical understandings of business-state relations and in how they envision the role of the state in both contributing to and preventing corporate crime. Instrumentally oriented Marxists following Mills (1956), Domhoff (1967), and Miliband (1969) favor agency theory, seeing the state as interlocked with the business class and its interests, as a contributing partner in economic domination and, by extrapolation, corporate crime. For instance in the state-corporate theory of crime, the state by commission, facilitation or negligence directly or indirectly expedites corporate crime (Kramer & Michalowski, 1990; Kauzlarich & Kramer, 1993; Aulette & Michalowski, 1995; Barak, 1991).

On the other hand, structural Marxists describe the role of the state as more autonomous, linked not instrumentally to the corporate class, not by the direct control and participation of corporate class members, but rather linked structurally to the corporate class by mutual survival interests, particularly the protection of capital accumulation and private property (Balbus, 1973; Poulantzas, 1975; Block, 1977). The state, as an agent of social control and stability polices the consequences caused by the capitalism's contradictions (crime) and periodic crises (deep recession). Though it disproportionately directs its policing at the lower class and labor unrest (Harring & McMullen,

1975; Hall Critcher, Jefferson, Clarke & Roberts, 1978; Spitzer, 1979; MacLean, 1986), it sometimes mediates on the side of labor, and always projects itself as representing the "general will of the people," which is the basis for its hegemonic control (Poulantzas, 1975; Gramsci, 1971, 1977).

However, for many thinkers this role as mediator is limited, it does not intrinsically generate real social change. Even during periods when the state seems progressive and sympathetic to labor, such as during the 1930s' New Deal and the 1960s' War on Poverty, ultimately the state ameliorated crises that spared capitalism and itself from the consequences of swelling political discontent (Piven & Cloward, 1972; O'Connor, 1973). Significant social change occurs as a result of class struggle, which is waged not by the state but by civil society, by workers, unions, consumers, environmentalists, human rights activists, and other social movements. It is the confrontation of these groups and the capitalist class that leads the state to adjust to a new social formation (Block, 1976/77, 1977; Snider, 1987, 1991; Curran, 1993). The improvements in health and safety, consumer products, and the environment are attributed to class struggle and conflict not to a progressive, intervening state. In this model, the control of corporate criminality must originate from outside the power blocs of the state and the corporate class. Thus, only class activism can change corporate crime.

The strength of this model is its identification of the root causes of corporate criminality in the capitalist structure of the economy and the effects this has on the state's level of willingness to maintain and enforce regulations and criminal laws against corporate wrongdoing. Its weakness lies in the impracticality of relying on class conflict or grass roots social movements to reshape corporate decisionmaking and the state's role in punishing corporate criminals.

Interventionistic Radicalism: New Left Realism

In this approach, reducing victimization and empowering the community are envisioned as coexisting with social control agencies (Young, 1986, 1992; Matthews, 1992). The state is seen as an integral ally in the struggle of workers' groups, environmentalists, and consumer activists to prevent corporate criminality. While the state's interests in maintaining capital accumulation dovetail with those of the capitalist class, its need to maintain legitimacy and rationalized social control compels it to contain destructive social contradictions such as corporate crime. Concessions made to civil society, to labor, and to activists in the regulation and punishment of corporate transgressors can profoundly alter class relations and hegemony, ushering in a new social formation of post industrial society. Ironically, while criminal, civil, and administrative law are the arms of rationalized social control of the population, they are the potential avenues for reducing corporate crime and eliciting social change. Punitive sanctions against corporate officials, particularly the sanctioning and stigmatizing effects of criminal trials and imprisonment have a delegitimating effect on the corporate class (Pearce, 1993; Pearce & Tombs, 1990, 1992).

While many fear that greater uses of the criminal justice system will reinforce an ominously powerful state, left-realists argue that the state can be an advocate of a more democratized criminal justice system which protects victims and involves the community in exacting justice. In short, the criminal justice system and the state can be socialized in both meanings of the term. Left realists have argued that the state is not locked into the interests of the ruling class; that the state and the criminal justice system are not the sole constructors of laws, rules, and definitions of who is criminal; and that state policy and policing can be reformed to be accountable to communities and to protect people from the very real victimization that they experience from street crime (Young, 1986, 1992; Matthews, 1992). In this view, the state and policing can be made more socialistic, more responsive, and accountable to the working and lower classes. Crime and victimization occur in a social, economic, and ideological context. The poor require economic change to reduce crime but they also require protection from victimization (Young, 1986, 1992; Matthews, 1992). Similarly corporate wrongdoing requires policing and criminalization precisely because the powerful continue to hide behind a business ideology that defines their victimization of workers and consumers as rare and unavoidable while defining themselves as good corporate citizens who can regulate themselves and eliminate the few "bad apples" among them (Reasons, Ross & Patterson, 1981; Pearce, 1993; Pearce & Tombs, 1990, 1992; Tombs, 1992).

Some radicals argue that if punitive fines and civil judgements were assessed on both primary and secondary participants, that is both the primary corporate agents involved in the fateful decisions and all other members and beneficiaries of the organization, including owners, stockholders, and workers, there would be an insurrection against the organization that, with judicial backing, could produce reorganization and potentially elicit the socialization of the company, that is, more worker involvement in decisionmaking (Pepinsky, 1974; Kennedy, 1985).

For radical social reform as for liberal social reform, organizational change is as crucial as individual accountability. However, radicals see state approaches such as organizational probation as a way to introduce more economic democracy in companies, more worker and citizen involvement. Ultimately these strategies are a mechanism to destabilize corporate class control over production, to socialize the corporation, to end the economic causes of corporate criminality.

The strengths of this position are that it identifies and attempts to change the root causes of corporate criminality. It sees the ideological importance of individual punishment and the structural importance of organizational punishments. It may, however, be somewhat unrealistic to assume that the state is willing or even able to serve as witness and conduit for the socialization of the corporation, and to assume that workers and activist groups have the consciousness to accept such deep changes in economic organizations and in the society. The state itself might facilitate or even contribute directly to corporate criminality, and thus might not be a reliable agent of change. And historically, activism is as likely to occur on the right as it is on the left, retrogressive as it is progressive. Abortion and gun control are cases in point.

THEORIES IN ACTION

Can an interventionistic regulatory apparatus, which is unhesitant to use punitive and adversarial measures, and which is supplemented by the criminal justice system's willingness to prosecute egregious cases and use traditional sanctions, reduce corporate crime considering how entrenched it is? As the evidence presented below will show, state interventionism at local, regional, and national levels has an impact on corporate crime. When regulatory controls have had teeth, have been backed by criminal prosecutions, there has been a reduction in corporate victimization. Local and state jurisdictions have filled in some of the gaps created when federal support for regulation wanes, but, in general the diminishment of punitive regulatory controls is regressive. What will become clear is that state intervention is vitally necessary to stem the devastation caused by business crime, and that holding corporate agents accountable, and, where appropriate, criminally responsible is critical to crime reduction and social change. The agency-based, interventionistic approach, conservative, liberal, or radical, holds more hope for the victims of business crime.

Workplace Deaths and Injuries

Consider the decrease in the number of employee deaths since the passage of the Occupational Health and Safety Act in 1970. According to Labor Department figures, traumatic workplace deaths from unsafe conditions have decreased by more than 50 percent from over 14,000 in 1971 to under 7,000 in 1991 (see U.S. Department of Labor, 1993; National Traumatic Occupational Fatality Project, 1990). Even using the higher estimates of the AFL-CIO and the National Safety Council, which place the figure at about 10,000 employee deaths, there still would be nearly a 40 percent decrease since 1971. Compared to the intractability of street homicides, which have hovered around 20,000 persons, this a significant decline.

However, these figures represent traumatic deaths and not the thousands of serious and fatal diseases such as black lung, brown lung, asbestosis, mesothelioma, and other cancers contracted by workers. The figure would jump to at least 100,000 persons if these cases could be systematically counted (Reasons, Ross & Patterson, 1981). Unfortunately, they are not. And there is no reliable research on the trends of these "uncounted" deaths. Given the complexity of disease etiology, especially the obvious contributions of cigarettes and environmental toxins, the estimation of workplace generated diseases or the workplace's contribution to disease is problematic. At the very least, there is an unquestionable need for a national survey for worker victimization much like the NCVS (National Criminal Victimization Survey) for conventional crimes.

The trends that we have measured do show some consistency. As with traumatic deaths, there is a parallel decline in workplace injuries. In the early period of federal OSHA, the injury and illness rates declined from 11 per 100 workers in 1973 to 7.6 per 100 in 1983. This steady decline was jolted by the deregulation policies and funding cuts of the Reagan/Bush administrations. Consistent with our assumptions, when regulatory diligence wanes, the injury rates rise (see Figure 8.1).

As Figure 8.1 illustrates, the next substantial decline in injuries does not occur until after 1992 and the election of a more liberal president. However, the deregulatory torch has been taken up by the present Congress and a policy confrontation is underway with the Clinton administration, the resolution of which will have a significant impact on the death and injury rates of workers.

The descriptive statistics that we have presented above are of course illustrative rather than conclusive. The scant research on the relationship between regulatory diligence and corporate violations lends some support for our assumptions, but only when criminal prosecutions back regulatory law. For instance, research comparing the injury rates of companies which were inspected and cited by OSHA and those which were not showed significant differences in companies with over 200 employees (Cooke & Gautschi, 1981) and regarding injuries that occurred in and between machines (Mendeloff, 1979). Yet, in all of the other categories and jobs, no significant differences were found (Smith, 1976, 1979; Vicusi, 1979).

However, these studies did not control for several important factors. First, there might be a general deterrent effect that inspections and regulatory diligence have on firms whether they have been inspected or not. Second, OSHA, by law, can assess fines only on the corporation, not on culpable individuals. The fines themselves are usually minuscule. In a sample of 80 cases that I drew from the LEXIS database on OSHA administrative hearings, the median OSHA fine, after review, for an employee death on the job is under $400, the mean is $1,312. These averages are roughly one-half of what the fines are for unsafe conditions. On the other hand, the median criminal fine given by the Department of Justice is $10,000, over 20 times the median civil fine OSHA gave after review. Further, OSHA issues fines in only one-third of its citations (*Corporate Crime Reporter*, May 3, 1993) partly because it rewards those companies which implement a self-enforced abatement program. However, OSHA usually does not follow up on corrective action orders. Rather, it requests written documentation of the changes and rarely punishes cited companies when they do not comply with the orders (*Corporate Crime Reporter*, May 3, 1993:5). Almost identical practices exist in coal industry regulation. Curran (1993) found that as the federal regulatory bureaucracy increased during the 1970s, the number of site inspections actually declined, and by the end of the Reagan deregulation period the average fine per violation after review was $84.

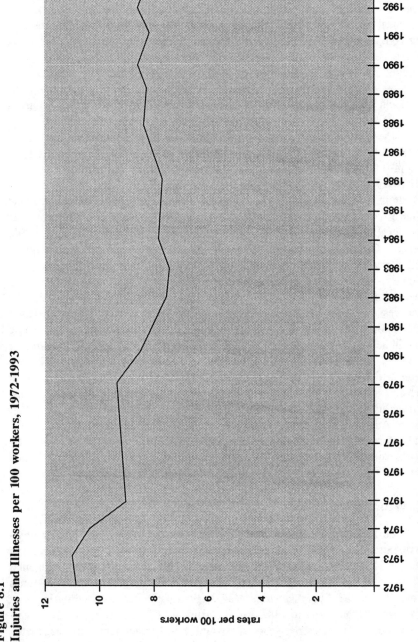

Figure 8.1
Injuries and Illnesses per 100 workers, 1972-1993

rates per 100 workers

Data adapted from: Bureau of Labor Statistics, 1995, Feb. Summary 95-5; and 1996 Aug. Bulletin 2366.

Finally, the role played by the state regulators and local criminal prosecutors may be more significant than the federal regulatory apparatus. Curington (1988) points out that many states had interventionistic regulators prior to the existence of OSHA. California, for instance, had more stringent safety regulations, 99 to be exact, than federal OSHA had initially. More importantly, state and local jurisdictions have generally been more active in criminally prosecuting companies and agents than has the federal government. During the heart of the deregulation battle waged by the Reagan administration, state courts brought 200 cases against businesses for worker victimization from 1985 to 1988, an average of 50 per year (Maakestad, 1990:46). During the same period, local criminal prosecutions of businesses for workplace offenses occurred in 11 percent of local districts (Benson, Cullen & Maakestad, 1993). By contrast, the federal government, during a span nearly four times as long, from 1978 to 1993, adjudicated a meager 28 cases out of only 102 referrals from federal OSHA, less than two cases per year (OSHA, 1993). A similar pattern exists with respect to environmental crimes (See Figure 8.2).

It is possible then that the success in decreasing workplace deaths and injuries could be attributed as much, or more, to the deterrent effects of state and local criminal prosecutions as to the regulatory system (Dutzman, 1990; Benson, Cullen & Maakestad, 1993). It is little wonder then that legal scholars call for a greater use of criminal prosecutions for workplace hazards (Korprowicz, 1986; McDonnell, 1989) or for company recklessness that leads to deaths (Miester, 1980; Reilly, 1987; Edelman, 1987; Maakestad, 1990). Even the Congress in 1989 (House Committee on Government Operations) chastised OSHA for never having used its imprisonment provision for companies whose willful actions led to an employee's death (Corporate Criminal Liability Reporter, 1989, v.2-3:85). Similarly, the Immigration and Naturalization Service (INS) has been criticized for not pursuing cases of slave labor conditions in the garment industry such as the El Monte, California sweat shop that forced 70 illegal Thai immigrants to work 18 hours per day for 50 cents per hour (The New York Times, Aug. 5, 1995:p.6). A whistleblower at INS claimed that while the agency had information on several sweat shops in California, it reneged on investigating because of the difficulties in prosecution, preferring simple cases in which nominal fines and voluntary abatement could be easily arranged.

Environmental Cases

The federal government has been far more zealous in prosecuting environmental violations in criminal court than cases involving workers' lives and health. The federal government has spent 20 times more for environmental crimes than for worker health and safety, while states have spent 16 times more (Corporate Crime Reporter, May 3, 1993:4-5). For instance during a 7-year period from 1983 to 1989, the Department of Justice prosecuted an average of nearly 60 cases per year, had obtained 520 indictments, 400 negotiated

Figure 8.2
Criminal Prosecutions of Labor and Environmental Violations in Federal vs. State & Local Courts
(Yearly averages, 1985-1995 data)

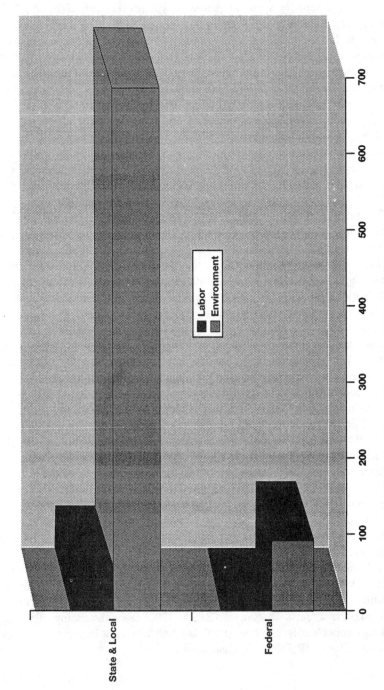

Data adapted from: OSHA, 1993; Maakestad, 1988; Revobich and Nixon, 1994; DOJ, Fedworld Information, 1995 (All figures represent actual, not projected, cases).

pleas, and 248 years of sentenced prison time, 86 years of which company agents had actually spent in prison (*Corporate Liability Reporter*, 1989, v.2-3:27). By contrast, during the 16-year period from 1978 to 1991, the Department of Justice had sentenced company agents (for OSHA referred workplace deaths) to a combined 1,000 hours of community service and a paltry total of 16½ months of confinement for workplace crimes, including 5 months in halfway houses, 10 months in home confinement, and 45 days in jail (OSHA, 1993). (The actual time served in jail is not reported by OSHA.) In a similar vein, the coal industry's Mine Safety and Health Administration sentenced 45 of its 64 convicted individuals (70%) to home detention (*Corporate Crime Reporter*, February 15, 1993:1).

Regarding the prosecution of environmental destruction, federal and state courts have had little problem in assessing both corporate and agent criminal liability (Niekamp, 1987; Milne, 1988/89; Cleaves, 1990; Humphreys, 1990; Goldberg, 1991; Rapson, 1991; Addison & Mack, 1991; Barnett, 1993). Environmental laws such as the Resource Conservation and Recovery Act (RCRA) which specifies up to 15 years imprisonment, the Superfund Act, and the Clean Water Act which specify heavy monetary fines, armed prosecutors with enabling statutes to pursue corporations and their agents, such as the president of Borjohn Optical Technology who received a 26-month prison sentence for violating the Clean Air Act (Gold, 1991; Korpics, 1991). In 1993, the Environmental Crimes Section of DOJ using RCRA convicted the chairman of the board and the president of the largest ceramic tile company, Dal Tile Corporation. They were sentenced to a fine of $6 million out of their personal funds and given 5 years probation for lead contamination.

State criminal and civil prosecutions of environmental violations are several times higher than federal prosecutions and are increasing steadily during the 1990s (see Figure 8.3).

While some criminologists are unenthusiastic about environmental prosecutions, describing them as having little effect on the levels of pollution, illegal dumping, and the restoration of the environment (Yeager, 1987; Farrier, 1990), Easterbrook (1995) finds that there were substantial improvements in environmental quality from social activism and regulatory diligence. Airborne sulfur dioxide has been cut by more than one-half since 1970, the number of people exposed to air that has failed federal standards has been reduced by one-half since 1982, airborne lead has decreased by 96 percent since the ban on leaded gasoline, and there has been a 40 percent increase in wooded areas in New England since 1950. The improvements are definitely linked to environmental law, the regulatory apparatus and criminal prosecutions, the debacle of Superfund mismanagement (Szasz, 1986) notwithstanding. The improvements could easily come to stumbling halt if severe budgetary cutbacks and deregulatory policies are implemented.

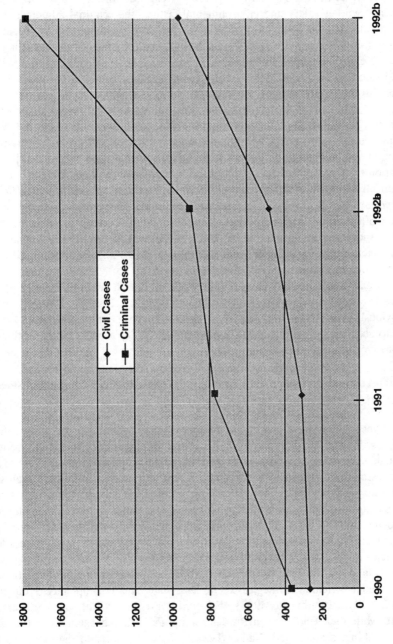

Figure 8.3
State Prosecutions of Environmental Law Violations

Source: Adapted from data in D. Rebovich & R.T. Nixon, 1994. "Environmental Crime Prosecution." Washington, DC: National Institute of Justice NCJ 150043.
Note: 1992a=cases for first 6 months of the year; 1992b=projected cases for the full year.

No Regulatory Unreasonableness in Financial Crimes

There is little doubt that, despite the great costs in life and health to victims of worker safety and environmental crimes, the criminal adjudication of corporate and white-collar misdeeds is virtually monopolized by financial crimes. The greatest amount of prison time served by business agents for corporate crime has been for property crimes such as fraud, misrepresentation, and stock manipulation. When scams involve the pocketbooks of stockholders and investors, the notion of regulatory unreasonableness is conveniently ignored. The voices for education and counseling were noticeably silent when the top 20 executives convicted in the 1980s' savings and loan scandal were sentenced to more prison time than the federal courts had given for environmental and workplace crimes combined. Nobody suggested enforced self-regulation for Charles Keating who was given a 151-month prison sentence, more than all of the federal time served by workplace offenders (*Corporate Crime Reporter,* July 12, 1993:9). Prosecutors proceeded with tenacity. Of the more than 500 savings and loan cases that the federal attorneys prosecuted, they were successful in 93 percent of them (Pontell & Calavita, 1993). If only the same tenacity existed with violent corporate crime there would significant reductions in deaths, diseases, and injuries.

Consistent with our assumptions, weak regulation from eviscerated agencies wreaked havoc in the savings and loan industry. The "good apples" were obviously worm-eaten and required a dose of interventionism. Regulatory diligence backed by criminal sanctioning proved to be a better antidote than a nonadversarial, nonintervening state.

Differential Prosecution and the Stratification of Businesses: No Vice Presidents for Going to Jail

Not all corporate agents are created equally when criminal prosecution occurs. Hagan and Parker (1985) find that managers receive the disproportionate share of sentencing, not owners or employers who are more likely to be processed in administrative court rather than criminal court even though the offenses that they committed are identical. Hagan and Parker's findings seem to support the contention of some thinkers that when companies, employers, and higher executives are faced with criminal prosecution they will sacrifice managers, "vice presidents for going to jail," regardless of how much their policies might have facilitated the criminal activity (Needleman & Needleman, 1979), and will insulate themselves from prosecution, making confrontational, deterrence oriented strategies seem less viable than compliance strategies (Stone, 1975; Braithwaite, 1993). Weisburd, Waring, and Wheeler (1990) argue that, while their findings confirm Hagan and Parker's, managers are not, strictly speaking, scapegoated. Rather, because they are closer to the daily operations of the company, they are more likely to be closely connected to the criminal activity. Nonetheless, managers are held more blameworthy and are punished more often than higher level officers of their companies, at least in large firms with hierarchic and fairly decentralized managerial organizations.

Jamieson (1994) finds a stratification of enforcement in antitrust violations. While large companies are predictably more likely to be prosecuted for these offenses, those charged and found guilty of the most serious violations are in competitive, nonconcentrated economic sectors, with flat management and lower technical sophistication. By contrast, those firms with highly delegated management and technical sophistication are charged with more minor violations. The DOJ largely avoids the vertical violations of these latter firms, leaving them to private suits which are very often unsuccessful.

The stratification of enforcement is most obvious in workplace offenses. The majority of corporate agents who are criminally prosecuted in these cases come from small firms, with flat management. Criminal responsibility squarely sits on owner-operators. There are no vice presidents for going to jail. Differential prosecution occurs partly because small companies have far higher worker fatalities and much shoddier workplaces than larger companies. A study of 500,000 federal and state inspection records from 1988 through 1992 found that the death rate in the smallest companies (under 20 employees) was nearly 200 per 100,000 workers compared with less than .4 per 100,000 workers in the largest companies (over 2,500 workers) (Marsh, 1994). While OSHA is much more likely to fine the largest companies such as General Electric and General Motors, smaller companies in the peripheral economic sector, with small profit margins, high competition, and more volatile markets generate the greater devastation and are more likely to be charged by local criminal prosecutors. Typical are the Film Recovery case in Illinois in which the president and a manager pleaded guilty to manslaughter in a worker's death (the president received a three-year sentence), the Pymm Thermometer case in New York in which owner-operator brothers were found guilty of assault in a worker's injury,[3] and the Imperial Foods Company disaster in which the company's owner was sentenced to 19½ months for involuntary manslaughter in the deaths of 25 workers.

I have found a similar pattern at the federal level. OSHA is more likely to refer smaller companies for criminal prosecution to the Justice Department. Since its inception OSHA has referred around 120 cases to the Department of Justice for possible criminal prosecution. Without a Freedom of Information Act request I was able to compile information on the specific businesses charged in only 25 of the 82 nonpending cases. These preliminary data show that the median sales of companies that OSHA refers to DOJ for criminal prosecution is $16 million whereas the median sales of the companies that it handles administratively is $50 million. This pattern of referring smaller companies was confirmed in my interviews with the Counsel for Legal Litigation of OSHA, whose belief it was that businesses with sole proprietors were easier to convict because they lacked the layers of organization that would normally insulate employers.[4] Further, he contended that the attorneys for smaller companies tended to negotiate plea bargains more readily than did those for larger companies. This was his working ideology in recommending referrals for criminal prosecution. Note that the similarity to the INS seems more than casual. With so few criminal referrals in its history to begin with, is OSHA, like the INS, taking on the more "normal" violations, using fines and voluntary abatement to avoid involved investigations of and drastic actions against the thousands of small and truly criminal worksites? Or is it being realistic, considering the fact that the U.S. Attorneys decline the majority (nearly 60%) of the cases that it refers (OSHA, 1993), and considering that its staff size and budget are comparatively small? After all, OSHA has under 300 employees for over six million worksites.

In either case, we are faced with a fundamental issue—economic stratification is related to business violence and to the likelihood of criminal prosecution. Smaller companies operating in the more competitive and uncertain secondary sector operate more dangerous worksites and are more likely to be criminally prosecuted not only because of the deaths and injuries that occur but also because their owner-operation is more amenable to assigning criminal blameworthiness and thus prosecution. By contrast, even when large companies are responsible for deaths and injuries, their layers of bureaucracy and technical sophistication make them more amenable to administrative hearings, regulatory fines, and voluntary abatement. Those advocating for a greater criminalization of corporate crime and the prosecution of corporate agents must deal with the asymmetrical advantage of big companies.

DISCUSSION

There are certainly other factors besides regulatory diligence and criminal prosecutions that have affected the downward trend in workers' deaths and injuries and in environmental destruction, factors such as deindustrialization, advances in technology, a decline in smoking, improvements in medical science, fuel efficient cars, automation, and outsourcing of many labor intensive jobs. However, it is safe to say from the data above that the connection between state interventionism—criminal and regulatory sanctioning—and corporate crime is not coincidental. Hence, interventionistic strategies, be they conservative, liberal, or radical, are superior to non-interventionistic approaches.

I believe that the left-realist approach offers the best of the crime control and social reform models with the additional crucial goal of social structural change. In a radical left position there is at least some attempt to deal with the great leverage of large companies and their asymmetrical advantage in investigations, hearings, and prosecutions. Admittedly, the radical left's ultimate solution to corporate crime is to democratize the workplace, socialize the economy, and eliminate private capital accumulation. Given today's conservative political climate and the historically antisocialist themes in U.S. ideology and economic policy, this strategy might seem chimeric. However, as we have shown above with improvements in work conditions and the environment, the state's responsiveness to popular activism can lead to some controls of corporate decision-making and to improvements in health and safety. Whether or not they seem to some thinkers like unreasonable intrusions into corporate activity, absolute standards for toxins such as lead, coal dust, cotton dust, and asbestos, enforced by an uncompromising regulatory apparatus and an adversarial criminal justice system have made a huge difference in the quality of life for the society.

The left-realist perspective has three main objectives: protecting potential victims, democratizing the criminal justice system, and socializing the economy. Criminalizing the acts of corporate agents is a first step. Similar to the desert/deterrence approaches, the criminal punishment of corporate officers is seen as a public condemnation of behavior that is violent and deadly, it partly redresses the grievances of victims, increases the costs of crime opening deterrence possibilities, and pierces the hegemonic armor protecting corporate agents by treating them like street criminals for equivalent acts of mayhem. It is true that studies of corporate agents in criminal court find them indignant, insulted, angry, embittered by status degradation, and rationalizing their acts (Benson, 1990; Paternoster & Simpson, 1993; Makkai & Braithwaite, 1994). Yet, I think that they suffer from feelings of relative deprivation. Samuel Stouffer found that people feel more relatively deprived if they fail to be promoted in an unit that promotes many (Stouffer et al., 1949). Presumably then corporate agents feel indignant when they are punished because so many others reap rewards for similar acts. Hence, corporate agents will feel less angry and indignant if more of their kind are punished and fewer benefit from corporate crime. Certainly more criminalization for corporate agents will make those prosecuted feel less relatively deprived, less singled out.

Left-realism also incorporates some elements of the liberal reform approach, particularly the recommendation to use court orders for organizational probation to resocialize decisionmaking in the company, to tune the organization and its officers to the concerns of the society, and to make the corporation more accountable for its victimizing actions, opening it to influence from concerned professional and community groups. Like the liberal reform approach, it advocates using the state's power to integrate the organized pressure from workers, environmentalists, consumer groups, the community, and other interest groups not only to modify corporate decisionmaking, but more importantly to confront the root causes of corporate crime in the economy, and in the long run to socializing the economy.

There is a glimmer of hope for such change. Even in a retrograde, antiregulatory period of American politics and regarding an industry that is an integral part of the economy—tobacco—the state, responding to health activism and the medical costs of lung cancer and heart disease, is attempting to restrict the marketing of cigarettes and encourage civil action against cigarette companies. While this and the criminal punishment of corporate officers for violations are embryonic motions by the state, they are necessary to dent the ideological armor protecting corporate class interests.

SIX PROPOSALS

To strengthen the regulatory apparatus, to criminalize acts of corporate victimization, and to attack the root causes of corporate crime, I present the following six proposals. Some are quite practical, others more radical, but any of them would advance the prevention of corporate crime.

1. Enact a Model Corporate Penal Code at Federal and State Levels. The lack of a separate corporate criminal code, the equivalent of conventional criminal statutes, is a distinct disadvantage, allowing many company agents and the companies themselves to escape the most serious sanctions for aggravated assault and homicide. Appellate courts, in numerous cases in which corporate agents have been criminally charged for wrongful deaths and injuries, have remarked that regulatory law and state statutes are inadequate to deal with corporate criminal liability. A corporate penal code would clearly delineate levels of criminal responsibility for individuals and organizations for willful, negligent, and reckless acts that lead to the physical harm of workers, consumers, and the environment. It would specify levels of punishment which include imprisonment for corporate agents and equivalent punishments for the organization such as decertification, quarantining, debarment from government contracts, delicensing, shutting down, intensive probation with restructuring, or receivership to workers or to a state agency. It would clearly address the issues of intent and vicarious liability while making sentences reflect the seriousness of the acts.

While the U.S. Sentencing Guidelines for Organizations is a first step, Orland (1993) argues that there is no statutory underpinning for criminal liability, and no criminal sentence to suspend if organizational probation is violated. Orland recommends a "Model Federal Corporate Criminal Code," establishing, in addition to what I have described above, mandatory public acknowledgment and compliance, and discretionary intermediate sentences such as, community service, notice to the victim, restitution, fine, and asset forfeiture. While Orland's proposal is progressive, I think that a corporate criminal code ought to go further. For serious cases, it should contain provisions for radically resocializing decisionmaking and restructuring the company. For example, intensive supervision probation orders could require the establishment of permanent monitoring committees composed of workers, consumers, community members, and other relevant constituents that would review a company's decisions. Extending this intervention, such committees could be made a permanent feature of regulatory statutes or a requirement of companies over a certain size or above a certain asset threshold. Thus, these committees would serve as a preventive measure before any violations were discovered. (In very serious cases, vital industries central to the economy or national security, could be nationalized.) Corporate crime could be treated like organized crime. A version of RICO for corporations would allow prosecutors to charge corporate agents and companies with conspiracy, to seize their assets, and to cumulatively sentence agents for the crimes of the organization. Seizing assets is a gateway to restructuring the organization.

2. Establish Enforcement Agencies for Corporate Crime and Liaisons with Regulatory and Local Prosecutors. There truly are a lack of prosecutors for corporate crime, particularly workplace violations. At the federal level, either the Justice Department ought to designate U.S. attorneys for handling this type of corporate violence, or OSHA lawyers need a statutory change so that they can try criminal cases. Similarly at the state level, the attorney general's office could be expanded to include a division for corporate violence. Many states already have environmental crimes divisions in the state's attorney general's office to fight crimes against the environment, and units dedicated to white-collar and organized crime. Either of these units could have a corporate violence department. No doubt budgetary cutbacks have hit these specialized units the hardest. Hence, a corporate criminal code might justify the need for a specialized unit with assigned prosecutors.

Vital to fighting corporate crime would be the establishment of liaisons to aid local, state, and federal regulatory and criminal investigations and prosecutions. Regional task forces, like those for organized crime and drug dealing, could be established to share investigators, legal staffs, expert witnesses, and information, and to elicit support from whistleblowers and involve the community.

3. Establish a National Center for Data Collection on Organizational Crimes. There is a virtual anarchy in the information gathering on crimes against health and safety, the environment, and consumers. No reliable database exists. Imagine criminologists without access to the UCR and the NCVS. We need the equivalent of the UCR and NCVS for organizational crimes. Presently, the Department of Justice, the Department of Labor, the EPA, OSHA FDA, the Department of Commerce, the National Safety Council, and other organizations collect bits and pieces of information on corporate crime and health and safety. This information needs to be collected by one agency which could also conduct public surveys and collect reports from local jurisdictions of police, courts, district attorney offices, regulatory agencies, the mass media, and other sources.

4. Regulatory Contingencies in International Trade Agreements. While the incipient globalization of the economy, the deindustrialization in the United States, and decline of manufacturing union membership appear to wrench away the control of corporate crime, new opportunities for international influence might actually arise. Regional trade arrangements across nations, such as NAFTA and

GATT, could allow countries with more stringent regulatory, civil and crime control systems to influence countries with few regulations and lax enforcement. Where business officers were accustomed to operating with impunity toward the law and cold indifference toward the safety of workers and the health of the community and the environment, the economic benefits of the agreement and the pressure from trading partners might lead to adjustments in operating practices, the adoption of a neutral monitoring body, and perhaps the gradual percolation of civil, criminal, and regulatory control systems.

5. Stock Fund Leverage. A relatively untapped area of influence is the financial leverage (in billions of dollars) of the stock market funds of workers and other interested groups. Some retirement fund managers, such as the huge TIAA-CREF, offer "social choice" funds. But a more aggressive attempt to pressure a victimizing company by organizing a massive boycott of its stock might get a company to modify its activities or agree to adopt a monitoring safety committee.

6. Socialize the Economy. Ultimately it is the structure and dynamics of the economy and market that drive crime. Of all the industrialized nations, we are among the worst in even attempting to equalize some of the gross inequalities in wealth. We do not attempt to control profit or professional salaries, yet we could. The $178 billion that is funneled to companies in the form of tax breaks, depreciation, contracts, and supplements from the government ought to have some strings attached. Corporate welfare should have transformed into corporate workfare. Companies ought to accept worker involvement not only in safety committees but also in board and managerial decisions. Community and environmental groups should be able to present yearly impact statements that are considered by an impartial regulatory agency. Businesses are licensed at the discretion of the state and the state can use some of that discretion to control inequality.

NOTES

[1]   Sections of this chapter have been adapted from material in the author's paper, "The Case for Radical Intervention into the Corporate Victimization of Workers," presented at the annual meetings of the American Society of Criminology, November, 1995, Boston, MA; and from the author's article, "Why Not Lock 'Em Up: A Realist Humanist Approach to Preventing Corporate Crime," Quarterly Journal of Ideology, December, 1995.

[2]   In some cases, ostensibly legitimate businesses cross the line and involve illegitimate organizations to execute frauds and other crimes. For example, Passas and Nelken (1993) find that companies were falsely claiming and acquiring farm subsidies from the European Economic Community's agricultural fund and cheating

on the value added taxes by having an illegitimate business generate fabricated documents, false invoices, and even entire artificial operations. One could say that many so-called "good corporate citizens" are actually "better organized criminals."

3   *New York v. Pymm Thermometer Corporation,* 135 Misc. 2d 565; 515 N.Y.S.2d 949; *People v. William Pymm, Edward Pymm Jr. Pymm Thermometer Corporation and Pak Glass Machinery Corporation,* 151 A.D.2d 133; 546 N.Y.S.2d 871; 1989 N.Y. App. Div.; People v. O'Neill, 194 Ill. App. 3d 79 (1990). Both of these cases were remanded for retrial on technicalities. Ten years after the Film Recovery case began, two corporate agents pleaded guilty to manslaughter to avoid a second trial.

4   See the similarity in my findings with Peter Yeager's (1987) findings of the EPA's stricter stance toward smaller firms which it presumed had lower technical sophistication, less ability to comply with the standards, and a substantially less intimidating legal staff compared to big firms. The biases, he claims, are structurally built into seemingly neutral regulatory agencies that end up sparing big corporations and contributing to the reproduction of not only class relations but also corporate crime rates.

9

Structure Model: Reforming Regulation

Bridget M. Hutter
London School of Ecomonics & Political Science

The use of the law to regulate the ill-effects of industrial and business activities has increased dramatically since the nineteenth century. New categories of criminal law, criminal behaviour, and enforcement agencies have been created, many of them directed to the regulation of corporate activity. There has been a recent increase in literature on the crimes of business, literature that considers a wide range of issues including corporations and criminal responsibility, white-collar crime and regulation (Kagan, 1994; Nelken, 1994; Wells, 1993). These terms need defining. Snider (1987) distinguishes between corporate crime and white-collar crime. Corporate crime refers to the crimes *of* business (and laws which regulate business) whereas white-collar crime refers to crimes *against* business (and laws in the interest of business). It is the former category, that of corporate crime, which is the subject matter of this chapter. In particular, it refers to breaches of regulatory offences rather than the transgression of criminal laws which are of general application (Wells, 1993:1). Regulation refers to the use of the law to constrain and organise the activities of business and industry. This encompasses, for example, laws protecting the environment, consumers, and employees. It concerns the regulation of industrial processes which may cause harm to workforces, the public, and the environment (Hawkins & Hutter, 1993).[1]

The use of the criminal law and criminal sanctions to control regulatory behaviour has proved controversial. The arguments cut across debates about the extent to which governments should adopt a "laissez-faire" approach to markets and their activities and the extent to which they should intervene to protect particular groups (Hutter & Sorensen, 1993). They are also central to debates about the nature of the relationship between the law and morality and the law and class. Theories of regulation divide on these issues and place very different interpretations upon the emergence, framing, and enforcement of legislation which is designed to regulate corporations. Accommodative theorists portray regulatory legislation as the result of an accommodation between interest groups. They adhere to a consensual, pluralist model of society and argue that the legislation is neither as interventionist as the reformers would want it to be nor as lax as business would prefer (Carson, 1974; Paulus, 1974). Conflict theorists, who tend to adopt a dominant power group model of society, regard economic interests as paramount. They argue that the dominant class has ensured that their interests are not seriously affected by regulation. For example, they argue that business and industry are well represented in government and are therefore significant in shaping the legislation (Gunningham, 1974; Yeager, 1993).

Divisions also emerge over the criminality of corporate offending. Some classes of corporate offending, notably regulatory offences, are often referred to as "quasi-criminal" offences, others distinguish between "real crimes" and "regulatory offences."[2] Proponents of these views argue that regulatory offences are administratively and morally distinct from traditional crimes. Not surprisingly, the role of regulatory agencies is caught up in these debates. Some authors consider it significant that regulatory offences are often handled differently from traditionally criminal offences—by different enforcement agencies and by administrative (as well as criminal) procedures. Different theories give varying interpretations of enforcement activity. Accommodative theorists regard low levels of prosecution as a rational response to limited agency resources, ambiguous legislation, and weak sanctions (Cranston, 1979; Hutter, 1988; Richardson, 1983). Conflict theorists, however, cite a reluctance to prosecute as evidence of ineffective legislation, the "capture" of the regulatory agency by business and the power of business (Bernstein, 1955; Box, 1983; Clinard & Yeager, 1980; Gunningham, 1974; Yeager, 1991). Consensual theories regard regulatory agencies as protecting a less powerful majority from the activities of relatively powerful groups. Conflict theorists, however, believe that regulatory laws and policies do nothing to curb seriously the activities of business and industry, who they believe to be both major players in the shaping of regulatory policies and players who are deemed to be favoured in the implementation process (Carson, 1974, 1980; Gunningham, 1974; Snider, 1987; Yeager, 1991).[3] What they all agree upon is that there are fundamental tensions between regulatory systems and corporate interests, and that it is the job of the enforcement agency to gain the compliance of potentially unwilling business organisations to bear costs they are reluctant to incur.

The arguments surrounding corporate crime embrace a complexity of political and academic views and raise a variety of interesting research questions about the nature of the relationship between the law and morality and the law and class. We need to know the reasons for the differential handling of offences and whether or not large companies can (and do) use their power to manipulate the labelling process and minimise sanctions.[4] How independent is the regulatory process? What are the complexities posed by regulating corporations? How can regulatory responsibility be satisfactorily assigned within large corporate bodies? (Wells, 1992). Moreover, is moral ambivalence encouraged by regulatory legislation?[5]

This chapter argues that corporations cannot be regarded as a homogeneous group of monolithic entities. Regulatory officials deal with highly diverse organisations that require—even demand—different regulatory responses and varying regulatory controls. The chapter is therefore consistent with accommodation theory in its identification of a complex, politicised regulatory environment in which regulatory officials are left to resolve the tensions surrounding the regulation of corporations in the absence of strong regulatory law and ambiguous government leadership.

REGULATORY RELATIONS

Much of the empirical work that has been undertaken into the relationship between regulators and the regulated in the control of corporate crime, has been undertaken from the perspective of the enforcement agency.[6] The implementation stage of regulation involves a division between policymaking and enforcement. The policymaking effort is very much directed to standard setting and organizational interpretations of the law,[7] whereas the enforcement aspect of implementation is focused on inspectors and their decisionmaking about the law and agency policies.[8] These officials are in the front line of regulatory enforcement, and it is they who have the discretion (perhaps even sometimes create the discretion) to determine how government regulation is ultimately translated into action—they are the "gatekeepers" to the regulatory process. An understanding of how these officials approach and regard the regulation of corporations is important for a variety of reasons. As Hawkins and I have explained elsewhere (1993:200):

> An enforcement perspective is important because it is the set of beliefs of regulatory officials about business. . . . that plays a large part in agency policymaking and agency enforcement practices, with all that is implied in this for the costs imposed on, and the benefits gained by business, and the corresponding level of protection offered to those at risk and society generally.

Enforcement Patterns

A number of patterns emerge from the growing body of research into the relationship between enforcement agencies and corporations. The starting point of many of the early studies of regulatory enforcement was to understand how the law and criminal sanctions are used to control business and industrial activities (Carson, 1970; Cranston, 1979; Hawkins, 1984; Richardson et al., 1983). Each of these studies identified the adoption of common enforcement practices by officials from a variety of backgrounds. Enforcement of the law, it was argued, did not refer simply to legal action but to a wide array of informal enforcement techniques including education, advice, persuasion, and negotiation. These were used by all law enforcement officials, but came into particular prominence in the regulatory arena.

The enforcement style approximating to that often adopted by regulatory officials is variously referred to as the accommodative (Richardson, 1983) or compliance (Hawkins, 1984; Reiss, 1984) strategy of enforcement. Compliance is of central importance to this strategy since securing compliance is its main objective, through both the remedy of existing problems and, above all, the prevention of others. The preferred methods to achieve these ends are co-operative and conciliatory. So where compliance is less than complete than persuasion, negotiation and education are the primary enforcement techniques. Thus, compliance is not necessarily regarded as being achievable immediately, but may rather be seen as a long-term aim. The use of formal methods, especially prosecution, is regarded as a last resort, something to be avoided unless all else fails to secure compliance. This model of enforcement is contrasted with another termed the sanctioning strategy by Hawkins (1984) and the deterrent model by Reiss (1984). This is a penal style of enforcement which accords prosecution an important role. Indeed, the number of prosecutions initiated may be regarded as both a sign of success and as an indicator of work undertaken.

While it was always emphasised that in reality all enforcement agencies would use both styles, albeit with differing levels of commitment, it remains the case that the majority of studies, especially the earliest ones, identified the accommodative style as characteristically a regulatory enforcement style. The first studies to document any significant deviation from this pattern were of American regulatory agencies in the 1970s. Kelman's study of OSHA and Shover et al.'s study of the Office of Surface Mining both describe regulatory agencies which adopted enforcement strategies closely approximating the sanctioning style. My research into the law enforcement procedures of Environmental Health Officers mapped out further evidence of variations in the enforcement strategies of regulatory officials (Hutter, 1988).

Cultural Variations

There also appear to be cultural differences in regulatory theory. American scholars tend to subscribe to rather more extreme theories than do, for example, those in Britain and Australia. At one extreme the United States has given us "capture" theory, that is the theory that regulatory agencies have been "captured" by business. According to this theory "captured" regulatory agencies share the world-view of business, partly because they are in close, co-operative and possibly dependent relations with business and partly because the agency can only recruit specialist staff from the regulated community. The result, it is argued, is regulatory failure (Bernstein, 1955; Nader, 1980). At another extreme, a different form of regulatory failure is identified by American theorists, namely that of over-regulation or regulatory excess. Wilson (1985:24) explains that this theory suggests first, that regulations were laying onerous burdens on industry and second, that they were sanctioning even the most trivial offences. This inflexibility, it is suggested, both alienated business and imposed unreasonable costs upon it (Bardach & Kagan, 1982).

British and Australian authors, in contrast to their American counterparts, tend to advocate the pluralist (Carson, 1974; Grabosky & Braithwaite, 1985), or occasionally the conflict (Gunningham, 1974, 1987), models of regulatory theory. These countries are very similar because they share very similar regulatory laws and structures. Much Australian health and safety legislation, for example, is based upon the British model. In 1985, for instance, the State of Victoria enacted legislation based upon Britain's overhaul of its health and safety system in 1974. The differences between these theorists and those from the United States have largely been explained in cultural terms. For example, the American system is said to be more adversarial and litigious than the British and Australian systems that place much more emphasis upon discretion than rules, and upon conciliation and compromise rather than coercion and compulsion (Hawkins & Hutter, 1993; also Hawkins, 1992; Kelman, 1981; Vogel, 1986).

Corporate Differences

Variations also emerge according to the type of corporation subject to regulation. Regulatory authorities deal with a wide range of corporations, ranging from large, complex multinationals to small, simple businesses which are not incorporated. Inspectors differentiate the regulatory population according to a variety of criteria. For example, the way in which different companies are regarded by inspectors is closely related to the type of activity in which they are involved. In some companies, attention to regulatory objectives may be imperative to the viability of the whole operation so there is a self-interest in compliance (Genn, 1993). For example, chemical and petroleum works could precipitate a disaster if they paid insufficient attention to their safety and environmental operations. Other activities have less impressive images attached to them. For example, the building industry, scrap metal merchants, and second-hand car dealers have a reputation for paying scant attention to regulatory requirements (Cranston, 1979; Hawkins, 1984; Hutter, 1997). Also of relevance are the skills of those employed by a corporation and the levels of supervision they receive. One assumption seems to be that people with steady, professional jobs are more likely to be law abiding and compliant than those in manual work, especially those without secure long-term employment.

The ownership and size of a company can also be significant in determining inspectors' interactions with a company. Regulatory officials may spend large portions of their time educating and advising the self-employed and small businesses as these are the least likely to know about the law and how to comply. Indeed, Dawson et al. (1988:261) found that the gap between standards of health and safety in large and small firms was considerable. Large companies, by contrast, were likely to have their own health and safety or environmental departments and even legal departments. Differential enforcement according to size of organisation is a persistent feature of regulatory enforcement. Researchers in the United States, Australia, and the United Kingdom (Grabosky & Braithwaite, 1986; Lynxwiler et al., 1983; Snider, 1987) have all noted a tendency for formal legal enforcement action to figure less prominently in regulatory officials' dealings with larger and more powerful organisations than in their dealings with small organisations. Yeager (1991:282) for example, found that in one region of the U.S. Environmental Protection Agency large companies were twice as likely to receive no action determinations and one-half as likely to receive warning letters as small firms.

The reasons for this are various. Grabosky and Braithwaite (1986:215ff) found that Australian regulatory officials believed that big business was more law abiding than small business. Snider (1987:49) similarly identified ideological reasons for this tendency, namely that "regulators tend to believe that only 'fly by night' organizations typically stoop to crime" (cf. Carson, 1982; Braithwaite, 1984). This belief may be partially related to the capacity of organisations to comply. For instance, larger companies are most likely to support compliance staff in a safety or environmental department (Grabosky & Braithwaite, 1986), and they may also enjoy regulatory economies of scale (Yeager, 1991:42ff, 291ff). Larger companies also have a greater capacity to challenge compliance, including negotiation with other regulatory officials, appeals against legal action, and influence over the political process (Snider, 1987; Yeager, 1991).

Large companies can pose problems for regulatory officials because they have "too much" knowledge. Thus they may be less susceptible to "bluffing" and inspectors may also tend against legal action since they perceive it to be more difficult to construct a case against a larger, well-informed company than a smaller, ill-informed one. Indeed, to the extent that larger companies are more complicated than smaller business, it can be more difficult and more time-consuming to construct a legal case against them (Snider, 1987:49). Moreover, as DiMento points out "size correlates with differentiation in a firm and the greater the differentiation the greater the possibility of non-compliance" (1986:156; see also Vaughan, 1982). It should also be noted that inspectors have greater opportunities to develop relationships with staff from larger companies, which typically received more frequent and lengthier visits from inspectors than smaller sites (see below). All of these factors contribute to officials' characterisations of companies.

Bardach and Kagan (1982) refer to "good apples" and "bad apples" when characterising the types of companies inspectors encounter. In between these extremes they operate with much finer gradations, referring to "poor," "reasonable," "fairly good," "responsible," "very good," and "exemplary" companies. Factors contributing to such characterisations are inspectors' perceptions of the company's commitment to regulatory objectives as demonstrated, for instance, by the time, energy, and finances the company devoted to regulatory objectives; the attitude of corporate staff towards compliance; the quality of management on site; and a company's ability to comply, including both its financial position and the degree of technical knowledge it possesses. Typically inspectors would characterise a company on the basis of several of the above criteria (Hutter, 1997). Also of relevance are regulatory officials' perceptions of why corporations comply or fail to comply with regulatory objectives.

REASONS FOR COMPLIANCE AND NON-COMPLIANCE

Different theoretical traditions have identified different reasons for compliance. As Olsen (1992:16ff) explains, political theorists, lawyers, and economists, among many others, have come up with their own explanations of compliance, but as Olsen points out, "It is clear that no single theoretical tradition could offer a complete interpretation of all the consequences of all the total regulatory process and its effects at the company level" (1992:17). There are a variety of reasons why corporations seem to comply with laws which regulate their activities. Self-interest was regarded as the main reason for compliance. There may be a coincidence of interest between corporate and regulatory goals, so strict compliance may be necessary to the viability of the business. Alternatively compliance could increase the profits of the corporation, for instance some companies have a great incentive to prevent emissions to the atmosphere because these emissions could involve the loss of profitable substances, such as valuable metals from metal recovery works or costly chemicals from chemical works.

Another variant on the self-interest theme is compliance motivated by a concern to protect corporate reputation. Essentially companies do not want to be seen as non-compliant either because of a major incident or accident or because of any legal action initiated by the regulatory agency (Olsen, 1992). Large companies are seen as particularly concerned to protect their image and so are those whose relationships with the general public are already or potentially strained. These are largely instrumental reasons for compliance. Other authors, notably Bardach and Kagan (1982:60ff), have detailed a range of instrumental reasons for compliance in addition to those already mentioned. These include the threat of private lawsuits; increased insurance premiums, and worry about compensation payments and claims; intra-organisational pressures to comply; and avoiding the indirect costs of accidents, including "down-time" and labour dissatisfaction. There are also symbolic reasons for compliance, for example a genuine concern for regulatory objectives, such as the environment or the health and safety of the workforce, which some might refer to as a moral reason for compliance. Others might just feel an obligation to comply with the law.

Reasons for non-compliance are also elaborated upon in the literature. Cost is, perhaps not surprisingly, referred to, but few authors would simply relate compliance and non-compliance to cost. Wilson (1980:359) notes that profit maximisation is "an incomplete statement of corporate goals." Likewise, DiMento (1986:137) emphasises that financial resources alone are an insufficient explanation of compliance—and one might add, non-compliance. Nevertheless calculation may be involved, for example, an estimate of the likelihood of the law being enforced. The basic argument here is that the threat of the law and formal sanctions must be credible for legal regulation to be effective and compliance to be achieved. Snider (1987:51) sums up the argument by stating that regulatory enterprises:

> . . . have no incentive to make substantial and costly
> improvements, knowing that the most the inspector is likely
> to do is to issue a formal letter suggesting changes with no
> follow-up or likelihood of further action.

Other companies may be either negligent or ignorant of the law's demands. Indeed, this is often the perception of regulatory officials who often adopt an educational and advisory role (Cranston, 1979; Hawkins, 1984; Hutter, 1988, 1997). Of course there is also intentional or malicious non-compliance. This may be indicated, for example, by persistent or repeated non-compliance. Indicators of intent commonly lead to the prosecution of regulatory offenders. Grabosky and Braithwaite (1986:188), for example, discovered that 18 percent of the regulatory agencies they examined in Australia had a written enforcement policy that suggested that *mens rea* was important (see also, Cranston, 1979; Hawkins, 1984; Hutter, 1988; Richardson et al., 1983).

We should, however, be cautious about simplifying inspectors' views about and reactions to non-compliance. As Kagan and Scholz (1984:68) point out, regulatory officials do not choose among theories of non-compliance, but may combine them and make case-by-case judgments. Certainly the matter is a complex one and probably the only thing we know for certain is that there is no simple explanation of compliance. Businesses vary in their ability and motivation to comply, and they also differ over time and across issues.

IMPLICATIONS

The characterisations regulatory officials have of corporations have implications for the interpretation of events and general regulatory responses, with the compliance strategy most likely to be evoked by "good" corporations and the sanctioning strategy for so-called "bad" organisations. The ways in which regulatory officials interpret non-compliance vary according to their general views of a company, so "good" companies have "accidents" whereas "bad" companies "fail" to comply (Hawkins, 1984). But characterisations are not immutable, they change. Inspectors and corporations have a reflexive relationship (Hawkins & Hutter, 1993). Often they are in a long-term relationship in which each party adapts to the other. The degree to which each party adapts to specific rather than general stereotypes varies according to the degree of contact between the two. Generally the larger companies have greater contact because the volume of activity, size of site, and consequent risks.

Regulatory philosophy may also be important. Where regulatory authorities adopt a legalistic and sanctioning enforcement style they tend to ". . . treat business corporations as monolithic legal entities, with a single will and an internally consistent attitude towards social and legal responsibility" (Bardach & Kagan, 1982:81). But where an accommodative stance is adopted then regulatory officials seem to regard corporations in much the same way as Bardach and Kagan's corporate managers, so ". . . the corporation is a loose conglomeration of separate departments and managers, each with distinct problems, some very responsible and some less so" (Bardach & Kagan, 1982:81; see Hutter, 1997). Within large companies inspectors may differentiate between areas, both across sites and within sites. They also differentiate between individuals. Within companies there are a wide range of participants in the regulatory relationship, namely owners, directors, management, employees, and possibly a regulatory organisation, comprising specialist committees and personnel. The extent to which these groups work together to promote regulatory objectives or come into conflict about them is largely unknown, although there do seem to be cultural differences (Kelman, 1989).

Regulatory officials' characterisations of sites and whole corporations include their opinions of the individuals in the company. Determining how "good" or "bad" individuals are depends on a variety of criteria which in many respects mirror the criteria used for judging how a company is characterised. This includes, for example, acceptance of regulatory recommendations; ability to detect and remedy problems on their own; and the state of the business. All of these give regulatory officials some clues about the calibre of corporate management and employees and hence the total organisation. All regulatory officials rely heavily on a company's internal regulatory system to secure compliance. Again this increases the importance of their confidence in the individuals comprising a corporation plus, of course, the internal rules and systems the company has in place to promote compliance.

EXPLANATIONS[9]

Explanations of the variations in regulatory relations between enforcement officials and corporations range from an emphasis upon the regulated activity through to the motives of the regulated firms (Rees, 1988); or more broadly upon the social, political, and organisational contexts of enforcement (Hutter, 1988, 1997). As the discussion above has indicated, part of the explanation lies in the cultural environments within which regulation takes place; and in the interactions between regulators and corporate employees. Also relevant is the whole structure of regulatory law. In Britain, for instance, regulatory legislation comprises duties rather than commands and administrative discretion takes on central importance (Baldwin, 1995; Hawkins, 1984; Hutter, 1988, 1997). This contrasts with the United States where the law is typically very detailed and specific and where the emphasis is upon rules and the restriction of discretion (Hawkins, 1992; Kelman, 1981; Vogel, 1986).

At another level, the nature of the activities controlled by regulatory officials may lead to an accommodative approach. This has a number of facets as Hawkins (1984) explains. He draws a distinction between forms of deviance which are "continuing, repetitive, or episodic in character" and deviance which consists of isolated discrete and bounded incidents (1984:6), his argument being that a negotiating strategy is more likely in the former and a sanctioning strategy in the latter. He contends that this is largely because the former type of deviance is "amenable to strategies of correction or control in a way that most forms of isolated crime cannot be" (1984:6) because they are unpredictable as to timing and location.[10]

The complexity of the problems encountered by enforcement officials may also be significant (Hawkins, 1984:108). A technically complex situation may demand constant negotiation and renegotiation about the source of a problem and how it might be remedied. Enforcement officials dealing with these types of deviance are able to develop a social relationship with those they regulate. Hawkins (1984:123) argues that the establishment of such relationships is more likely to cultivate the "sense of mutual trust" which is "important in sustaining the bargaining relationship." Also of relevance is Galanter's (1974) distinction between "one-shotters" and "repeat players," the point being that "repeat players" are able to gain knowledge of each other's practices and expectations. Moreover, they have greater incentives to enter a co-operative relationship than do "one-shotters" who may not meet again.

Organisational factors may intervene, notably enforcement agency resources and policies. Typically accommodative strategies of control occur where there is a high ratio of regulatory officials to regulated corporations. A variety of mechanisms are at work here, key among which is the frequency of interaction between the regulators and regulated (Grabosky & Braithwaite, 1986; Hutter, 1988, 1997; Scholz, 1984; Shover et al., 1984). But while high levels of interaction facilitate a persuasive enforcement strategy, it also carries with it the danger of capture. It is partly for this reason that some agencies have policies which directly or indirectly discourage the development of relationships between inspectors and corporate employees.

Political factors are also relevant, especially when the control of corporate activity, is often inherently ambiguous. For example, while governments want the economic benefits of corporate activity, they do not always want the social costs associated with it. Typically the resolution of these tensions is left to the agency, particularly where the legislation accords enforcement officials high levels of discretion. Moreover, different political regimes have varying political agendas concerning the control of corporate activity, agendas which change according to political party, economic climate and high profile cases (Carson, 1982; Hutter & Lloyd-Bostock, 1990; Kagan, 1994; Kelman, 1981).

THEORETICAL AND POLICY ISSUES

Empirical research into the regulation of corporations has emphasised the complexity of regulation. Different models of regulation "fit" varying substantive examples at varying time periods and in different cultures (Cotterrell, 1992). Regulation is undoubtedly a complex and complicated process. Hence, it is difficult to be too prescriptive about what does and does not work in corporate control. This is especially so when there is so much that we do not know. In particular, we need to learn more about the impact of regulation upon corporations. For example, we need to know how much corporations know about regulatory laws and controls; how and to what extent they adapt to regulation; and which regulatory strategies are more or less likely to induce compliance. Similarly, we need to establish the accuracy of some of the commonly held assumptions about corporate behaviour, for example, reasons for compliance and non-compliance and the extent to which corporations do fear criminal sanctions, if at all.

Establishing the efficacy of enforcement strategies is bedeviled with difficulties relating to inadequate data and the complexity of regulation. For example, there are problems in differentiating the effects of regulation from wider changes, such as changes in an industry, occupational structure or public expectations (Wilson, 1985). This underlines the difficulties of proclaiming the efficacy of any particular enforcement approach.

Ayres and Braithwaite (1992:20) refer to "a long history of barren disputation" between "staunch advocates of deterrence and defenders of the compliance model." Generally such arguments have reached stalemate with the work of academics across the world being misrepresented in the interests of argument and polemic. All of this serves, once again, to highlight the tensions surrounding regulatory control. Certainly there are times when corporations seem to "get off lightly" and there is undoubtedly a need for regulatory tools and sanctions to deal with what Bardach and Kagan refer to as the "bad apples." But we also need to appreciate that corporations vary. Hence the argument for "responsive regulation" (Ayres & Braithwaite, 1992) or "flexible enforcement" (Rees, 1988), which can accommodate different enforcement styles and techniques.

Finally, in addition to all of these complexities, we must add the legal and social difficulties associated with assigning liability to corporations. All too often legal and social responsibility and blame is attributed to individuals, often relatively junior individuals, who may have been the immediate cause of a corporate misdemeanours, rather than attention and responsibility being attributed to the structural and systemic problems which may have given rise to or allowed the problem to emerge. In part this a matter of perception, for both the law and society find it easier to blame tangible individuals than intangible corporations (Wells, 1992). Individuals may easily be attributed intentions, meanings, and faults in a way that organisations, especially large ones, cannot. It is perhaps for similar reasons that "criminal" offences are often seen as distinct from "regulatory" ones. Moreover, as I have argued elsewhere (1988), there is often a lack of appreciation about the nature of corporate offending and the harmful effects which can follow a breach of the law.[11] This is partly because the effects may emerge in the long-term and not be immediately tangible. For example, the effects of breaches in health and safety legislation may be poor health. It may take some considerable time for the ill-effects of such breaches to manifest themselves. Asbestosis, for example, may take decades to develop following exposure to crocidolite. Appreciation of the nature of corporate offending may also be hindered because the offending is technically complex and difficult to understand. Financial frauds often fall into this category. Moreover, routine breaches of the law by corporations are often not regarded as newsworthy or worthy of other forms of public condemnation. This is partly because of the factors already mentioned, namely the long-term consequences of the breach or its complexity. Conversely, it may be because the offences are seemingly mundane and undramatic, for example, failing to fill in a tax return, failing to wash hands prior to food preparation, or failing to use safety equipment. The effects may individually or cumulatively *actually* prove quite harmful but on their own it may be easy to trivialise them.

Corporate crime remains an ill-understood and poorly appreciated form of criminal activity. This is partly because of a relative dearth of research into the topic and partly because this form of criminal activity is often trivialised and perceived as something separate from "traditional" crimes involving individuals. Reforming regulations requires a greater understanding of the dynamics of regulatory corporate activities, most especially the impact of regulation upon corporations. Moreover, it also requires a greater public understanding of the harms which may be caused by corporate crime. This could be fostered by education programmes and by more media publicity and public shaming about corporate offending and its effects (Braithwaite, 1989). But once again we need to know more about strategies that are likely to include corporate compliance.

NOTES

[1] Regulatory offences may be committed by individuals and a wide range of businesses and industries, not just by corporations. Indeed regulatory laws pertain to a wide range of small businesses, such as corner shops, market traders, farms, and workshops, none of which fit easily our stereotypes of "the corporate criminal" (Croall, 1988).

[2] See, for example, *Lord Reid in Warner v. Metropolitan Police Commissioner [1968] 2 All ER 356. Council of the Law Society* (1967), Jackson (1967), Justice (1980), Smith and Hogan (1978).

[3] Sociological theories of regulations are mirrored in other social science approaches to regulation, for example, by economic theory. See Ogus (1994).

[4] See generally, Hutter (1988), Chapter 2.

[5] This legislation is notable for abandoning the concept of *mens rea* and accepting the principle of strict liability. Arguably this dilutes the moral force of the legislation (Justice, 1980; Paulus, 1974). Yet there is increasing evidence that regulatory officials give the strict liability provisions at their disposal pragmatic value only in relation to serious offences. In other cases they reintroduce at the operational level the notion of *mens rea* (Hartung, 1950; Hawkins, 1984; Hutter, 1988; Richardson et al., 1983).

[6] Relatively little work has been undertaken on the impact of regulations upon business. See Brittan (1984), Genn (1993), Gricar (1983), Hutter (1993). See Hawkins and Hutter (1993), for a discussion of how and why research into regulation has developed in the ways it has.

[7] Very few studies of policymaking have been undertaken to date. Notable exceptions include Mashaw and Harfst (1990), Cheit (1990), Rock (1986, 1990).

[8] In contrast to the scarcity of studies of policymaking there is a long tradition of research into the activities of field-level police officers and regulatory officials. (See, for example, Banton, 1964; Bittner, 1967; Cain, 1973; Cranston, 1978; Hawkins, 1984; Hutter, 1988, 1997; Jamieson, 1985; Manning, 1977; Piliavin & Briar, 1964; Richardson et al., 1983; Skolnick,1975.)

[9] See Kagan (1994), for a comprehensive and detailed account of regulatory variability.

[10] These categories are best regarded as "ideal-types" as some types of law breaking do not fall easily into one category or the other.

[11] As Phil Sorensen and I have argued elsewhere (Sorensen & Hutter, 1993:173-174), the stakes in corporate offending may be high involving financial collapse, fatalities, or environmental damage, depending upon the type of breach involved.

10

The Risks and Rewards of an Interdisciplinary Inquiry into the Causes and Consequences of Corporate Misconduct

Mark A. Cohen
Vanderbilt University

William S. Lofquist
SUNY College at Geneseo

If there is only one lesson to be learned from this book, it is that the study of corporate crime is necessarily interdisciplinary. The boundaries of any single discipline are simply inadequate to address all of the complexities of this most controversial subject. To the editors, coordinating and editing such a truly interdisciplinary volume has been an exciting and informative experience. Although the disciplinary boundaries set up in academia are often impenetrable, we have brought together an extremely diverse set of academics, including criminologists, sociologists, economists, and lawyers. Primarily because of these disciplinary boundaries, these scholars seldom have an opportunity to meet at conferences, discuss each other's theories, or even to read each other's writings.

The ability of society to design a rational public policy to punish and/or deter future corporate wrongdoing depends heavily on the degree to which we understand both the causes and consequences of corporate crime. However, the diverse views expressed by the authors we have convened for this volume highlight an even more basic issue that must be addressed in formulating public policy—we need to come to a common understanding of the definition of corporate crime itself. The term "corporate crime" means different things to different disciplines. To some, corporate crime is approached behaviorally, and is equated with corporate misconduct or any action by a corporation that is either legally prohibited or that causes harm to individuals. To others, corporate crime is a legal concept with boundaries that are both circumscribed by the criminal law and that are to be debated by legal scholars. Why corporate crime occurs, how harmful it is, and what to do about it all depends to some extent on what it is!

Going beyond these definitional issues, even the best theory is only a "hypothesis" until it is subjected to rigorous empirical analysis and testing. Unfortunately, corporate crime is not something that is easily measured. We often have little evidence of the extent of corporate crime and are left to infer the scope of the problem by examining companies that have been caught and prosecuted. Even those data have only recently been available to researchers, and then only in a very limited format. Gaining access to the names, personnel, and records of these companies often requires overcoming substantial barriers not confronted in the study of street crime. In this brief conclusion, we attempt to distill the areas of agreement and disagreement on these issues, and to examine the sources of the disagreements that exist. Finally, we suggest areas of future research that might enhance our understanding of corporate crime and punishment.

THE CAUSES OF CORPORATE CRIME

Our first debate centers around the causes of corporate crime. This topic appears to be the least controversial subject in the book, since there is much common ground. Cohen and Simpson (Chapter 2) model crime as the outcome of rational decisions based on agency theory. Yet, they also consider the fact that rational agents are influenced by organizational and environmental factors such as corporate culture and moral norms. Ermann and Rabe (Chapter 3) believe that organizational structure is the overriding factor contributing to corporate crime, but allow for rational actors within the organization who affect outcomes. The difference thus appears to be a matter of degree and emphasis.

Even though it appears the two approaches do not differ dramatically, they may lead to vastly different policy implications. For example, if one believes that individuals have little effect on corporate crime and are instead highly influenced by the organizational structure in which they find themselves, there is little deterrent value to punishing individuals and much to be gained from more interventionist policies that involve restructuring the corporation or other forms of corporate "probation." As was seen in Chapters 6 and 7, the appropriate form of punishment will depend a great deal on the underlying cause of crime.

CORPORATE CRIMINAL LIABILITY

In contrast to the first issue, the second debate we encountered—when corporations should be held criminally liable for the actions of its agents—is highly controversial. Both Parker (Chapter 4) and Jörg (Chapter 5) agree that corporate criminal liability hinges on whether a corporation can be held "morally" responsible for its actions. However, the answer to this question is primarily a philosophical/moral one. To Parker, only individuals can have moral culpability and should thus be subject to criminal laws. To Jörg, the very fact that the individuals who take illegal actions do so within the organizational structure and operating procedures of the company suggests that organizations can take on a moral character of their own.

The question of corporate criminal liability can be addressed on two different levels. As a philosophical issue, both sides of the issue must resign themselves to agree to disagree. No amount of empirical evidence would likely convince Parker that corporations should be routinely held criminally liable for actions of their employees, or convince Jörg that they should not. At a more pragmatic level, those who do not hold strong philosophical views on liability may appeal to empirical evidence to help guide their beliefs. The question of whether corporations should be held criminally liable for their agent's actions will then critically depend on factors such as: how the crime occurred, what role top management played in the offense, what harm was done, and what punishment the corporation faces. These are questions addressed in most of the other chapters in the book.

CORPORATE CRIMINAL SANCTIONING

The first two issues are largely debated in academia even if they have profound policy implications. In contrast, the third issue—corporate criminal sanctioning—has been the subject of considerable public debate due to recently enacted Sentencing Commission Guidelines for Organizations. Guidelines were first proposed in 1988, and the public debate continued unabated through 1991 when they were finally enacted. This topic was the subject of public hearings, articles in the popular business media and major newspapers, conferences, and other public forums. In addition, several law journals published full issues devoted to the topic of organizational sanctions. Despite all of the public debate, there is still little consensus about the role of criminal sanctions in deterring corporate crime.

Much of the controversy over whether fines are adequate can be traced to a lack of solid empirical evidence on both sides of the issue. How can we determine the appropriate size of a penalty, or whether monetary penalties alone are large enough to deter illegal activity if we do not know how much illegal activity is taking place? One interesting phenomenon that occurred during the drafting process of the Sentencing Guidelines for organizations was that both proponents and opponents of the proposals cited the same basic statistics to make their point. Were existing penalties too high or too low? Few objective measures existed in order to either defend or attack the current penalty structure.

In addition to the paucity of useful data, the sanctioning debate is enlivened by theoretical differences of opinion. Some structure theorists, for example, view fines as secondary to more interventionist measures, regardless of the accounting of loss and gain, due to the organizational origins of corporate crime. Further, although neither chapter author focused on this point, some of the debate over the proper type of criminal sanction may hinge on the philosophy behind sanctions. Both Ulen and Gruner focus primarily on deterrence and examine the conditions under which monetary penalties are likely to be adequate to deter illegal behavior. Neither considers the possibility that penalties serve another role—to educate, display moral outrage, and to "punish," irrespective of any deterrent value.

The importance of understanding an author's perspective and assumptions is apparent when reading Chapter 4 (Parker) and Chapter 6 (Ulen). As noted above, how one views the origins of corporate crime or corporate liability will affect the type of sanction ultimately chosen. Perhaps more intriguing, however, is the fact that these two authors who both start from an agency theory perspective can come to such diametrically opposed views of corporate sanctions. Although Parker is primarily addressing the issue of criminal liability and arguing strongly against imposing criminal liability in most instances, one of the major reasons he cautions against using the criminal law is the severity of punishment that is meted out to corporate criminals. Thus, to Parker, it is partly the fact that "punishment" is an "ugly, brutal thing" that causes him to question the advisability of imposing criminal liability on all but the most egregious corporate actions. In contrast, Ulen does not consider criminal fines to be a form of "brutal punishment." Instead, society is told to choose an "optimal" penalty that provides incentives to optimally deter illegal behavior. He advocates criminal sanctions when existing civil enforcement mechanisms are inadequate.

Why do these two authors appear to have such different views about the role of punishment? The fact is, they are not as far apart as it might seem. Ulen cautions that the criminal law should only be used for "intentional" acts, and to impose criminal sanctions on unintentional acts might result in overdeterrence. Parker argues that few (if any) corporate crimes are "intended" by the organization, even if intended by their agents. Thus, one cannot cite Ulen in support of criminal sanctions for vicarious and strict liability offenses. Neither can one cite Parker as having entirely eliminated corporate criminal liability from consideration as a viable form of legal punishment. Nevertheless, it is also true that these two authors reach different policy conclusions about the role of criminal sanctions, even though they start from the same basic premise of rational individual behavior.

REGULATORY RELATIONS

The final debate concerns the role of government regulatory authorities in working with or against organizations. In taking an agency theory perspective, Barrile (Chapter 8) believes that only through strict criminal enforcement and punitive sanctions will the profit-motivated harms generated by corporations be controlled. In contrast, Hutter (Chapter 9) argues that the complexity of corporate structures calls for ongoing cooperative regulatory relations between firms and their regulators.

As this final debate makes clear, the distinction between agency theorists and structuralists is not a debate between liberals and conservatives, leftists versus right wing theorists, or interventionists versus libertarians. Rather, the essential difference between them is rooted in their opposing views on the relative importance of individual agency and organizational structure in understanding behavior within organizations. This is most obvious in Chapter 8, where Barrile espouses a radical leftist perspective based on agency theory. Although Barrile is also in favor of some limited forms of intervention primarily at the probationary stage, after a prosecution and punishment, he argues strongly for more criminal liability and stricter enforcement and punishment of corporations that cause harm. Contrast this view with Parker (Chapter 4), who believes that corporations are generally involved in socially desirable activities and that government enforcement agencies are not generally to be trusted in using their discretion to come up with appropriate punishments that are not themselves socially harmful. Parker argues that there is likely to be a lack of information and the ability of the government to find and/or use that information wisely in fashioning an appropriate structural sentence.

THE BOTTOM LINE: WHAT HAVE WE LEARNED?

There are both risks and rewards in undertaking a volume with such an interdisciplinary approach to corporate crime and bringing together such a diverse set of scholars with opposing views, methodologies, and academic traditions. The risk is that the reader is left with more questions than answers. The reward, however, is also that the reader is left with more questions than answers! No one discipline or paradigm can have all the answers. The causes, consequences, and control of corporate crime are complex issues requiring sophisticated analysis.

Having made the argument in favor of more interdisciplinary research and collaboration, it is also important to keep in mind that there is often tremendous value in the simplistic approach that a single discipline can bring to bear on a problem. For example, as Cohen and Simpson (Chapter 2) point out, a simple model of rational individuals maximizing their own personal satisfaction can help explain the existence of corporate crime even when the owners of a corporation would prefer that crime not be committed. On the other hand, Ermann and Rabe (Chapter 3) argue that organizational structure and cultures help define the conditions under which we expect corporate crime to occur. In reality, there is likely to be some truth to both views; that both individual decisions and organizational structure affect the likelihood of corporate crime. Which one is a more influential factor is an empirical issue that will largely depend on the nature of the crime and the organization.

Despite its purely objective appearance, research into corporate crime (as with any other field of inquiry) is necessarily value-laden. For example, to someone who believes corporate power is so great it must be closely checked and so dispersed such checks must encompass organizational interventions, a strong case can be made for imposing corporate probation and allowing the government to become involved in the management structure of organizations. On the other hand, to someone who believes that corporations will respond to moral and legal incentives and that there are strong market forces and government penalties available to those who do wrong, corporate probation is a socially costly form of intervention that should be avoided except in the most corrupt organizations.

Interpretation of data may vary considerably across disciplines and according to the values one brings to the analysis. For example, as Barrile (Chapter 8, Figure 8.1) points out, worker safety rates have improved since 1971, the year that the Occupational Safety and Health Administration (OSHA) was established. Further, there appears to have been a slight upward trend in injury rates during the Reagan years, which Barrile interprets as an argument in favor of more stringent enforcement and higher penalties for workplace injuries. Yet other authors have looked at the same data, and noted that worker injury rates had been declining over the 30- to 40-year period prior to the establishment of OSHA, and that any increase in injury rates during the Reagan years paled in comparison to the secular trends (see, e.g., Kniesner & Leeth, 1995). They interpret these same data as being evidence that OSHA did not lead to significant improvements in worker safety and that those improvements would have taken place even without OSHA. In fact, Kniesner and Leeth (1995) point out that due to the limited liability offered employers under workplace safety laws, the establishment of OSHA (coupled with sporadic enforcement), may lead to more workplace injuries than a system without direct regulation but in which workers can sue for pain, suffering, and punitive damages in cases where employers display a reckless disregard for safety. Other authors have pointed out that despite some improvement in safety rates following OSHA, the cost of compliance with OSHA greatly exceeds the measurable benefits (Hahn & Hird, 1990).

Thus, the same basic source of data has been used by both sides of an ongoing policy debate. Ultimately, the questions that both sides of this debate must ask are: (1) whether society has too many workplace injuries, (2) if the cost of preventing further injuries is acceptable to society, and (3) if there are other less costly ways to achieve the same level of safety. These are difficult empirical questions that we leave open to further study and debate. They are also generic questions that policymakers need to address in formulating an effective policy to deter and control corporate crime of any form.

Bibliography

Abel, C.F. (1985). "Corporate Crime and Restitution." *Journal of Offender Counseling, Services and Rehabilitation,* 9,3:71-94.

Adams, J. (1996). "Principals and Agents, Colonialists and Company Men: The Decay of Colonial Control in the Dutch East Indies." *American Sociological Review,* 61:12-28.

Addison, F.W. III & E.E. Mack (1991). "Creating an Environmental Ethic in Corporate America: The Big Stick of Jail Time." *Southwestern Law Journal,* 44:1427-1448.

Advisory Group on Environmental Sanctions (1993). *Final Report to the Sentencing Commission.* Washington, DC: U.S. Sentencing Commission.

Alexander, C.R. & M.A. Cohen (1996). "New Evidence on the Origins of Corporate Crime," *Managerial and Decision Economics,* 17(4):421-435.

Alexander, C.R. & M.A. Cohen (1995). "Why Do Corporations Become Criminals?" Unpublished Manuscript. Vanderbilt University.

Allen, M.P. (1991). "Capitalist Response to State Intervention: Theories of the State and Political Finance in the New Deal." *American Sociological Review,* 56:679-689.

Allison, G. (1971). *Essence of Decision: Explaining the Cuban Missile Crisis.* New York, NY: Harper Collins.

———— (1969). "Conceptual Models and the Cuban Missile Crisis." *American Political Science Review,* 63,3:689-718.

American Law Institute (1985). *Model Penal Code and Commentaries.* Philadelphia, PA: American Law Institute.

American National Standards Institute and American Society for Quality Control (ANSI and ASQC) (1987). *Quality Management and Quality System Elements—Guidelines.* Milwaukee WI: American Society for Quality Control.

Anderson, J. & L. Whitten (1976). "Auto Maker Shuns Safer Gas Tank." *Washington Post,* December 30:B-7.

Arlen, J. (1994). "The Potentially Perverse Effects of Corporate Criminal Liability." *Journal of Legal Studies,* 32:833-867.

219

Arrow, K. (1985). "The Economics of Agency." In J. Pratt & R. Zeckhauser (eds.) *Principals and Agents: The Structure of Business*. Boston, MA: Harvard Business School Press.

Aulette, J.R. & R. Michalowski (1995). "Fire in Hamlet: A Case Study of State-Corporate Crime." In G. Geis, R.F. Meier & L.M. Salinger, *White-Collar Crime: Classic and Contemporary Views*, Third Edition, pp. 166-190. New York, NY: Free Press.

Ayres, I. & J. Braithwaite (1992). *Responsive Regulation: Transcending the Deregulation Debate*. New York, NY: Oxford University Press.

Balbus, I. (1973). *The Dialectics of Legal Repression*. New York, NY: Russell Sage.

Baldwin, R. (1995). *Rules and Government*. Oxford: Clarendon Press.

Baldwin, R.W. (1974). "The Application of the Federal Probation Act to the Corporate Entity." *Baltimore Law Review*, 3:294-306.

Ball, H.V. & L.M. Friedman (1965/1977). "The Use of Criminal Sanctions in the Enforcement of Economic Legislation: A Sociological View." In G. Geis & R.F. Meier (eds.) *White Collar Crime*, pp. 318-336. New York, NY: Free Press.

Ballam, D.A. (1988). "The Occupational Safety and Health Act's Preemptive Effect on Criminal Prosecutions of Employers for Workplace Deaths and Injuries." *American Business Law Journal*, 26:1-27.

Banton, M. (1964). *The Policeman in the Community*. London: Tavistock.

Barak, G. (ed.) (1991). *Crimes by the Capitalist State: An Introduction to State Criminality*. Albany, NY: State University of New York Press.

Bardach, E. & R. Kagan (1982). *Going by the Book: The Problem of Regulatory Unreasonableness*. Philadelphia, PA: Temple University Press.

Barnard, C.I. (1938). *The Functions of the Executive*. Cambridge, MA: Harvard University Press.

Barnett, H.C. (1993). "Crimes Against the Environment: Superfund Enforcement at Last." *Annals of the American Academy of Political and Social Science*, 525:119-133.

——— (1992). "Hazardous Waste, Distributional Conflict, and a Trilogy of Failure." *Journal of Human Justice*, 3:91-110.

——— (1981). "The Production of Corporate Crime in Corporate Capitalism." *Crime & Delinquency*, 27,1:4-23.

Barrile, L.G. (1994). "Strategies for Combatting Corporate Victimization of Workers." Paper presented at the Annual Meeting of the American Society of Criminology. Miami, FL.

_____ (1993). "A Soul to Damn and a Body to Kick: Imprisoning Corporate Criminals." *Humanity and Society,* 17:2.

Baucus, M.S. & J.P. Near (1991). "Can Illegal Corporate Behavior Be Predicted? An Event History Analysis," *Academy of Management Journal*, 34:9-36.

Baysinger, B.D. (1991). "Organization Theory and the Criminal Liability of Organizations." *Boston University Law Review,* 71,2:341-376.

Beccaria, C. (1986). *On Crimes and Punishments*. Indianapolis, IN: Hackett.

Beckenstein, A., H. Gabel & L. Roberts (1983). "An Executive's Guide to Antitrust Compliance," *Harvard Business Review,* 94:Sept-Oct.

_____ (1985). "Tailoring Punishment to White Collar Crime: A Mix of Fines and Lawsuits—with the Occasional Prison Term—Would Remove the Profit Motive from Corporate Crime." *Business Week,* October 28:20.

_____ (1981). *A Treatise on the Family*. Cambridge, MA: Harvard University Press.

_____ (1968). "Crime and Punishment: An Economic Approach." *Journal of Political Economy,* 76:169-217.

Bedau, H. (1982). *The Death Penalty in America*, Third Edition. New York, NY: Oxford University Press.

Belbot, B.A. (1992). "Corporate Criminal Liability." In M. Blankenship (ed.) *Understanding Corporate Criminality*. New York, NY: Garland Publishing.

Benson, M.L. (1990). "Emotions and Adjudication: Status Degradation Among White-Collar Criminals." *Justice Quarterly,* 7:515-527.

Benson, M.L. & E. Moore (1992). "Are White-Collar and Common Offenders the Same? An Empirical and Theoretical Critique of a Recently Proposed General Theory of Crime." *Journal of Research in Crime and Delinquency,* 29:251-272.

Benson, M.L. & E. Walker (1988). "Sentencing the White-Collar Offender." *American Sociological Review,* 53:294-302.

Benson, M.L., F.T. Cullen & W.J. Maakestad (1993). *Local Prosecutors and Corporate Crime*. Washington, DC: National Institute of Justice.

_____ (1990). "Local Prosecutors and Corporate Crime." *Crime & Delinquency,* 36:356-372.

Benson, M.L., W.J. Maakestad, F.T. Cullen & G. Geis (1988). "District Attorneys and Corporate Crime: Surveying the Prosecutorial Gatekeepers." *Criminology,* 26:501-514.

Bentham, J. (1970). *An Introduction to the Principles of Morals and Legislation*. London: Althone.

Bergman, D. (1990). "Recklessness in the Boardroom." *The New Law Journal,* October 26,140:1496.

Berle, A. & G.C. Means (1932). *The Modern Corporation and Private Property.* New York, NY: Macmillan.

Bernard, T.J. (1984). "The Historical Development of Corporate Criminal Liability." *Criminology,* 22,1:3-17.

Bernstein, M.H. (1955). *Regulating Business by Independent Commission.* Princeton, NJ: Princeton University Press.

Bittner, E. (1967). "The Police on Skid-Row: A Study of Peace Keeping." *American Sociological Review,* 32:600-715.

Bixby, M.B. (1990). "Was it an Accident or Murder? New Thrusts in Corporate Criminal Liability for Workplace Deaths." *Labor Law Journal,* 41:417-422.

Black, D. (1976). *The Behavior of Law.* New York, NY: Academic Press.

Blakey, G.R. (1991). Professor of Law, Notre Dame University. Former Staff Member of Brown Commission and Former Counsel to Senate Judiciary Committee, Subcommittee on Criminal Laws and Procedures. Interview with W.S. Lofquist. August 2.

Block, F. (1977). "The Ruling Class Does Not Rule: Notes on the Marxist Theory of the State." *Socialist Revolution,* 33:6-28.

———— (1976/77). "Beyond Corporate Liberalism." *Social Problems,* 24:350.

Block, M.K. (1991). "Optimal Penalties, Criminal Law, and the Control of Corporate Behavior." *Boston University Law Review,* 71:395.

———— & V.E. Gerety (1995). "Some Experimental Evidence on Differences Between Student and Prisoner Reaction to Monetary Penalties and Risk." *Journal of Legal Studies,* 24:123-138.

———— & R. Lind (1975). "An Economic Analysis of Crimes Punishable by Imprisonment." *Journal of Legal Studies,* 4:479.

———— F.C. Nold & J.G. Sidak (1981). "The Deterrent Effect of Antitrust Enforcement," *Journal of Political Economy,* 89:429-445.

Blum-West, S. & T.J. Carter (1983). "Bringing White-Collar Crime Back In: An Examination of Crimes and Torts." *Social Problems,* 30,5:545-554.

Bosch, J.C. & E.W. Eckard, Jr. (1991). "The Profitability of Price-Fixing: Evidence from Stock Market Reaction to Federal Indictments." *Review of Economics and Statistics,* 73:309-317.

Boston College Law School (1988). "Pursuit of the Corporate Criminal: Employer Criminal Liability for Work Related Deaths as a Method of Improving Workplace Safety and Health." *Boston College Law Review,* 29:451-480.

Box, S. (1987). *Recession, Crime and Punishment.* Totowa, NJ: Barnes and Noble.

————— (1983). *Power, Crime and Mystification.* London: Tavistock.

Braithwaite, J. (1993). "Transnational Regulation of the Pharmaceutical Industry." *Annals of the American Academy of Political and Social Sciences,* 525:12-30.

————— (1989a). *Crime, Shame, and Reintegration.* New York, NY: Cambridge University Press.

————— (1989b). "Criminological Theory and Organizational Crime." *Justice Quarterly,* 6,3:333-358.

————— (1985a). *To Punish or Persuade: Enforcement of Coal Mine Safety.* Albany, NY: State University of New York Press.

————— (1985b). "White Collar Crime." *Annual Review of Sociology,* 11:1-25.

————— (1985c). "Taking Responsibility Seriously: Corporate Compliance Systems." In B. Fisse & P.A. French (eds.) *Corrigible Corporations and Unruly Law,* pp. 39-61. San Antonio, TX: Trinity University Press.

————— (1984). *Corporate Crime in the Pharmaceutical Industry.* London: Routledge & Kegan Paul.

————— (1982). "Enforced Self-Regulation: A New Strategy for Corporate Crime Control." *Michigan Law Review,* 80:1466-1507.

————— (1981-1982). "The Limits of Economism in Controlling Harmful Corporate Conduct." *Law & Society Review,* 16,3:481-504.

Braithwaite, J. & B. Fisse (1985). "Varieties of Responsibility and Organizational Crime." *Law & Policy* 7,3:315-343.

Braithwaite, J. & G. Geis (1982). "On Theory and Action for Corporate Crime Control." *Crime & Delinquency,* 28:292-314.

Braithwaite, J. & T. Makkai (1990). "Testing An Expected Utility Model of Corporate Deterrence." Paper presented at American Society of Criminology Annual Meeting. Baltimore, MD.

Braithwaite, J. & P. Pettit (1990). *Not Just Deserts: A Republican Theory of Criminal Justice.* Oxford: Clarendon Press.

Brenner, S.N. & E.A. Molander (1977). "Is the Ethics of Business Changing?" *Harvard Business Review,* 55,1:57-71.

Breyer, S.J. (1993). *Breaking the Vicious Circle: Towards Effective Risk Regulation.* Cambridge, MA: Harvard University Press.

Brickey, K.F. (1984). *Corporate Criminal Liability.* Three volumes. Wilmette, IL: Callaghan & Company.

Brittan, Y. (1984). *The Impact of Water Pollution Control on Industry.* Oxford: Centre for Socio-Legal Studies.

Bros, C.L. (1989). "A Fresh Assault on the Hazardous Workplace: Corporate Homicide Liability for Workplace Fatalities in Minnesota." *William Mitchell Law Review,* 15:287-326.

Brown, M. (1981). *Laying Waste: The Poisoning of America by Toxic Chemicals.* New York, NY: Washington Square Press.

Bucy, P.H. (1991). "Corporate Ethos: A Standard For Imposing Corporate Criminal Liability." *Minnesota Law Review,* 75:1095-1184.

Byam, J. (1982). "Comment: The Economic Inefficiency of Corporate Criminal Liability." *Journal of Criminal Law & Criminology,* 73:582-603.

Byrne, J. & S.M. Hoffman (1985). "Efficient Corporate Harm: A Chicago Metaphysic." In B. Fisse & P.A. French (eds.) *Corrigible Corporations and Unruly Law*, pp. 101-136. San Antonio, TX: Trinity University Press.

Cain, M. (1973). *Society and the Policeman's Role.* London: Routledge and Kegan Paul.

Calavita, K. (1990). "Employer Sanctions Violations: Toward a Dialectical Model of White-Collar Crime." *Law & Society Review,* 24:1041-1069.

——— (1983). "The Demise of the Occupational Safety and Health Administration: A Case Study in Symbolic Action." *Social Problems,* 30:437-448.

——— & H.N. Pontell (1990). "'Heads I Win, Tails You Lose:' Deregulation, Crime, and Crisis in the Savings and Loan Industry." *Crime & Delinquency,* 55:309-341.

Carney W. et al. (1978). "The Optimal Amount of Fraud." *Journal of Law and Economics,* 16:67-88.

Carney, W. & J. Arlen (1992). "Vicarious Liability for Fraud on Securities Markets: Theory and Evidence." *University of Illinois Law Review,* 92:691-740.

Carnoy, M. & D. Shearer (1980). *Economic Democracy.* White Plains, NY: M.E. Sharpe.

Carson, W.G. (1982). *The Other Price of Britain's Oil.* Oxford: Martin Robertson.

——— (1980). "The Institutionalization of Ambiguity: Early British Factory Acts." In G. Geis & E. Stotland (eds.) *White Collar Crime: Theory and Research*, Beverly Hills, CA: Sage.

_____ (1974). "Symbolic and Instrumental Dimensions of Early Factory Legislation: A Case Study in the Social Origins of Criminal Law." In R. Hood (ed.) *Crime, Criminology and Public Policy*. London: Heineman.

Chambliss, W. & R. Seidman (1982). *Law Order and Power*. Reading MA: Addison-Wesley.

Chandler, A. (1962). *Strategy and Structure*. Cambridge, MA: MIT Press.

Cheit, R.E. (1990). *Setting Safety Standards: Regulation in the Public and Private Sectors*. Berkeley, CA: University of California Press.

Chubb, J.E. & T.M. Moe (1990). *Politics, Markets, and America's Schools*. Washington, DC: Brookings Institute.

Clarke, M. (1990). *Business Crime: Its Nature and Control*. New York, NY: St. Martin's Press.

Cleaves, R.E. IV (1990). "White-Collar Environmental Crime: Emerging Trends in Corporate Criminal Liability." *Maine Bar Journal*, 5:28-35.

Clinard, M.B. (1946). "Criminological Theories of Violations of Wartime Regulations." *American Sociological Review*, 11:258-270.

_____ & P.C. Yeager (1980). *Corporate Crime*. New York, NY: Free Press.

_____ P.C. Yeager, J.M. Brissette, D. Petrashek & E. Harries (1979). *Illegal Corporate Behavior*. Washington, DC: U.S. Government Printing Office.

Coase, R.H. (1960). "The Problem of Social Cost." *Journal of Law and Economics*, 3:1-44.

Coffee, J.C., Jr. (1992). "Paradigms Lost: The Blurring of the Criminal and Civil Law Models—And What Can Be Done About It." *Yale Law Journal*, 101:1875-1892.

_____ (1991). "Does 'Unlawful' Mean 'Criminal'?: Reflections on the Disappearing Tort/Crime Distinction in American Law." *Boston University Law Review*, 71:193.

_____ (1990). "Levy Corporate Fines in Stock, Not Cash." *Wall Street Journal*, March 22:A14.

_____ (1986). Testimony Before the United States Sentencing Commission. June 10.

_____ (1981). "'No Soul to Damn, No Body to Kick:' An Unscandalized Inquiry into the Problem of Corporate Punishment." *Michigan Law Review*, 79:386-459.

_____ (1980). "Making the Punishment Fit the Corporation: The Problem of Finding the Optimal Corporate Criminal Sanction." *Northern Illinois University Law Review*, 3:3-26.

———— (1979-1980). "Corporate Crime and Punishment: A Non-Chicago View of the Economics of Criminal Sanctions." *American Criminal Law Review,* 17:419-478.

———— (1978). "The Repressed Issues of Sentencing: Accountability, Predictability, and Equality in the Era of the Sentencing Commission." *Georgetown Law Journal,* 66:975.

———— (1977). "Beyond the Shut-Eyed Sentry: Toward a Theoretical View of Corporate Misconduct and an Effective Legal Response." *Virginia Law Review,* 63:1099-1278.

———— R. Gruner & C. Stone (1988). "Draft Proposal on Standards for Organizational Probation." *Discussion Materials on Organizational Sanctions.* Washington, DC: United States Sentencing Commission.

———— (1988). "Standards for Organizational Probation: A Proposal to the United States Sentencing Commission." *Whittier Law Review,* 10:77-102.

Cohen, L.E. & M. Felson (1979). "Social Change and Crime Rate Trends: A Routine Activities Approach." *American Sociological Review,* 44:588-607.

Cohen, M.A. (1992). "Environmental Crime and Punishment: Legal/Economic Theory and Empirical Evidence on Enforcement of Federal Environmental Statutes." *Journal of Criminal Law and Criminology,* 82,4:1054-1108.

———— (1991). "Corporate Crime and Punishment: An Update on Sentencing Practice in the Federal Courts, 1988-1990." *Boston University Law Review,* 71:247-280.

———— (1989a). "Corporate Crime and Punishment: A Study of Social Harm and Sentencing Practice in the Federal Courts, 1984-1987." *American Criminal Law Review,* 26:605-660.

———— (1989b). "The Role of Criminal Sanctions in Antitrust Enforcement." *Contemporary Policy Issues,* 7:36-46.

———— (1987). "Optimal Enforcement Strategy to Prevent Oil Spills: An Application of a Principal-Agent Model with Moral Hazard." *Journal of Law and Economics,* 30:23-51.

———— D.T. Scheffman (1989). "The Antitrust Sentencing Guideline: Is the Punishment Worth the Costs?" *American Criminal Law Review,* 27-331.

———— C.C. Ho, E.D. Jones III & L.M. Schleich (1988). "Report to the U.S. Sentencing Commission on Sentencing of Organizations in the Federal Courts, 1984-1987." *Discussion Materials on Organizational Sanctions.* Washington, DC: United States Sentencing Commission.

Coleman, J.S. (1982). *The Asymmetric Society.* Syracuse, NY: Syracuse University Press.

———— (1974). *Power and the Structure of Society.* New York, NY: Norton.

Coleman, J.W. (1987). "Toward an Integrated Theory of White-Collar Crime." *American Journal of Sociology,* 93:406-439.

Comptroller General of the United States (1994). *Government Auditing Standards.* Washington, DC.

Conklin, J. (1977). *Illegal but Not Criminal: Business Crime in America.* Englewood Cliffs, NJ: Prentice-Hall.

Conley, J. (1977). "Is It Time for Corporations to be on the Federal Charter?" *National Journal,* 9:1772-1774.

Cooke, W.N. & F.H. Gautschi III (1981). "OSHA, Plant Safety Programs, and Injury Reduction." *Industrial Relations,* 20:245-247.

Cooter, R. & T. Ulen (1996). *Law and Economics,* Second Edition. Glenview, IL: Scott Foresman.

—————— (1988). *Law and Economics.* Glenview, IL: Scott Foresman.

Cornish, D.B. & R.V.G. Clarke (eds.) (1986). *The Reasoning Criminal: Rational Choice Perspectives on Offending.* New York, NY: Springer-Verlag.

Corporate Crime Reporter (1991). "Interview with Jeffrey Parker, Associate Professor of Law, George Mason University School of Law." November 25:18-21.

—————— (1989). "Interview with Leonard Orland, Professor of Law, University of Connecticut." March 13:11-16.

—————— (1988). "Interview with Professor John C. Coffee, Jr." September 5:11-20.

—————— (1987). "Interview with John Braithwaite, Senior Research Fellow, Australian National University, Canberra, Australia, and Peter N. Grabosky, Senior Criminologist, Australian Institute of Criminology, Phillip, Australia." June, 22:4-10.

Cotterrell, R. (1992). *The Sociology of Law,* Second Edition. London: Butterworth.

Council of the Law Society (1967). "First Memorandum to the Royal Commission on the Penal System in England and Wales." In *Written Evidence from Government Departments: Miscellaneous Bodies and Individual Witnesses,* Vol II. London: HMSO.

Cranston, R. (1979). *Regulating Business: Law and Consumer Agencies.* London: Macmillan.

Cressey, D.R. (1989). "The Poverty of Theory in Corporate Crime Research." In W.S. Laufer & F. Adler (eds.) *Advances in Criminological Theory,* Volume 1. New Brunswick, NJ: Transaction Books.

—————— (1953). *Other People's Money: A Study in the Social Psychology of Embezzlement.* Glencoe, IL: Free Press.

————— (1950). "The Criminal Violation of Financial Trust." *American Sociological Review,* 15:738-743.

Croall, H. (1988). "Mistakes, Accidents and Someone Else's Fault: The Trading Offender in Court." *Journal of Law and Society,* 15:293-315.

Cullen, F.T. & P.J. Dubeck (1985). "The Myth of Corporate Immunity to Deterrence: Ideology and the Creation of the Invincible Criminal." *Federal Probation,* 49,3:3-9.

Cullen, F.T., W.J. Maakestad & G. Cavender (1987). *Corporate Crime Under Attack.* Cincinnati, OH: Anderson Publishing Co.

Curington, W.P. (1988). "Federal Versus State Regulation: The Early Years of OSHA." *Social Science Quarterly,* 69:341-360.

Curran, D.J. (1993). *Dead Laws for Dead Men: The Politics of Federal Coal Mine Health and Safety Legislation.* Pittsburgh, PA: University of Pittsburgh Press.

Curran, J.D. (1986). "Probation for Corporations Under the Sentencing Reform Act." *Santa Clara Law Review,* 26:785-808.

Cyert, R.M. & J.G. March (1963). *A Behavioral Theory of the Firm.* Englewood Cliffs, NJ: Prentice-Hall.

Dawson, S., P. Willman, M. Bamford & A. Clinton (1988). *Safety at Work: The Limits of Self-Regulation.* Cambridge, MA: Cambridge University Press.

DeMott, D.A. (1977). "Reweaving the Corporate Veil: Management Structure and the Control of Corporate Information." *Law and Contemporary Problems,* 41,3:182-221.

Dershowitz, A. (1961). "Increasing Community Control Over Corporate Crime—A Problem in the Law of Sanctions." *Yale Law Journal,* 71:280-306.

DeVos, T. (1985). "Toward More Effective Regulation of Corporate Behavior." In B. Fisse & P.A. French (eds.) *Corrigible Corporations and Unruly Law,* pp. 85-99. San Antonio, TX: Trinity University Press.

DiMaggio, P.J. & W.W. Powell (1983). "The Iron Cage Revisited: Institutional Isomorphism and Collective Rationality in Organizational Fields." *American Sociological Review,* 48:147-160.

DiMento, J.F. (1986). *Environmental Law and American Business: Dilemmas of Compliance.* New York, NY: Plenum Press.

Domhoff, W.G. (1986). "Corporate-Liberal Theory and the Social Security Act: A Chapter in the Sociology of Knowledge." *Politics and Society,* 15:297-329.

————— (1967). *Who Rules America?* Englewood Cliffs, NJ: Prentice-Hall.

Dowie, M. (1977). "Pinto Madness." *Mother Jones,* 2:21.

Downes, A. (1967). *Inside Bureaucracy*. Boston, MA: Little, Brown.

Dunmire, T.D. (1989). "The Problems With Using Common Law Criminal Statutes to Deter Exposure to Chemical Substances in the Workplace." *Northern Kentucky Law Review,* 17:53-81.

Dutzman, J. (1990). "State Criminal Prosecutions: Putting Teeth in the Occupational Safety and Health Act." *George Mason University Law Review,* 12:737-755.

Easterbrook, F.H., W.M. Landes & R.A. Posner (1980). "Contribution Among Antitrust Defendants: A Legal and Economic Analysis." *Journal of Law and Economics,* 23.

Easterbrook, G. (1995). *A Moment on Earth: The Coming Age of Environmental Optimism.* New York, NY: Viking.

Edelman, P.T. (1987). "Corporate Criminal Liability For Homicide: The Need to Punish Both the Corporate Entity and its Officers." *Dickinson Law Review,* 92:193-222.

Elis, L. & S.S. Simpson (1995). "Informal Sanction Threats and Corporate Crime: Additive versus Multiplicative Models." *Journal of Research in Crime and Delinquency,* 32:399-424.

Elkins, J.R. (1976). "Corporations and the Criminal Law: An Uneasy Alliance." *Kentucky Law Journal,* 65:73-129.

Elzinga, K.G. & W. Breit (1976). *The Antitrust Penalties: A Study in Law and Economics.* New Haven, CT: Yale University Press.

Engel, D.L. (1979). "An Approach to Corporate Social Responsibility." *Stanford Law Review,* 32,1:1-98.

Epstein, S., S.L. Brown & C. Pope (1982). *Hazardous Waste in America.* San Francisco, CA: Sierra Club Books.

Ermann, M.D. (forthcoming). "Hiding Hazards." Unpublished manuscript, University of Delaware.

————— (1991). "Ordinary Deadly Decisions: Why People, Organizations, and Events Cause Hazard Concealment." Unpublished Manuscript. University of Delaware.

————— (1986). "How Managers Unintentionally Encourage Corporate Crime." *Business and Society Review,* 59:30-34.

Ermann, M.D. & R.J. Lundman (1992). "Overview." In M.D. Ermann & R.J. Lundman (eds.) *Corporate and Governmental Deviance,* Fourth Edition, pp. 3-43. New York, NY: Oxford University Press.

————— (1987). "Overview." In M.D. Ermann & R.J. Lundman (eds.) *Corporate and Governmental Deviance,* Third Edition, pp. 3-33. New York, NY: Oxford University Press.

————— (1982). *Corporate Deviance*. New York, NY: Holt, Rinehart and Winston.

————— (1978). "Deviant Acts by Complex Organizations: Deviance and Social Control at the Organizational Level of Analysis." *Sociological Quarterly,* 19:55-67.

Etzioni, A. (1988). *The Moral Dimension*. New York, NY: The Free Press.

Farley, J.E. (1990). *Sociology*. Englewood Cliffs, NJ: Prentice-Hall.

Farrier, D. (1990). "Criminal Law and Pollution Control: The Failure of the Environmental Offenses and Penalties Act 1989 [N.S.W.]." *Criminal Law Journal,* 14:317-341.

Field, S. & N. Jörg (1991). "Corporate Liability and Manslaughter: Should We Be Going Dutch?" *Criminal Law Review,* 156-171.

Fiss, O. (1978). *The Civil Rights Injunction*. Bloomington, IN: Indiana University Press.

Fisse, B. (1986). "Sanctions Against Corporations: Economic Efficiency or Legal Efficacy." In W.B. Groves & G. Newman (eds.) *Punishment and Privilege*. New York, NY: Harrow and Heston.

————— (1985). "Sanctions Against Corporations: The Limitations of Fines and the Enterprise of Creating Alternatives." In B. Fisse & P.A. French (eds.) *Corrigible Corporations and Unruly Law*, pp. 137-153. San Antonio, TX: Trinity University Press.

————— (1983). "Reconstructing Corporate Criminal Law: Deterrence, Retribution, Fault, and Sanctions." *Southern California Law Review,* 56:1141-1246.

————— (1978). "The Social Policy of Corporate Criminal Responsibility." *Adelaide Law Review,* 6:361-412.

————— (1973). "Responsibility, Prevention, and Corporate Crime." *New Zealand University Law Review,* 5:250-279.

————— (1971). "The Use of Publicity as a Criminal Sanction Against Business Corporations." *Melbourne University Law Review,* 8,1:1733-1777.

————— & J. Braithwaite (1993). *Corporations, Crime and Accountability*. New York, NY: Cambridge University Press.

————— (1983). *The Impact of Publicity on Corporate Offenders*. Albany, NY: State University of New York Press.

Foerschler, A. (1990). "Corporate Criminal Intent: Toward a Better Understanding of Corporate Misconduct." *California Law Review,* 78:1287-1311.

Fletcher, G. (1978). *Rethinking Criminal Law*. Boston, MA: Little, Brown.

Fligstein, N. (1990). *The Transformation of Corporate Control*. Cambridge, MA: Harvard University Press.

Frank, N. (1993). "Maiming and Killing: Occupational Health Crimes." *Annals of the American Academy of Political and Social Sciences,* 525:107-118.

_____ (1984). "Choosing Between Criminal and Civil Sanctions for Corporate Wrongs." In E. Hochstedler (ed.) *Corporations as Criminals*. Beverly Hills, CA: Sage Publications.

_____ (1983). "From Criminal to Civil Penalties in the History of Health and Safety Laws." *Social Problems,* 30,5:532-544.

_____ & M. Lombness (1988). *Controlling Corporate Illegality*. Cincinnati, OH: Anderson Publishing Co.

French, P.A. (1984). *Collective and Corporate Responsibility*. New York, NY: Columbia University Press.

Friedlander, S.L. (1990). "Using Prior Corporate Convictions to Impeach." *California Law Review,* 78:1313-1339.

Friedman, H.M. (1979). "Some Reflections on the Corporation as a Criminal Defendant." *Notre Dame Lawyer,* 55:173-202.

Friedman, M. (1970). "The Social Responsibility of Business is to Increase its Profits." *New York Times Magazine*, September 13:32-33.

_____ (1962). *Capitalism and Freedom*. Chicago, IL: University of Chicago Press.

Galanter, M. (1974). "Why the 'Haves' Come Out Ahead: Speculations on the Limits of Legal Change." *Law and Society Review,* 9:95-160.

Galbraith, J.K. (1967/1985). *The New Industrial State*, Second Edition. Boston, MA: Houghton Mifflin Company.

_____ (1977). *Organization Design*. Reading, MA: Addison-Wesley.

_____ (1971). *The New Industrial State*, Second Edition. Boston, MA: Houghton Mifflin.

_____ (1956). *American Capitalism: The Concept of Countervailing Power*. Boston, MA: Houghton Mifflin.

Gans, H.J. (1962). *The Urban Villagers: Group and Class in the Life of Italian-Americans*. New York, NY: Free Press.

Garbade, K.D., W.L. Silber & L.J. White (1982). "Market Reaction to the Filing of Antitrust Suits: An Aggregate and Cross-Sectional Analysis." *Review of Economics and Statistics,* 64:686-691.

Gattozzi, L.M. (1986/87). "Charitable Contributions as a Condition of Probation for Convicted Corporations: Using Philanthropy to Combat Corporate Crime." *Case Western Reserve Law Review,* 37:569-588.

Gautschi, F.H., III & T.M. Jones (1987). "Illegal Corporate Behavior and Corporate Board Structure." *Research in Corporate Social Performance and Policy,* 9:93-106.

Geis, G. (1972). "Criminal Penalties for Corporate Criminals." *Criminal Law Bulletin,* 8:377-392.

————— (1967). "The Heavy Electrical Equipment Antitrust Cases of 1961." In R. Quinney & M. Clinard (eds.) *Criminal Behavior Systems.* New York, NY: Holt, Rinehart and Winston.

Genn, H. (1993). "Business Responses to the Regulation of Health and Safety in England." *Law and Policy,* 15,3:219-234.

Geraghty, J.A. (1979). "Structural Crime and Institutional Rehabilitation: A New Approach to Corporate Sentencing." *Yale Law Journal,* 89:353-375.

Gerber, J. (1990). "Enforced Self-Regulation in the Infant Formula Industry: A Radical Extension of an 'Impractical' Proposal." *Social Justice,* 17:98-112.

Gierke, O. (1887). *Die Genossenschaftstheorie und die deutsche Rechtsprechung,* Berlin: Weidmannsche Buchhandlung.

Glasbeek, H.J. (1984). "Why Corporate Deviance is Not Treated as a Crime—The Need to Make 'Profits' a Dirty Word." *Osgoode Hall Law Journal,* 22,3:393-439.

Goff, C. & C. Reasons (1978). *Corporate Crime in Canada.* Scarborough, Ontario: Prentice-Hall.

Goffman, E. (1973). *The Presentation of Self in Everyday Life.* Woodstock, NY: Overlook Press.

Gold, A.R. (1991). "Increasingly, Prison Term is the Price for Polluters." *The New York Times,* Friday, Feb. 15.

Goldberg A.M. (1991). "Corporate Officer Liability For Federal Environmental Statute Violations." *Boston College Environmental Affairs Law Review,* 18:357-379.

Gottfredson, M.R. & T. Hirschi (1990). *A General Theory of Crime.* Stanford, CA: Stanford University.

Grabosky, P. & J. Braithwaite (1986). *Of Manners Gentle.* Melbourne: Oxford University Press.

Gramsci, A. (1977). *Selections from the Political Writings: 1910-1920.* New York, NY: International Publishers.

_____ (1971). *Selections from the Prison Notebooks*. New York, NY: International Publishers.

Gricar, B.G. (1983). "A Primary Theory of Compliance with OSHA Regulation." In L.E. Preston (ed.) *Research in Corporate Social Performance and Policy* Vol. 5, Greenwich, CT: JAI Press.

Griffin, C.L. (1989). "Corporate Scienter Under the Securities Exchange Act of 1934." *Brigham Young University Law Review,* 1227-1259.

Griffith, W.B. & R.S. Goldfarb (1991). "Amending the Economist 'Rational Egoist' Model to Include Moral Values and Norms." In K.J. Koford & J.B. Miller (eds.) *Social Norms and Economic Institutions.* Ann Arbor, MI: University of Michigan Press.

Gruner, R. (1994a). *Corporate Crime and Sentencing.* Charlottesville, VA: Michie.

_____ (1994b). "Towards an Organizational Jurisprudence: Transforming Corporate Criminal Law Through Federal Sentencing Reform." *Arizona Law Review,* 36:407-472.

_____ (1993). "Beyond Fines: Innovative Corporate Sentences Under Federal Sentencing Guidelines." *Washington University Law Quarterly,* 71,2:261-328.

_____ (1992). "Just Punishment and Adequate Deterrence for Organizational Misconduct: Scaling Economic Penalties Under the New Corporate Sentencing Guidelines." *Southern California Law Review,* 66:225-288.

_____ (1990). "Corporate Criminals." *National Law Journal,* April 2:13-14.

_____ (1988). "To Let the Punishment Fit the Organization: Sanctioning Corporate Offenders Through Corporate Probation." *American Journal of Criminal Law,* 16:1-106.

Gunningham, N. (1987). "Negotiated Non-Compliance: A Case Study of Regulatory Failure." *Law and Policy,* 9,1:69-95.

_____ (1974). *Pollution, Social Interest and the Law.* London: Martin Robertson.

Habermas, J. (1973). *Legitimation Crisis.* Translated by T. McCarthy. Boston, MA: Beacon Press.

Hagan, J. (1989). *Structural Criminology: Social Structure Crime and Punishment.* New Brunswick, NJ: Rutgers University.

_____ (1982). "The Corporate Advantage: A Study of the Involvement of Corporate and Individual Victims in a Criminal Justice System." *Social Forces,* 60:993-1032.

Hagan, J., I.H. Nagel-Bernstein & C. Albonetti (1980). "Differential Sentencing of White-Collar Offenders." *American Sociological Review,* 45:802-820.

Hagan, J. & P. Parker (1985). "White-Collar Crime and Punishment." *American Sociological Review,* 50:302-316.

Hall, J. (1960). *General Principles of Criminal Law*, Second Edition. Chicago, IL: LaSalle Extension University.

Hall, S., C. Critcher, T. Jefferson, J. Clarke & B. Roberts (1978). *Policing the Crisis: Mugging, the State, and Law and Order*. London: Macmillan.

Hamilton, L.C. (1985). "Who Cares About Water Pollution? Opinions in a Small-Town Crisis." *Sociological Inquiry,* 55:170-179.

Hans, V.P. & W.S. Lofquist (1992). "Jurors' Judgments of Business Liability in Tort Cases: Implications for the Litigation Explosion Debate." *Law & Society Review,* 26,1:85-115.

Harring, S. & L.M. McMullen (1975). "The Buffalo Police 1872-1900: Labor Unrest, Political Power and the Creation of the Police Institution." *Crime and Social Justice* 4:5-15.

Harris, C., P.O. Cavanaugh & R.L. Zisk (1988). "Criminal Liability For Violations of Federal Hazardous Waste Law: The 'Knowledge' of Corporations and Their Executives." *Wake Forest Law Review,* 23:203-236.

Harris, R. & S.M. Milkis (1989). *The Politics of Regulatory Change*. New York, NY: Oxford University Press.

Hart, H.L.A. (1968). *Punishment and Responsibility*. Oxford: Clarendon.

Hartung, F.E. (1950). "White-Collar Offenses in the Wholesale Meat Industry in Detroit." *American Journal of Sociology,* 56:25-34.

Harvard Law Review (1979). "Developments in the Law—Corporate Crime: Regulating Corporate Behavior Through Criminal Sanctions." 92:1227-1375.

Hawkins, K. (1992). *The Regulation of Occupational Health and Safety: A Socio-Legal Perspective*. Report to the Health and Safety Executive. London.

———— (1984). *Environment and Enforcement: Regulation and the Social Definition of Pollution*. New York, NY: Oxford University Press.

———— & B.M. Hutter (1993). "The Response of Business to Social Regulation in England and Wales: An Enforcement Perspective." *Law and Policy,* 15,3:199-218.

———— & J.M. Thomas (1989). "Making Policy in Regulatory Bureaucracies." In K. Hawkins & J.M. Thomas (eds.) *Making Regulatory Policy*. Pittsburgh, PA: University of Pittsburgh Press.

Heider, J. (1991). Vice President and General Counsel, B.F. Goodrich, and Attorney, Business Roundtable. Interview with W.S. Lofquist. July 16.

Hembroff, L.A. (1987). "The Seriousness of Acts and Social Contexts: A Test of Black's Theory of the Behavior of Law." *American Journal of Sociology,* 93:322-347.

Henry, F. (1989). "Drug Testing in the Pharmaceutical Industry: Its Faults and Its Victims." In E.C. Viano (ed.) *Crime and Its Victims: International Research and Public Policy Issues,* pp. 257-266. New York, NY: Hemisphere Publishing.

_____ (1982). "Capitalism, Capital Accumulation, and Crime." *Crime and Social Justice,* 9:79-86.

Henry, S. (1985). "Community Justice, Capitalist Society, and Human Agency: The Dialectics of Collective Law in the Cooperative." *Law and Society Review,* 19:303-327.

_____ & D. Milovanovic (1991). "Constitutive Criminology: The Maturation of Critical Theory." *Criminology,* 29:293-316.

Hill, C.W.L., P.C. Kelley, B.R. Agle, M.A. Hitt & R.E. Hoskisson (1993). "An Empirical Examination of the Causes of Corporate Wrongdoing in the United States." *Human Relations,* 45:1055.

Hindelang, M.J., M. Gottfredson & J. Garofalo (1978). *Victims of Personal Crime: An Emperical Foundation for a Theory of Personal Victimization.* Cambridge, MA: Ballinger.

Hirschi, T. & M. Gottfredson (1987). "Causes of White-Collar Crime." *Criminology,* 25, 4:949-974.

Holmes, O. (1963). *The Common Law,* M. Howe (ed.). Boston, MA: Little, Brown.

Hopkins, A. (1980). "Controlling Corporate Deviance." *Criminology,* 18,2:198-214.

Horowitz, D. (1977). *The Courts and Social Policy.* Washington, DC: Brookings Institute.

Horwitz, M.J. (1980). "Law and Economics: Science or Politics?" *Hofstra Law Review,* 8:905-912.

Howard, P.K. (1994). *The Death of Common Sense: How Law is Suffocating America.* New York, NY: Random House.

Hughes, E.C. (1962). "Good People and Dirty Work." *Social Problems,* 10:3-10.

Humphreys, S.L. (1990). "An Enemy of the People: Prosecuting the Corporate Polluter as a Common Law Criminal." *The American University Law Review,* 39:311-354.

Hutter, B.M. (1997). *Compliance: Interpretation in Health, Safety and Environmental Regulation.* Oxford: Clarendon Press.

_____ (1993). "Regulating Employers and Employees: Health and Safety in the Workplace." *Journal of Law and Society,* 20,4:452-470.

————— (1988). *The Reasonable Arm of the Law?: The Law Enforcement Procedures of Environmental Health Officers*. Oxford: Clarendon Press.

Hutter, B.M. & S. Lloyd-Bostock (1990). "The Power of Accidents: The Social and Psychological Impact of Accidents and the Enforcement of Safety Regulations." *British Journal of Criminology* 30,4:409-422.

Hutter, B.M. & P. Sorenson (1993). "Business Adaptation to Legal Regulation." *Law and Policy,* 15,3:169-178.

Jackall, R. (1988). *Moral Mazes: The World of Corporate Managers*. New York, NY: Oxford University Press.

Jackson, R.M. (1967). *Enforcing the Law*. London: Macmillan.

Jacobs, D. (1988). "Corporate Economic Power and the State: A Longitudinal Assessment of Two Explanations." *American Journal of Sociology,* 93:852-881.

Jamieson, H. (1985). "Persuasion or Punishment: The Enforcement of Health and Safety at Work Legislation by the British Factory Inspectorate." M. Litt. dissertation, University of Oxford.

Jamieson, K.M. (1994). *The Organization of Corporate Crime: Dynamics of Antitrust Violations*. Thousand Oaks, CA: Sage.

Jemison, D.B., S.B. Sitkin (1986). "Corporate Acquisitions: A Process Perspective." *Academy of Management Review*, 11:145-163.

Jones, S.D. (1990/91). "State Prosecutions for Safety-Related Crimes in the Workplace: Can D.A.'s Succeed Where OSHA Failed?" *Kentucky Law Journal,* 79:139-158.

Jones, K. (1982). *Law and Economy*. New York, NY: Academic Press.

Judson, F.N. (1906). "The Control of Corporations." *The Green Bag,* 18,12:662-666.

Justice (1980). *Breaking the Rules*. London: Justice.

Kadish, S.H. (1963). "Some Observations on the Use of Criminal Sanctions in Enforcing Economic Regulations." *University of Chicago Law Review,* 30,3:423-449.

Kagan, R.A. (1994). "Regulatory Enforcement." In D.H. Rosenbloom & R.D. Schwartz (eds.) *Handbook of Regulation and Administrative Law*. New York, NY: Marcel Dekker.

Kagan, R.A. & J.T. Scholz (1984). "The 'Criminology of the Corporation' and Regulatory Enforcement Strategies." In K. Hawkins & J.M. Thomas (eds.) *Enforcing Regulation*. Boston, MA: Kluwer-Nijhoff.

Karpoff, J.M. (1991). "Reputation Disciplines Corporate Crimes, Too (Sometimes Better than Criminal Penalties)." Paper Presented at the Cato Institute Symposium on Corporate Sentencing, Washington DC.

————— & J.R. Lott, Jr. (1993). "The Reputational Penalty Firms Bear from Committing Criminal Fraud." *Journal of Law and Economics,* 36:757.

Katz, J. (1980). "The Social Movement Against White-Collar Crime." In E. Bittner & S.L. Messinger (eds.) *Criminology Review Yearbook.* Volume 2. Beverly Hills, CA: Sage.

Katzman, R.A. (1980). "Judicial Intervention and Organization Theory: Changing Bureaucratic Behavior and Policy." *Yale Law Journal,* 89,3:513-537.

Kauzlarich, D. & R.C. Kramer (1993). "State-Corporate Crime in the U.S. Nuclear Weapons Production Complex." *Journal of Human Justice,* 5:4-28.

Kelley, D. (1991). "Worker Participation and Economic Democracy: The Potential and Limitation of Two Separate Movements in Reducing Corporate and Occupational Crime." Paper presented at the American Society of Criminology Annual Meetings. San Francisco, CA.

Kelman, H.C. & V.L. Hamilton (1989). *Crimes of Obedience: Toward a Social Psychology of Authority and Responsibility.* New Haven, CT: Yale University Press.

Kelman, M.G. (1983). "Misunderstanding Social Life: A Critique of the Core Premises of 'Law and Economics.'" *Journal of Legal Education,* 33:274-284.

Kelman, S. (1981). *Regulating America, Regulating Sweden: A Comparative Study of Occupational Safety and Health Policy.* Cambridge, MA: MIT Press.

Kennedy, C. (1985). "Criminal Sentences for Corporations: Alternative Fining Mechanisms." *California Law Review,* 443-482.

King, R. (1986). *The State in Modern Society.* London: Macmillan.

Kniesner, T.J. & J.D. Leeth (1995). "Abolishing OSHA." *Regulation,* 4:46-56.

Kolko, G. (1963). *The Triumph of Conservatism: A Reinterpretation of American History, 1900-1916.* New York, NY: Free Press of Glencoe.

Koprowicz, K.M. (1986). "Corporate Criminal Liability For Workplace Hazards: A Viable Option for Enforcing Workplace Safety?" *Brooklyn Law Review,* 52:183-227.

Korpics, J.J. (1991). "United States v. Protex Industries, Inc.: Corporate Criminal Liability Under RCRA's 'Knowing Endangerment' Provision." *Houston Law Review,* 28:449-486.

Kraakman, R.H. (1984). "Corporate Liability Strategies and the Costs of Legal Controls." *Yale Law Journal,* 93:857-898.

Kramer, R.C. (1992). "The Space Shuttle Challenger Explosion: A Case Study of State-Corporate Crime." In K. Schlegel & D. Weisburd (eds.) *White Collar Crime Reconsidered,* pp. 214-243. Boston, MA: Northeastern University Press.

————— (1989). "Criminologists and the Social Movement Against Corporate Crime." *Social Justice,* 16:146-164.

————— (1987). "The Space Shuttle Disaster as Organizational Deviance." Paper presented at the Society for the Study of Social Problems Annual Meetings, Chicago.

————— & R. Michalowski (1990). "State-Corporate Crime." Paper presented at the Annual Meetings of the American Society of Criminology.

Kriesberg, S.M. (1976). "Decisionmaking Models and the Control of Corporate Crime." *Yale Law Journal,* 85,8:1091-1129.

Kruttschnitt, C. (1985). "Are Businesses Treated Differently? A Comparison of the Individual Victim and the Corporate Victim in the Criminal Courtroom." *Sociological Inquiry,* 55:225-238.

Kunen, J. (1994). *Reckless Disregard.* New York, NY: Simon and Schuster.

Kynes, J.H. & S.C. Markman (1989). "Corporate Internal Investigations for Federal Criminal Wrongdoing." *The Florida Bar Journal,* 63:57-59.

LaFave W. & J. Israel (1992). *Criminal Procedure,* Second Edition. St. Paul, MN: West.

LaFave W. & A. Scott (1986). *Criminal Law,* Second Edition. St. Paul, MN: West.

Laitinen, A. (1991). "The Problems of Controlling Organizational Crime." Paper presented at the American Society of Criminology Annual Meetings. San Francisco, CA.

Landes, W.M. & R.A. Posner (1994). "The Influence of Economics on Law: A Quantitative Study." *Journal of Law and Economics,* 36:385-424.

Lansing, P. & D. Hatfield (1985). "Corporate Control Through the Criminal System— An Alternative Proposal." *Journal of Business Ethics,* 4:409-414.

Laurell, A.C. (1989). "The Role of Union Democracy in the Struggle for Workers' Health in Mexico." *International Journal of Health Services,* 19:279-293.

Lederman, E. (1985). "Criminal Law, Perpetrator and Corporation: Rethinking a Complex Triangle." *Journal of Criminal Law and Criminology,* 76,2:285-340.

Leigh, L.H. (1982). "The Criminal Liability of Corporations and Other Groups: A Comparative View. *Michigan Law Review,* 80:1508-1528.

Levin, M.L. (1984). "Corporate Probation Conditions: Judicial Creativity or Abuse of Discretion?" *Fordham Law Review,* 52:637-662.

Lindblom, C.E. (1977). *Politics and Markets.* New York, NY: Basic Books.

Lipset, S.M. & W. Schneider (1987). *The Confidence Gap: Business, Labor, and Government in the Public Mind.* Baltimore, MD: Johns Hopkins University Press.

Liska, A.A., M.B. Chamlin & M.D. Reed (1985). "Testing the Economic Production and Conflict Models of Crime Control." *Social Forces,* 64:119-138.

Lofquist, W.S. (1993a). "Organizational Probation and the U.S. Sentencing Commission." *Annals of the American Academy of Political and Social Science,* 525:157-169.

———— (1993b). "Legislating Organizational Probation: State Capacity, Business Power, and Corporate Crime Control." *Law & Society Review,* 27,4:741-783.

———— (1992). "Crafting Corporate Crime Controls: The Development of Organizational Probation and its Implications for Criminology." Ph.D. dissertation. University of Delaware.

Lorsch, J. & P. Lawrence (eds.) (1970). *Studies in Organization Design.* Homewood, IL: Irwin.

Los Angeles Times (1979). "Drive to Curb Big Business Launched." December 13: C19.

Lott, J.R., Jr. (1992). "An Attempt at Measuring the Total Monetary Penalty from Drug Convictions: The Importance of an Individual's Reputation." *Journal of Legal Studies,* 21:159-187.

———— (1991). "Will Consumers Be Haunted by the U.S. Sentencing Commission Corporate Guidelines?" Paper presented at the Cato Institute Symposium on Corporate Sanctioning. Washington, DC.

Lynxwiler, J., N. Shover & D.A. Clelland (1983). "The Organization and Impact of Inspector Discretion in a Regulatory Bureaucracy." *Social Problems,* 30,4:425-436.

Maakestad, W.F. (1990). "Corporate Homicide." *The New Law Journal,* 140:356-357.

Macey, J.R. (1991). "Agency Theory and the Criminal Liability of Organizations." *Boston University Law Review,* 71,2:315-340.

MacLean, B.D. (1986). "Critical Criminology and Some Limitations of Traditional Inquiry." In B.D. MacLean (ed.) *The Political Economy of Crime: Readings for a Critical Criminology,* pp. 1-20. Toronto, CN: Prentice-Hall.

Magat, W.A. & W.K. Viscusi (1990). "Effectiveness of the EPA's Regulatory Enforcement: The Case of Industrial Effluent Standards" *Journal of Law and Economics,* 33:331-360.

Magnuson, J.C. & G.C. Leviton (1987). "Policy Considerations in Corporate Criminal Prosecutions After People v. Film Recovery Systems, Inc." *Notre Dame Law Review,* 62:913-939.

Makkai, T. & J. Braithwaite (1994). "The Dialectics of Corporate Deterrence." *Journal of Research in Crime and Delinquency,* 31:347-373.

Mann, K. (1992). "Punitive Civil Sanctions: The Middleground Between Criminal and Civil Law," *Yale Law Journal,* 101:1795-1802.

Manning, P.K. (1977). *Police Work: The Social Organisation of Policing*. Cambridge, MA: M.I.T. Press.

March, J.G. & H.A. Simon (1963). *Organizations*. New York, NY: John Wiley & Sons.

Marsh, B. (1994). "Chance of Getting Hurt Is Generally Far Higher At Smaller Companies." *The Wall Street Journal*, Feb. 3, 1994, A1,7.

Martin, W.F. & G.C. Lodge (1975). "Our Society in 1985—Business May Not Like It." *Harvard Business Review,* 53,6:143-148.

Mashaw, J.L. & D.L. Harfst (1990). *The Struggle for Auto Safety*. Cambridge, MA: Harvard University Press.

Matthews, M.C. (1989). *Strategic Interventions in Organizations: Resolving Ethical Dilemmas*. Newbury Park, CA: Sage Publications.

_____ (1984). "Corporate Crime: Internal vs. External Regulation." Ph.D. dissertation, University of California, Santa Barbara.

Matthews, R. (1992). "Replacing 'Broken Windows:' Crime, Incivilities and Urban Change." In R. Matthews & J. Young (eds.) *Issues in Realist Criminology*, pp. 19-50. Newbury Park, CA: Sage.

McBarnet, D. (1992). "Legitimate Rackets: Tax Evasion, Tax Avoidance, and the Boundaries of Legality." *Journal of Human Justice,* 3:56-74.

McCormick, A.E. (1977). "Rule Enforcement and Moral Indignation: Some Observations of the Effects of Criminal Anti-Trust Convictions upon Societal Reaction Processes." *Social Problems,* 25:30-39.

McDonnell, X.K. (1989). "Criminal Liability for Workplace Accidents." *New England Law Review,* 24:293-331.

McLelland, D. (1979). *Marxism after Marx*. New York, NY: Harper and Row.

McVisk, W. (1978). "Toward a Rational Theory of Criminal Liability for the Corporate Executive." *Journal of Criminal Law & Criminology,* 69,1:75-91.

Merryman, J. (1985). *The Civil Law Tradition*, Second Edition. Stanford, CA: Stanford University Press.

Messner, S.F. & R. Rosenfeld (1994). *Crime and the American Dream*. Belmont, CA: Wadsworth Publishing Co.

Metzger, M.B. (1984). "Corporate Criminal Liability for Defective Products: Policies, Problems, and Prospects." *Georgetown Law Journal,* 73,1:1-88.

_____ & C.R. Schwenk (1990). "Decision Making Models, Devil's Advocacy, and the Control of Corporate Crime." *American Business Law Journal,* 28:323-377.

Michalowski, R.J. & R.C. Kramer (1987). "The Space Between Laws: The Problem of Corporate Crime in a Transnational Context." *Social Problems,* 34:34-53.

Miester. D.J., Jr. (1990). "Criminal Liability For Corporations That Kill." *Tulane Law Review,* 64:919-948.

Miliband, R. (1969). *The State in Capitalist Society.* New York, NY: Basic Books.

Mills, C.W. (1956). *The Power Elite.* New York, NY: Oxford University.

Milne, R.A. (1988/89). "The Mens Rea Requirements of the Federal Environmental Statutes: Strict Criminal Liability in Substance but Not Form." *Buffalo Law Review,* 37:307-336.

Mitroff, I. & R. Manson (1980). "Structuring Ill-Structured Policy Issues: Further Explorations in the Methodology for Messy Problems." *Strategic Management Journal,* 1:331.

Mokhiber, R. (1988). *Corporate Crime and Violence.* San Francisco, CA: Sierra Club Books.

Moore, C.A. (1987). "Taming the Giant Corporation: Some Cautionary Notes on the Deterrability of Corporate Crime." *Crime & Delinquency,* 33,2:379-402.

Morris, N. (1974). *The Future of Imprisonment.* Chicago, IL: University of Chicago Press.

Mouritsen, J. (1994). "Rationality, Institutions and Decision Making: Reflections on March and Olsen's Rediscovering Institutions." *Accounting, Organizations, and Society,* 19:193-211.

Mueller, G. (1957). "Mens Rea and the Corporation." *University of Pittsburgh Law Review,* 19:21-50.

M.V. Herald of Free Enterprise (1987). Report of the (Sheen) Court, No. 8074, Department of Transport (UK), July.

Nader, L. (ed.) (1980). *No Access to Law: Alternatives to the American Judicial System.* New York, NY: Academic Press.

Nader, R. & M.J. Green (eds.) (1973). *Corporate Power in America.* New York, NY: Grossman.

———— & J. Seligman (1976). *Taming the Giant Corporation.* New York, NY: Norton.

Nagin, D.S. & R. Paternoster (1994). "Personal Capital and Social Control: The Deterrence Implications of a Theory of Individual Differences in Criminal Offending," *Criminology,* 32:581-606.

National Commission on Reform of Federal Criminal Laws (1971). *National Commission on Reform of Federal Criminal Laws Final Report: A Proposed New Federal Criminal Code.* Chapters 30-33. Washington, DC: Government Printing Office.

————— (1970). *Working Papers of the National Commission on Reform of Federal Criminal Laws*. Two Volumes. Washington, DC: Government Printing Office.

National Traumatic Occupational Fatality Project (1990). *Fatal Occupational Injuries in the United States, 1980 Through 1985*. Washington DC: U.S. Department of Labor.

Needleman, M.L. & C. Needleman (1979). "Organizational Crime: Two Models of Criminogenesis." *Sociological Quarterly,* 20:517-528.

Nelkin, D. (1994). "White-Collar Crime." In M. Maguire, R. Morgan & R. Reiner (eds.) *The Oxford Handbook of Criminology.*. Oxford: Oxford University Press.

Newman, D.J. (1958). "White-Collar Crime." *Law and Contemporary Problems,* 23:735-753.

Newman, G. (1983). *Just and Painful: A Case of Corporal Punishment for Criminals*. London: Macmillan.

Nichols, L.T. & A.F. Buono (1986). "Accounting for Corporate Deviance: Strategic Uses of Cultural Shields." Paper presented at 46th Annual Meeting of the Academy of Management, Chicago.

Nichols, T. (1990). "Industrial Safety in Britain and the 1974 Health and Safety at Work Act: The Case of Manufacturing." *International Journal of the Sociology of Law,* 18:317-342.

Niekamp, T.J. (1987). "Individual Liability of Corporate Officers, Directors, and Shareholders for Violations of Environmental Laws." *Ohio Northern University Law Review,* 14:379-391.

O'Connor, J. (1973). *The Fiscal Crisis of the State*. New York, NY: St. Martin's Press.

Office of Technological Assesment (1990). *Neurotoxicity: Identifying and Controlling Poisons in the Nervous Systems*. Washington, DC: U.S. Government Printing Office.

Ogus, A. (1994). *Regulation: Legal Form and Economic Theory*. Oxford: Clarendon Press.

Olsen, P. (1992). *Six Cultures of Regulation*. Copenhagen: Handelshøjskolen 1 København.

Ordeshook, P. (1986). *Game Theory and Political Theory: An Introduction*. Cambridge, MA: Cambridge University Press.

Orland, L. (1993). "Beyond Organizational Guidelines: Toward a Model Federal Corporate Criminal Code." *Washington University Law Quarterly,* 71:357-373.

————— (1980). "Reflections on Corporate Crime: Law in Search of Scholarship." *American Criminal Law Review,* 17,4:501-520.

Packer, H. (1968). *The Limits of the Criminal Sanction*. Stanford, CA: Stanford University Press.

Panitch, L. (1980). "Recent Theorizations of Corporatism: Reflections on a Growth Industry." *British Journal of Sociology,* 31,2:159-187.

Parker, J.S. (1996). "Doctrine for Destruction: The Case of Corporate Criminal Liability." *Managerial and Decision Economics,* 17:381-398.

_____ (1993). "The Economics of Mens Rea." *Virginia Law Review*, 79:741-811.

_____ (1993). "Rules Without . . .: Some Critical Reflections on the Federal Corporate Sentencing Guidelines." *Washington University Law Quarterly,* 71,2:397-442.

_____ (1991). "Doctrine for Destruction: The Case of Corporate Criminal Liability." Paper presented at the Cato Institute Conference on Corporate Sentencing, October 31.

_____ (1989). "Criminal Sentencing Policy for Organizations: The Unifying Approach of Optimal Penalties." *American Criminal Law Review,* 26:513-604.

_____ (1988). "Criminal Sentencing Policy for Organizations." *Discussion Materials on Organizational Sanctions*. Washington, DC: United States Sentencing Commission.

Passas, N. & D. Nelken (1993). "The Thin Line Between Legitimate and Criminal Enterprises: Subsidy Frauds in the European Community." *Crime, Law and Social Change,* 19:223-243.

Paternoster, R. (1987). "The Deterrent Effect of the Perceived Certainty and Severity of Punishment: A Review of the Evidence and Issues." *Justice Quarterly,* 4:173-217.

Paternoster, R., L.E. Saltzman, G.P. Waldo & T.G. Chiricos (1983). "Perceived Risk and Social Control: Do Sanctions Really Deter?" *Law & Society Review,* 17:457-479.

Paternoster, R. & S. Simpson (1993). "A Rational Choice Theory of Corporate Crime." In R.V. Clarke & M. Felson (eds.) *Routine Activity and Rational Choice: Advances in Criminological Theory,* Vol. 5, pp. 37-58. New Brunswick, NJ: Transaction Books.

Paulus, I. (1974). *The Search for Pure Food*. London: Martin Robertson.

Pearce, F. (1993). "Corporate Rationality as Corporate Crime." *Studies in Political Economy,* 40:135-162.

_____ & S. Tombs (1992). "Realism and Corporate Crime." In R. Matthews & J. Young (eds.) *Issues in Realist Criminology,* pp. 70-101. Newbury Park, CA: Sage.

_____ (1990). "Ideology, Hegemony, and Empiricism: Compliance Theories of Regulation." *British Journal of Criminology,* 30:423-443.

Pepinsky, H. (1974). "From White Collar Crime to Exploitation: Redefinition of a Field." *Journal of Criminal Law and Criminology,* 65:225-233.

Perry, S. & J. Dawson (1985). *Nightmare: Women and the Dalkon Shield.* New York, NY: Macmillan.

Phillips, K. (1990). *The Politics of Rich and Poor.* New York, NY: Random House.

Piliavin, T. & S. Briar (1964). "Police Encounters with Juveniles." *American Sociological Review,* 70:206-214.

Piven, F.F. & R. Cloward (1972/1993). *Regulating the Poor: The Functions of Public Welfare.* New York, NY: Vintage.

Polinsky, A.M. & S. Shavell (1992). "Enforcement Costs and the Optimal Magnitude and Probability of Fines." *Journal of Law & Economics,* 35:133-148.

Pontell, H.N. & K. Calavita (1993). "White-Collar Crime in the Savings and Loan Scandal." *Annals of the American Academy of Political and Social Science,* 525:31-45.

Porter, R.H. (1990). "Voluntary Disclosures to Federal Agencies: Their Impact on the Ability of Corporations to Protect from Discovery Materials Developed During the Course of Internal Investigations." *Catholic University Law Review,* 39:1007-1033.

Posner, R.A. (1995). *Aging and Old Age.* Cambridge, MA: Harvard University Press.

————— (1993). *Sex and Reason.* Cambridge, MA: Harvard University Press.

————— (1992). *Economic Analysis of Law,* Fourth Edition. Boston, MA: Little, Brown.

————— (1990). *The Problems of Jurisprudence.* Cambridge, MA: Harvard University Press.

————— (1985). "An Economic Theory of the Criminal Law." *Columbia Law Review,* 85,6:1193-1231.

————— (1980). "Optimal Sentence for White-Collar Criminals." *American Criminal Law Review,* 17:409-418.

Poulantzas, N. (1975). *Political Power and Social Classes.* London: New Left Books.

Poveda, T.G. (1992). "White-Collar Crime and the Justice Department: The Institutionalization of a Concept." *Crime, Law and Social Change,* 17:235-251.

Punch, M. (1990). "Business Crime in America and Europe: A Comparison of Control, Compliance, and Sanctions." Paper presented at American Society of Criminology Annual Meetings. Baltimore, MD.

Quinney, R. (1980). *Class, State and Crime.* New York, NY: Longmans.

_____ (1977a). *Class, State, and Crime*. Boston, MA: Little, Brown.

_____ (1977b). "The Study of White-Collar Crime: Toward a Reorientation in Theory and Research." In G. Geis and R.F. Meier (eds.) *White Collar Crime*, pp. 283-295. New York, NY: Free Press.

_____ (1974a). *Critique of Legal Order*. New York, NY: David McKay Company.

_____ (1974b). *Criminal Justice in America*. Boston, MA: Little, Brown.

Rabe, G.A. & M.D. Ermann (1995). "Corporate Concealment of Tobacco Hazards: Changing Motives and Historical Contexts." *Deviant Behavior*, 16:223-244.

_____ (1992). "Why Corporations Hide Smoking Hazards: Using 'Reverse Culture Lag' to Explain Product Hazard Concealment." Paper presented at the American Society of Criminology Annual Meetings. New Orleans, LA.

Rakoff, J.S., L.R. Blumkin & R.A. Sauber (1993). *Corporate Sentencing Guidelines: Compliance and Mitigation*. New York, NY: Law Journal Seminars-Press.

Rapson, R.R. (1991). "Mens Rea Requirements Under CERCLA: Implications For Corporate Directors, Officers and Employees." *Santa Clara Computer and High-Technology Law Journal,* 6:377-405.

Reasons, C., L. Ross & C. Patterson (1981). *Assault on the Worker*. Toronto, CN: Butterworth.

Rees, J. (1988). *Reforming the Workplace: A Study of Self-Regulation in Occupational Safety*. Philadelphia, PA: University of Pennsylvania Press.

Reich, M.R. (1991). *Toxic Politics: Responding to Chemical Disasters*. Ithaca, NY: Cornell University Press.

Reich, R.B. (1981). "Regulation by Confrontation or Negotiation?" *Harvard Business Review,* May-June:82-93.

Reichman, N. (1993). "Insider Trading" In M. Tonry & A.J. Reiss, Jr. *Beyond the Law: Crime in Complex Organizations*, pp. 55-96. Chicago, IL: University of Chicago Press.

Reilly, D.J. (1987). "Murder, Inc.: The Criminal Liability of Corporations for Homicide." *Seton Hall Law Review,* 18:378-404.

Reiner, I. & J. Chatten-Brown (1989). "When it is Not an Accident, but a Crime: Prosecutors Get Tough with OSHA Violations." *Northern Kentucky Law Review,* 17:83-103.

Reiss, A. (1984). "Selecting Strategies of Social Control Over Organisational Life." In K. Hawkins & J. Thomas (eds.) *Enforcing Regulation*. Boston, MA: Kluwer-Nijhoff.

Reiss, A.J., Jr. & M. Tonry (1993). "Organizational Crime." In M. Tonry & A.J. Reiss, Jr. (eds.) *Beyond the Law: Crime in Complex Organizations,* pp. 1-10. Chicago, IL: University of Chicago Press.

Ribstein, L. & P. Letsou (1995). *Business Associations,* Second Edition. New York, NY: Matthew Bender.

Richardson, G.M., A.I. Ogus & P. Burrows (1983). *Policing Pollution: A Study of Regulation and Enforcement.* Oxford: Oxford University Press.

Richberg, D.R. (1907). "The Imprisonment of Criminal Corporations." *The Green Bag,* 19,3:156-162.

————— (1906). "Imprisonment of Corporations." *The Green Bag,* 18,4:253-254.

Roberts, C. (1991). "Corporations Plan for Sentencing Guidelines." *LA Daily Journal,* Nov. 1, 1991:1.

Robinson, J.C. (1988). "Labor Union Involvement in Occupational Safety and Health, 1957-1987." *Journal of Health Politics, Policy and Law,* 13:453-468.

Rock, P. (1990). *Helping Victims of Crime.* Oxford: Clarendon Press.

————— (1986). *A View from the Shadows.* Oxford: Clarendon Press.

Ross, I. (1980). "How Lawless are Big Companies." *Fortune,* December 1:57-64.

Ross, J. & B.M. Staw (1986). "Expo 66: An Escalation Prototype." *Administrative Science Quarterly,* 31:274-297.

Rothschild, J. & R. Russell (1986). "Alternatives to Bureaucracy: Democratic Participation in the Economy." *Annual Review of Sociology,* 12:307-328.

Rothschild-Whitt, J. (1984). "Worker Ownership: Collective Responses to an Elite-Generated Crisis." *Research in Social Movements, Conflict and Change,* 6:167-194.

Rourke, N. (1990). "The Corporation as Defendant: Comments on the Proposed Sentencing Guidelines for Organizations." Paper submitted to the United States Sentencing Commission.

Rush, F.L., Jr. (1986). "Corporate Probation: Invasive Techniques for Restructuring Institutional Behavior." *Suffolk University Law Review,* 21:33-89.

Ryan, M. (1994). "Agency in Health Care: Lessons for Economists from Sociologists." *American Journal of Economics and Sociology,* 53:207-217.

Sampson, R. & J.H. Laub (1993). *Crime in the Making: Pathways and Turning Points Through Life.* Cambridge, MA: Harvard University.

Schlegel, K. (1990). *Just Deserts for Corporate Criminals.* Boston, MA. Northeastern University Press.

Schmitter, P. (1985). "Neo-Corporatism and the State." In W. Grant (ed.) *The Political Economy of Corporatism*. London: MacMillan.

_____ (1974). "Still the Century of Corporatism?" *Review of Politics,* 36,1:85-131.

Scholz, J.T. (1984). "Co-operation, Deterrence and the Ecology of Regulatory Enforcement." *Law and Society Review,* 18:601-646.

Schrager, L.S. & J.R. Short, Jr. (1978). "Toward a Sociology of Organizational Crime." *Social Problems,* 25,4:407-419.

Scott, D.W. (1989). "Policing Corporate Collusion." *Criminology,* 27:559-587.

Scott, W.R. (1992). *Organizations: Rational, Natural, and Open Systems*, Third Edition. Englewood Cliffs, NJ: Prentice-Hall.

Shapiro, S. (1990). "Collaring the Crime not the Criminal: Reconsidering White-Collar Crime." *American Sociological Review,* 55:346-365.

_____ (1984). *Wayward Capitalists*. New Haven, CT: Yale University Press.

Shavell, S. (1990). "Deterrence and the Punishment of Attempts." *Journal of Legal Studies* 19:435-466.

_____ (1987). "Optimal Use of Nonmonetary Sanctions as a Deterrent," 77:584-592. *American Economic Review*.

_____ (1985). "Criminal Law and the Optimal Use of Nonmonetary Sanctions as a Deterrent." *Columbia Law Review,* 85,6:1232-1262.

Shover, N., D. Clelland & J. Lynxwiler (1986). *Enforcement or Negotiation: Constructing a Regulatory Bureaucracy*. Albany, NY: State University of New York Press.

_____ (1982). *Constructing a Regulatory Bureaucracy: The Office of Surface Mining Reclamation and Enforcement*. Washington, DC: National Institute of Justice.

Shute, N. (1991). "Unfair Competition." *Amicus Journal,* 13,3:31-34.

Sigler, J.A. & J.E. Murphy (1991). "A Novel Approach to Business-Government Relationships." In J.A. Sigler & J.E. Murphy (eds.) *Corporate Lawbreaking and Interactive Compliance: Resolving the Regulation-Deregulation Dichotomy*, pp. 1-15. New York, NY: Quorum Books.

_____ (1988). *Interactive Corporate Compliance: An Alternative to Regulatory Compulsion*. New York, NY: Quorum Books.

Silets H.M. & S.W. Brenner (1986). "The Demise of Rehabilitation: Sentencing Reform and the Sanctioning of Organizational Criminality." *American Journal of Criminal Law,* 13:329-380.

Silk, L. & D. Vogel (1976). *Ethics and Profits*. New York, NY: Simon and Schuster.

Simon, D.R. & D.S. Eitzen (1993). *Elite Deviance,* Fourth Edition. Boston, MA: Allyn and Bacon.

———— (1982). *Elite Deviance,* First Edition. Boston, MA: Allyn and Bacon.

Simon, H.A. (1979). "Rational Decision Making in Business Organizations." *American Economic Review,* 69,4:493-513.

———— (1945). *Administrative Behavior.* New York, NY: Macmillan.

Simpson, S. (1992). "Corporate-Crime Deterrence and Corporate-Control Policies." In K. Schlegel & D. Weisburd (eds.) *White Collar Crime Reconsidered,* pp. 289-308. Boston, MA: Northeastern University Press.

———— (1986). "The Decomposition of Antitrust: Testing a Multi-Level Longitudinal Model of Profit Squeeze." *American Sociological Review,* 51:859-875.

———— & C.S. Koper (1995). "Top Management Team Characteristics, Organizational Strain, and Antitrust Offending." Working Paper.

———— & C.S. Koper (1992). "Deterring Corporate Crime." *Criminology,* 30,3:347-373.

Skocpol, T. (1980). "Political Response to Capitalist Crisis: Neo-Marxist Theories of the State and the Case of the New Deal." *Politics & Society,* 10,2:155-201.

———— & K. Finegold (1982). "State Capacity and Economic Intervention in the Early New Deal." *Political Science Quarterly,* 97,2:255-278.

Skolnick, J. (1975). *Justice Without Trial,* Second Edition. New York, NY: John Wiley & Sons.

Smith, R.S. (1979). "The Impact of OSHA Inspections on Manufacturing Injury Rates." *Journal of Human Resources,* 14:145-170.

———— (1976). *The Occupational Safety and Health Act: Its Goals and Achievements.* Washington, DC: American Enterprise Institute for Public Policy Research.

Snider, L. (1993). *Bad Business: Corporate Crime in Canada.* Ontario, CN: Nelson Canada.

———— (1991). "The Regulatory Dance: Understanding Reform Processes in Corporate Crime." *International Journal of the Sociology of Law,* 19:209-236.

———— (1990). "Cooperative Models and Corporate Crime: Panacea or Cop-Out?" *Crime & Delinquency,* 36,3:373-391.

———— (1987). "Towards a Political Economy of Reform: Regulation and Corporate Crime." *Law and Policy,* 19:37-68.

Spit, I.W.M. (1986). "Multisubjectieve activiteit en morele verantwoordelijkheid." Dissertation, Utrecht University.

Spitzer, S. (1979). "The Rationalization of Crime Control in Capitalist Society." *Contemporary Crises,* 3:187-206.

Staw, B.N. & E. Szawajkowski (1975). "The Scarcity-Munificence Component of Organizational Acts." *Administrative Science Quarterly,* 20:345.

Steinert, H. (1985). "The Development of 'Discipline' According to Michel Foucault: Discourse Analysis vs. Social History." *Crime and Social Justice,* 12:83-98.

Stern, Y.Z. (1987). "Corporate Criminal Personal Liability: Who is the Corporation?" *Journal of Corporation Law,* 13:125-143.

Stevenson, R.B., Jr. (1974). "Corporations and Social Responsibility: In Search of the Corporate Soul." *George Washington Law Review,* 42,4:706-736.

Stone, C.D. (1985). "Corporate Regulation: The Place of Social Responsibility." In B. Fisse & P.A. French (eds.) *Corrigible Corporations and Unruly Law*, pp. 13-37. San Antonio, TX: Trinity University Press.

_____ (1981). "Large Organizations and the Law at the Pass: Toward a General Theory of Compliance Strategy." *Wisconsin Law Review,* 861-890.

_____ (1980). "The Place of Enterprise Liability in the Control of Corporate Conduct." *Yale Law Journal,* 90,1:1-77.

_____ (1977). "Controlling Corporate Misconduct." *Public Interest,* 48:55-71.

_____ (1975). *Where the Law Ends: The Social Control of Corporate Behavior.* New York, NY: Harper & Row.

Strock, J.M. (1991). "Environmental Criminal Enforcement Priorities for the 1990s." *George Washington Law Review,* 59,4:916-937.

Sutherland, E. (1949/1983). *White Collar Crime: The Uncut Version.* New Haven, CT: Yale University Press.

_____ (1945). "Is 'White-Collar Crime'?" *American Sociological Review,* 10:132-139.

_____ (1940). "White Collar Criminality." *American Sociological Review,* 5:1-12.

Sykes, A. (1984). "The Economics of Vicarious Liability." *Yale Law Journal,* 93:1231.

Szasz, A. (1986). "The Process and Significance of Political Scandals: A Comparison of Watergate and the 'Sewergate' Episode at the Environmental Protection Agency." *Social Problems,* 33:202-217.

Thomas, C.W. & D.M. Bishop (1987). *Criminal Law: Understanding Basic Principles.* Newbury Park, CA: Sage Publications.

Thompson, B.T. (1991). Corporate Governance Section, National Association of Manufacturers. Interview with W.S. Lofquist. July 1.

Thornburg, D. (1991). "Criminal Enforcement of Environmental Laws—A National Priority." *George Washington Law Review,* 59,4:775-780.

Tigar, M.E. (1990). "It Does the Crime But Not the Time: Corporate Criminal Liability in Federal Law." *American Journal Criminal Law,* 17:211-234.

Toensing, V. (1990). "Corporations on Probation: Sentenced to Fail." *Legal Times*, February 12:21-22.

Tombs, S. (1992). "Stemming the Flow of Blood?: The Illusion of Self-Regulation." *Journal of Human Justice,* 3:75-92.

Tversky, A. & D. Kahneman (1981). "The Framing of Decisions and the Rationality of Choice." *Science,* 221:331.

Ulen, T.S. (1994). "Rational Choice and the Economic Analysis of Law." *Law & Social Inquiry,* 19:487.

U.S. Department of Commerce (1994). *Malcolm Baldrige National Quality Award Criteria.* Washington, DC.

U.S. Department of Defense (1963). *Quality Program Requirements MIL-Q-9858A.* Washington, DC.

———— (1960). *Inspection Requirements MIL-I-45208.* Washington, DC.

U.S. Department of Justice (1994a). Bureau of Justice Statistics, *Criminal Victimization in the United States: 1973-1992 Trends.* Washington, DC: U.S. Department of Justice.

———— (1994b). Bureau of Justice Statistics, *Sourcebook of Criminal Justice Statistics—1994,* Table 3.94. Washington, DC: U.S. Department of Justice.

———— (1991). "Factors in Decisions on Criminal Prosecutions for Environmental Violations in the Context of Significant Voluntary Compliance or Disclosure Efforts by the Violator." Washington, DC: U.S. Department of Justice.

U.S. Department of Labor (1993). *Fatal Workplace Injuries in 1991: A Collection of Data and Analysis.* Washington, DC: Bureau of Labor Statistics. Report # 845.

U.S. Environmental Protection Agency (1991). "Policy Regarding the Role of Corporate Attitude, Policies, Practices, and Procedures in Determining Whether to Remove a Facility from the EPA List of Violating Facilities." *Federal Register,* 56:64785-64788.

———— (1986). "Environmental Auditing Policy Statement." *Federal Register,* 51:25004-25010.

United States House of Representatives (1990a). *Federal Contract Crimes Sentencing Act of 1990*. Hearing before the Subcommittee on Criminal Justice. October 11. Washington, DC: U.S. Government Printing Office.

United States House of Representatives (1990b). Committee on the Judiciary 1990. *Oversight on the United States Sentencing Commission and Guidelines for Organizational Sanctions: Hearings Before the Subcommittee on Criminal Justice of the Committee on the Judiciary*. House of Representatives, 101st Cong., 2d Sess. 230-31, 439-78.

United States Occupational Safety and Health Administration (1993). *Criminal Referrals by OSHA to DOJ or U.S. Attorneys*. Washington, DC: OSHA, Office of Information and Consumer Affairs.

United States Senate, Committee on the Judiciary (1984). Senate Report No. 225, 98th Cong., 2nd Sess. 76, *reprinted in 1984 U.S. Code Congressional and Administrative News* 3182.

_____ (1983). *Comprehensive Crime Control Act of 1983*. Senate Report 98-225.

United States Sentencing Commission (1991a). "Sentencing Guidelines for Organizational Defendants." Washington, DC: United States Sentencing Commission. April 26.

_____ (1991b). *Supplementary Report on Sentencing Guidelines for Organizations*. Washington, DC.

_____ (1990a). Public Hearing on Organizational Sanctions. Washington, DC. February 14.

_____ (1990b). "Organizational Sanctions Working Group Memo on Methodology." November 16.

_____ (1988). Public Hearing on Organizational Sanctions. Pasadena, California. December 2.

University of Michigan Journal of Law Reform (1987). "Reckless Endangerment of an Employee: A Proposal in the Wake of Film Recovery Systems to Make the Boss Responsible For His Crimes." 20:873-905.

University of Toledo Law Review (1986). "Imposing Penal Sanctions on the Unwary Corporate Executive: The Unveiled Corporate Criminal." 17:383-96.

van Woensel, A.M. (1993). *In de daderstand verheven*. Beschouwingen over functioneel daderschap in het Nederlandse strafrecht. (Thesis University of Amsterdam.) Arnhem: Gouda Quint (with a summary in English).

Vandivier, K. (1972). "Why Should My Conscience Bother Me?" In R.L. Heilbroner (ed.) *In the Name of Profit: Profiles in Corporate Irresponsibility*. New York, NY: Doubleday.

Vaughan, D. (1996). *The Challenger Launch Decision: Risky Technology, Culture and Deviance at NASA*. Chicago, IL: University of Chicago Press.

————— (1990). "Autonomy, Interdependence, and Social Control: NASA and the Space Shuttle Challenger." *Administrative Science Quarterly,* 35:225-257.

————— (1983). *Controlling Unlawful Organizational Behavior: Social Structure and Corporate Misconduct*. Chicago, IL: University of Chicago Press.

————— (1982). "Transaction Systems and Unlawful Organizational Behavior." *Social Problems,* 29,4:373-379.

Vicusi, K.W. (1979). "The Impact of Occupational Safety and Health Regulation." *Bell Journal of Economics,* 10:117-140.

Vogel, D. (1986). *National Styles of Regulation: Environmental Policy in Great Britain and the United States*. Ithaca, NY: Cornell University Press.

Von Ebers, D. (1986). "The Application of Criminal Homicide Statutes to Work-Related Deaths: Mens Rea and Deterrence." *University of Illinois Law Review,* 3:969-999.

Von Hirsch, A. (1993). *Censures and Sanctions*. New York, NY: Oxford University Press.

————— (1985). *Past or Future Crimes: Deservedness and Dangerousness in the Sentencing of Criminals*. New Brunswick, NJ: Rutgers University Press.

————— (1976). *Doing Justice: The Choice of Punishments*. New York, NY: Hill & Wang.

von Savigny, F.C. (1840). *System des heutigen römischen Rechts*. Berlin: Bei Veit und Comp. II, §94,95.

Waldman, S. (1989). "The Revolving Door." *Newsweek,* February 6.

Walker, N. (1991). *Why Punish?* Oxford: Oxford University Press.

Wallace, M. (1987). "Dying for Coal: The Struggle for Health and Safety Conditions in American Coal Mining, 1930-82." *Social Forces,* 66:336-364.

Washington University Law Quarterly (1990). "Recent Developments in Corporate and White Collar Crime." 68:779-818.

————— (1986). "Can a Corporation Commit Murder?" 64:967-984.

Weisburd, D., E. Waring & S. Wheeler (1990). "Class, Status, and the Punishment of White-Collar Criminals." *Law & Social Inquiry,* 15:223-243.

Wells, C. (1992). *Corporations and Criminal Responsibility*. Oxford: Clarendon Press.

Wheeler, S. & M.L. Rothman (1982). "The Organization as Weapon in White-Collar Crime." *Michigan Law Review,* 80:1403-1426.

Wheeler, S., D. Weisburd & N. Bode (1982). "Sentencing the White-Collar Offender: Rhetoric and Reality." *American Sociological Review,* 47:641-659.

Williams, G. (1961). *Criminal Law.* London: Stevens & Son Limited.

Williams, R. (1961). *The Long Revolution.* London: Chatto and Windus.

Williamson, O. (1970). *Corporate Control and Business Behavior.* Englewood Cliffs, NJ: Prentice Hall.

Wilson, G.K. (1985). *The Politics of Safety and Health.* Oxford: Clarendon Press.

Wilson, J.Q. (1980). *The Politics of Regulation.* New York, NY: Basic Books.

_____ & R.J. Herrnstein (1985). *Crime and Human Nature.* New York, NY: Simon & Schuster.

Wilson, J.Q. & A. Abrahamse (1992). "Does Crime Pay?" *Justice Quarterly,* 9:359.

Wray, C. (1992). "Corporate Probation Under the New Organizational Sentencing Guidelines." *Yale Law Journal,* 101,8:2017-2042.

Wright, J.P., F.T. Cullen & M.B. Blankenship (1995). "The Social Construction of Corporate Violence: Media Coverage of the Imperial Food Products Fire." *Crime & Delinquency,* 41,1:20-36.

Wylie, M.I. (1991). "Corporations and the Non-Compellability Right in Criminal Proceedings." *The Criminal Law Quarterly,* 33:344-363.

Yale Law Journal (1982). "Constitutional Rights of the Corporate Person." 91:1641-1658.

Yeager, M.G. (1984). "Community Redress Against the Corporate Offender." *Crime and Social Justice,* 21-22:223-227.

Yeager, P.C. (1991). *The Limits of Law: The Public Regulation of Private Pollution.* New York, NY: Cambridge University Press.

_____ (1987). "Structural Bias in Regulatory Law Enforcement: The Case of the U.S. Environmental Protection Agency." *Social Problems,* 34:330-344.

_____ (1986). "Analyzing Corporate Offenses: Progress and Prospects." *Research in Corporate Social Performance and Policy,* 8:93-120.

Yoder, S.A. (1978). "Criminal Sanctions for Corporate Illegality." *Journal of Criminal Law and Criminology,* 69,1:40-58.

Young, J. (1992). "Ten Points of Realism." In J. Young & R. Matthews (eds.) *Rethinking Criminology: The Realist Debate*, pp. 24-68. Beverly Hills, CA: Sage.

———— (1986). "The Tasks of a Realist Criminology." *Contemporary Crises*, 11:337-356.

Zald, M.N. (1978). "On the Social Control of Industries." *Social Forces*, 57,1:79-102.

Zeitlin, M. (1989). *The Large Corporation and Contemporary Classes*. New Brunswick, NJ: Rutgers University Press.

Zey, M. (1992). *Decision Making*. Newbury Park, CA: Sage.

STATUTES AND GUIDELINES CITED

Model Penal Code and Commentaries §2.07 American Law Institute (1985)

Public Law 98-473, 98 Stat. 1837, 1976 (1984).

Sentencing Reform Act, 18 U.S.C. §3551 et seq. (Supp. III 1985).

Sentencing Guidelines (1994). In U.S. Sentencing Commission, *Sentencing Guidelines Manual*, Chapter 8. St. Paul, MN: West.

Index

255

About the Authors

Leo G. Barrile is a Professor of sociology at Bloomsburg University in Bloomsburg, PA. His areas of interest are corporate crime, attitudes about crime and punishment, the sociology of mass communication, and social theory. Recently, Barrile has published articles on the implications of imprisoning business agents for health and safety crimes, and has co-authored an introductory text, *Criminology and Justice*.

Mark A. Cohen is Associate Professor of Management, Owen Graduate School of Management, Vanderbilt University (Ph.D. Economics, Carnegie-Mellon University). Cohen was formerly senior economist with the U.S. Sentencing Commission and served as a consultant to the Commission in developing corporate sentencing guidelines. Current research projects related to corporate crime include: why firms become corporate criminals; the relationship between financial and environmental performance of firms (does it pay to be green?); and the effect of criminal and civil penalties on firm behavior. Cohen has recently published books and articles on corporate crime.

M. David Ermann is a Professor of sociology at the University of Delaware. His major research interest is organizational behavior, especially the organizational components of corporate crime. Ermann is currently studying why some usually nondeviant organizations and their employees can knowingly cause human injury and death.

Richard S. Gruner is a Visiting Professor of Law at the University of Southern California and a Professor of Law at the Whittier Law School. Gruner is a former inside counsel to the IBM Corporation and consultant to the U.S. Sentencing Commission concerning corporate sentencing standards. He has recently authored and co-authored works on corporate crime, including many articles on corporate compliance issues. He has also been a speaker at numerous ALI-ABA conferences on corporate law compliance and related forms of liability. Gruner is presently a member of the National Center for Preventive Law's Commission on Compliance Standards, which is developing standards for evaluating corporate law compliance programs. Gruner also serves as a trustee of the National Center for Preventive Law. He is a member of the New

York and California state bars and a graduate of the Columbia University School of Law (LL.M. 1982), the USC Law Center (J.D. 1978), and CalTech (B.S. 1975).

Bridget M. Hutter is a Lecturer in sociology at the London School of Economics & Political Science. Previously she was a Research Fellow at the Centre for Socio-Legal Studies and a Senior Research Fellow of Jesus College University of Oxford. She has a long-standing research interest in regulation, working primarily on environmental and occupational health and safety regulation. Hutter is the author of numerous reports and articles on regulation, and of two recent books. She is currently preparing a third book on the impact of occupational, health and safety regulation on the railway industry.

Nico Jörg is a judge in the Court of Appeals, Arnhem, The Netherlands. He is a former Associate Professor of criminal law and procedure at Utrecht University. Jörg's publications include "Corporate Liability and Manslaughter: Should we be Going Dutch?" (1991) *Criminal Law Review* (with Stewart Field).

William S. Lofquist is an Assistant Professor of sociology at SUNY College at Geneseo. His research interests include the causes and control of organizational wrongdoing and the death penalty. He recently co-authored (with Michael Radelet and Hugo Bedau) an article on wrongful convictions in death penalty cases that appeared in the *Cooley Law Review.* His present research focuses on wrongful convictions as a form of organizational wrongdoing; this research examines how and why police and prosecutorial agencies pursue convictions against innocent defendants. Lofquist's earlier research focused on the development of organizational probation and the federal organizational sentencing guidelines and on the performance of civil juries in cases involving corporations.

Jeffrey S. Parker is a Professor of law and Associate Dean for Academic Affairs at George Mason University School of Law. He has authored several articles examining issues in law and economics. Current research interests include experimental comparisons of the adversarial and inquisitional systems of civil procedure, an historical analysis of the Federal Rules of Civil Procedure from a public choice perspective, and a monograph on corporate criminal liability. Prior to joining GMU, Parker practiced law in New York City, with Sullivan & Cromwell and Sacks Montgomery, and served as Deputy Chief Counsel and Consulting Counsel to the United States Sentencing Commission.

Gary A. Rabe is an Assistant Professor at Minot State University. His research interests include corporate crime and the sociology of law. His research activities have included examining the sentencing of organizational offenders and studying organizational factors and processes which precipitated the concealment of tobacco hazards. Rabe is currently applying organizational perspectives to explain corporate crime. He is also conducting a comparative analysis death penalty discrimination cases and employment discrimination cases to see how the U.S. Supreme Court has used social science evidence to inform its decisions.

Sally S. Simpson is Graduate Director and Associate Professor in the Department of Criminology and Criminal Justice at the University of Maryland, College Park. She has published 12 articles and chapters that examine a range of corporate crime topics including theory, etiology, prevention, and control. She is finishing a book on corporate crime deterrence and control for Cambridge University Press. Simpson's current research (with Craig Smith at Georgetown) involves using a factoral survey to assess individual and organizational factors that inhibit and promote corporate crime. The survey will be administered to managers at various levels and assignments within six U.S. corporations.

Thomas S. Ulen received a BA in 1968 from Dartmouth College. He then served in the Peace Corps in Korea from 1968 to 1970. From 1970 to 1972 he studied at St. Catherine's College, University of Oxford, and then worked on a Ph.D. in economics at Stanford University. He joined the faculty at the University of Illinois in 1977 and specialized in United States economic history. He began teaching at the College of Law in 1983 and his principal appointment at the University is now in the College of Law. He is also a professor in the Institute of Government and Public Affairs. His research has been on law and economics topics in property, contracts, tort law, and criminal law. Ulen has co-authored (with Robert Cooter) a text on law and economics, and is currently working on an anthology of law and economics articles and a book on the relationship between cognitive psychology, the theory of rational choice, and the economic analysis of law.

Debating corporate crime

DA

INFORMATION RESOURCES CENTER
AMERICAN SOCIETY
FOR INDUSTRIAL SECURITY
1625 PRINCE STREET
ALEXANDRIA, VA 22314
(703) 519-6200

DEMCO